LONG-DISTANCE NATIONALISM

For Matija Stefan and Zala Ann

Dansk Center for Migration
og Etniske Studier

Long-distance Nationalism

Diasporas, homelands and identities

ZLATKO SKRBIŠ
Queensland University of Technology
Brisbane, Australia

LONDON AND NEW YORK

First published 1999 by Ashgate Publishing

Published 2017 by Routledge
2 Park Square, Milton Park, Abingdon, Oxon OX14 4RN
711 Third Avenue, New York, NY 10017, USA

Routledge is an imprint of the Taylor & Francis Group, an informa business

Copyright © Zlatko Skrbiš 1999

All rights reserved. No part of this book may be reprinted or reproduced or utilised in any form or by any electronic, mechanical, or other means, now known or hereafter invented, including photocopying and recording, or in any information storage or retrieval system, without permission in writing from the publishers.

Notice:
Product or corporate names may be trademarks or registered trademarks, and are used only for identification and explanation without intent to infringe.

British Library Cataloguing in Publication Data
Skrbiš, Zlatko
    Long-distance nationalism : diasporas, homelands and
    identities. - (Research in migration and ethnic relations
    series)
    1. Nationalism 2. Croats - Australia 3. Serbs - Australia
    I. Title
    320.5'4

Library of Congress Catalog Card Number: 99-73633

ISBN 13: 978-1-85972-672-3 (hbk)

Contents

Figures and tables ix
Acknowledgements xi
Preface xiii
List of abbreviations xv

1 Introduction 1

    1   The relativisation of distance   2
    2   Long-distance nationalism   5
    3   Methodology and research design   10
    3.1   Historical note   10
    3.2   Sample characteristics   11
    3.3   The size and representativeness of the research setting   13
    3.4   Fieldwork update   14
    4   The war and its impact on the outcome of this research   18
    5   Plan of the book   23
    6   Notes   26

2 History, homeland, nostalgia 28

    1   The European post-Second World War refugee problem   29
    1.1   Slovenians in Argentina   32
    2   Memory…   33
    3   Innocence…   34

	4	Political migrants and their contribution to the formation of a distinct diaspora identity in Australia	35
	5	Homeland, nostalgia and the myth of return	38
	5.1	The elusive concept of homeland	38
	5.2	The ethnic homeland: the questions of time and space	39
	5.3	Nostalgia	41
	6	Ideas about homeland	42
	6.1	Romanticism – second generation respondents	43
	6.2	Parents' romanticism through their children's eyes	45
	6.3	The second generation's critical attitudes towards the ethnic homeland	47
	6.4	The myth of return	48
		6.4.1 Second generation Croatian respondents' reflections on first generation Australian-Croatians: returning home	50
		6.4.2 Second generation Slovenian respondents' reflections on first generation Slovenians: returning home	52
		6.4.3 Second generation Croatians and Slovenians – returning home	54
	7	Notes	56

3 Diasporas and community sentiments 58

	1	Some limitations of the prevalent discourses on ethnic communities	60
	1.1	Ethnic community boundaries and the segmentation of ethnic community space	62
	2	Politics, otherness and diasporas	64
	3	Conforming to norms and standards in diaspora organisations	67
	4	From antagonism to schism	72
	5	Diaspora cohesion and the question of generations	74
	6	Concerns about the future of diaspora organisations	77
	7	The problem of representation in ethnic communities	78
	7.1	Whither community	80
	8	Notes	81

4		**The distant view**	**83**
	1	Mediation of information about the homeland	83
	2	'Tabloid' political culture as mainstream culture	87
	3	Invention, manipulation and legitimation	91
	3.1	*The maps*	91
	3.2	*The 'Tesla case'*	93
	3.3	*Myths of origin*	95
	4	Diaspora and party politics: the case of Australian-Croatians	97
	5	The contrast: the case of Australian-Slovenians	107
	6	The power of symbols	108
	6.1	*Religious...*	108
	6.2	*... and historical*	111
	7	Notes	113
5		**Constructing the Other**	**115**
	1	Slovenian respondents on other ethnic groups from the former Yugoslavia: Southerners – the generalised Other	118
	2	Croatian respondents on Slovenians	128
	3	Croatians on the 'practical identity' of Yugoslavs	129
	4	Croatian respondents on the Other: the Serbs	136
	5	Croatian respondents on Bosnian Muslims: search for 'true' ethnicity	147
	6	From 'public' to 'private'	151
	7	Notes	152
6		**Marriage choices**	**154**
	1	The key factors which impact on in(ter)marriage in diaspora settings	155
	2	'Pragmatism' in the functioning of intimacy	162
	3	The construction of marriage markets	167
	3.1	*Privileged marriage market*	169
	3.2	*Privileged marriage sub-market*	170
	3.3	*Deprivileged marriage market*	171
	3.4	*Anathema market and factors which influence its performance*	172
	4	The future of marriage choice	178
	5	Notes	181

7	**Conclusion**	183
	Post scriptum	186
8	**Bibliography**	188

Figures and tables

Table 1.1	Australia and South Australia: estimation of the number of Croatians and Slovenians	14
Table 1.2	Reactions of second generation respondents to the war in their ethnic homelands	23
Table 2.1	The first four countries of destination for refugees with Yugoslav citizenship, 1 July 1947 – 31 December 1951	31
Figure 3.1	External view of ethnic community: paradox of abstract inclusion	60
Figure 3.2	Schematic representation of Slovenian diaspora institutional framework in Adelaide, South Australia	80
Figure 4.1	Nationalist discourse: mediation between past and present	97
Figure 4.2	Homeland: from passive to an interactive agent	106
Table 5.1	Second generation responses to the question posed in the questionnaire: "What do you think about other ethnic groups in Yugoslavia and in Australia?"	117
Figure 5.1	Essentialising a 'Yugoslav'	133

Table 6.1	Marital status of respondents at the time of interviews	155
Table 6.2	Arguments against inmarriage: categorisation of respondents in relation to their use of assimilationist/hegemonist, libertarian and social status arguments	158
Figure 6.1	Reconstruction of marriage markets	168

Acknowledgements

The research used as the basis for this book was conducted between 1991 and early 1998. It began when I took up a Postgraduate Research scholarship offered by the Australian government. The core of this project came into being during my time as a doctoral candidate at Flinders University (1992-1994). It is more than a routine gesture to thank Flinders University for the many forms of support it has provided. Since mid-1995 I have worked at Queensland University of Technology, Brisbane. I would like to thank the former School of Social Science and the Centre for Community and Cross-Cultural Studies for their financial support which was instrumental in updating some of the information contained in this book.

My academic life has been blessed with a number of wonderfully supportive friends and colleagues. Bob Holton, my teacher, mentor and friend, deserves a very special mention. My life could have turned out very differently without his unfailing support in a myriad of ways – my heartfelt thanks. I also wish to thank Constance Lever-Tracy for her support and guidance. I am grateful to Gillian Bottomley who has always been ready to offer friendly comments and advice. Benedict Anderson has been a wonderfully constructive critic and is also the author of the term 'long-distance nationalism'. Rudi Rizman was my teacher when I was an undergraduate – I am still a grateful recipient of his useful and critical comments. My colleague and friend Loretta Baldassar generously found the time to read and comment on various drafts of this manuscript. Without her help and encouragement it would have been almost impossible to bring this work to fruition. I have learned a great deal from all these individuals. None of them, however, is responsible for the content or the quality of this book.

Waveney Croft was instrumental in helping me with the final editing and was always obliging in keeping up with my impossible deadlines.

During my study years my family and I were assisted by numerous friends who helped to ease our occasional hardships. To mention all of them would mean expanding this acknowledgment section into a separate chapter.

And just as I was blessed with academic colleagues, I was also blessed in my personal life. This book is dedicated to my children, Matija and Zala. They are the most generous children a parent could wish for: they offer love, joy and wit in plenitude. Marta, my life companion, has been a source of enormous support, patience and understanding for almost half my lifetime.

Last, but not least, I would like to thank the numerous individuals who were willing to share their thoughts and stories with me. Needless to say, this book would not have been possible without them.

Preface

This book sets out to explore specific aspects of the phenomenon of long-distance nationalism, i.e. nationalism which effectively spans the globe and which, by utilising modern global communications networks, crosses ethno-national boundaries with unprecedented ease. This phenomenon implicates a variety of groups and institutions, from ethno-national collectivities and the individuals who constitute them and who directly engage in ethno-national discourse, to more or less accidental participants in this process.

Ethno-nationalism, a phenomenon which characterised this century with its incredibly powerful consequences, shows no sign of withering away; ethnic cleansing, this late modern version of ethnic strife, is a case in point. It is heartening and theoretically essential, however, to realise that conflict is not the only mode of interaction between different ethno-national groups and states. Some complex contemporary processes such as the unification of Europe or the increasingly significant and active role of regional associations reveal of the possibility of at least partial (if not considerable) transcendence of narrow ethno-nationalisms. Such an optimistic remark, however, should in no way render irrelevant the contemporary significance of ethno-national sentiments.

It is mistaken to see globalisation, transnationalisation and nationalist processes as contradictory. Rather, they should be seen as complementing each other. This book tries to do precisely that by showing how ethno-nationalist sentiments in the ethnic homelands can draw their strength, ideas, material support or simply nationalist enthusiasm from diaspora settings. The reverse, of course, may also be true. The comparative content of this inquiry will show considerable variations in these practices in different groupings – knowledge about these processes is inevitably highly contextual. The increased global interdependence of the world makes long-distance nationalism an increasingly more likely and more important form of ethno-nationalist expression and an evermore potent phenomenon in international politics. It is therefore a topic which calls for academic attention and which needs to become a constitutive aspect of analyses of contemporary nationalist movements.

This book is an analysis of two Australian diaspora groups, Croatian and Slovenian, which have both experienced varying degrees of nationalist upheaval in their respective homelands in recent times. It follows two main themes. Firstly, it systematically compares and analyses differences in transnational exchanges and interactions between Croatian and Slovenian migrant groups in Australia and their respective homelands. Secondly, it examines the generational aspect of these interactive processes and analyses the crucial similarities and differences between members of the first and second generations in both groups.

In other words, this book explores the process of long-distance nationalism and its persistence over time: is long-distance nationalism something that affects first generation migrants only or does it have the potential to persist across migrant generations? If it has, what then are the mechanisms involved in such transmission? What roles – if any – are played by the host society's institutions and the political establishment in the homeland? Do different migrant groups respond differently to ethno-national challenges in their homelands? These and other questions are scrutinised in this work which elaborates on the intersections of homeland-diaspora interaction, the cultural and nationalist transmission between first and second generations of migrants, and collective-individual identity formation.

List of abbreviations

DP	Displaced Persons
HDZ	Hrvatska demokratska zajednica (Croatian Democratic Union)
HOP	Hrvatski oslobodilački pokret (Croatian Liberation Movement)
HSP	Hrvatska stranka prava (Croatian Rights Party)
IRO	International Refugee Organisation
SHAEF	Supreme Headquarters Allied Expeditionary Force
UNRRA	United Nations Relief and Rehabilitation Organisation

1 Introduction

This study is both an exploration into the phenomenon of long-distance nationalism and an analysis of Croatians and Slovenians in Australia with a particular focus on second generation individuals. The generational aspect of ethno-nationalist transmission in a diaspora context is a real test of the strength of ethno-nationalism. It is quite easy to understand why first generation migrants feel strongly about the developments in their homelands but to explain the nationalist sentiments of second and subsequent generations, a range of additional factors needs to be scrutinised. What are the factors which enable the successful transmission of ethno-nationalism across the generations? What is the difference between the intensity of ethno-national sentiments between migrant generations? Do these sentiments manifest differently (and above all more subtly) in subsequent generations? What is the role of the state in this process? Is an active and highly interactive relationship between the ethnic homelands and diaspora populations necessary for intense ethno-national sentiments to develop in the diaspora? How does an external threat (e.g. war in the parents' homeland) influence the nature and extent of these feelings? How do these feelings influence the way of thinking, pattern of behaviour and actions of second generation individuals in different social contexts of the 'host' society? Is their influence something which could potentially undermine the social cohesion of a country which hosts ethnic groups whose homelands are in conflict? These and similar questions deserve our intellectual curiosity because they provide one of the important keys to an understanding of the global social processes in the modern age. They are of particular importance for countries with a large intake of diverse groups of migrants (Australia, Canada, Germany, Israel, Sweden to name but a few).

Although an enormous amount of attention has been given to the phenomenon of nationalism in the past few decades, the above questions have not received adequate consideration. The belief that modernisation processes will eventually or inevitably bring about the demise of nationalism could be held partly responsible for this (e.g. Breuilly 1982, Hobsbawm 1990, Harris 1991). Closely related to this are the widely shared assumptions about the impact of globalisation, identified by Holton (1998) as globe-talk. He argues that alongside this process we witness "the continuing development of the nation-state and a revival of ethnicity" (ibid., p. 7). A.D. Smith (1995, p. 160) makes a similar point when he argues that both nationalism and the nation "remain indispensable elements of an interdependent world and a mass-communications culture." It appears that ethno-national mobilisation has successfully adapted to a new hi-tech environment and that it comfortably utilises modern media and global networks (Anderson 1994, Margolis 1995, Naficy 1991). Ethno-nationalism[1] and globalisation thus need to be viewed as complementary rather than contradictory processes.

The discrepancy between all too optimistic expectations about the gradual demise of the significance of nationalism and the global resurgence of nationalism since the mid-1980s, makes the question of the persistence of ethno-nationalism in diaspora settings particularly interesting. The extension of this question to include the persistence of ethno-nationalism in second generation diaspora settings makes the debate between the expectations of the modernisation theorists and the stubborn persistence of ethno-nationalism even more complex.

1 The relativisation of distance

'Distance', 'isolation', 'space' and 'time' are concepts which require thorough re-evaluation. The processes causing and effecting these changes have been at work throughout a relatively long historical period. According to some (e.g. Anderson 1993 rev.ed.), this would be the invention of print which enabled the imagining of national collectivities, for others, the attempts at standardisation of time (Nowotny 1994), or the discovery of the New World. Regardless of any particular answer, migratory movements of unprecedented scale are also to be considered as significant factors in these changes. Reflecting on the massive movements of the population, Benedict Anderson (1992a, p. 13) observes that over the past 150 years the market, war and political oppression "have profoundly disrupted a once seemingly 'neutral' coincidence of national sentiment with lifelong residence in fatherland or motherland." Interactions between groups and individuals who reside in different countries or even continents are becoming increasingly regular and geographical location has become a relatively minor obstacle in such transnational exchanges. To be sure, these massive movements of populations represent nothing radically new as such movements have been in existence for centuries. What is new, however, is the ease and frequency with which people transgress the political and physical constraints of time and space. Standardised time regulates every aspect of social, cultural, economic and political life on the planet, and distance has been obliterated. As Holton (1998, p. 1) puts it: "[G]eography has, in this sense, been pronounced dead."

It is precisely in this context of relativisation of time and space that one can understand a rather presumptuous statement made by a Greek Consul in Melbourne: "Australia is the first line of defence in the battle for Macedonia" (Danforth 1995, pp. 7-8). The Consul's statement, referring to an old dispute over 'Macedonia', which is half a world away, astutely captures the obscurity of physical distance which is becoming of minor relevance in modern nationalist struggles. This quotation is also revealing of the interference of the state and its representatives in the construction and sustenance of ethno-nationalist hegemonic narratives. In other words, to understand the multidimensionality of contemporary nationalist conflicts, one needs to examine thoroughly the nature of interactions between diasporas and homelands.

Migrant groups *are* affected by events in their homelands. Eugen Weber (1977, p. 103) wrote about "how little impact" the 1870-71 Franco-Prussian war had "on the popular mind in the [French] countryside." Nothing apparently had changed "apart from the departure of a few soldiers." If the 'countryside' in this case represents the lack of synchronisation with the contemporary world, then one might feel tempted to say that 'countryside' in that sense no longer exists. Physical distance nowadays neither removes visual images of the homeland (because of media hi-tech), nor does it prevent physical interaction (because of transport). More than three decades ago, Charles Price (1963, p. 305) wrote about Greek islanders in Australia who, "thumping down glasses of liquor", discussed issues that stirred them up, such as, for example, "the proper time and method for Greek Cypriots to obtain Union with Greece." By the same measure, Catalan settlers in Melbourne "were concerned with the policy of the Franco government toward Catalonian independence" (ibid.). Kuropas (1991, p. 132), in his study of Ukrainians in the United States, discusses the ecstatic feelings of some segments of American-Ukrainian communities at the beginning of the First World War conflict, when the "long-awaited opportunity for national emancipation from Russia had finally come." He also examines the actual support for resistance of the various Ukrainian communities regarding the Soviet occupation of Ukraine. Campbell and Sherrard (1968, p. 301) claim that "(t)he War of Independence (1821-29) and the Balkan Wars of 1912 brought emigrants back to fight for Greece." Similarly, although much more remarkably, according to Glazer and Moynihan's (1965, p. 242) interpretation, when the American Irish "discovered they were Celts, locked in ageless struggle with Saxons", the following happened:

> The speeches were grand; the rallies grander. One hundred thousand persons attended a Fenian gathering in Jones' Wood in New York in 1866 – against the wishes of the Archbishop! The Fenians hoped to free Ireland by capturing Canada. From their New York headquarters they raised an army, and prepared for the invasion, with the full regalia of a modern government-in-exile.
> [...] Nothing came of it. A thousand men or so marched into Canada. And marched right out again. In the one battle of the whole fiasco, eight Irishmen were killed.

Last but not least, in Australia, the Australian Gallipoli legend[2] was – in addition to the support of a large proportion of the Australian citizenry – *also* made possible by those Australian British migrants and their children who believed the call to arms by the British Monarch had to be obeyed. These are but a few examples of this not unusual phenomenon of long-distance 'obedience' which is so commonly found in diaspora settings.

In order to proceed with this discussion, I first need to deal with the ambiguity of meaning of the term diaspora. Although a variety of definitions of diaspora are available in the literature (Connor 1986, Safran 1991, Klausner 1991), I would like to make two comments in relation to its existence at this point.[3] Firstly, a diaspora population *may* result from the disappearance of a homeland from the world political map. A classical example of this kind is the existence of the Jewish diaspora from the period of the Bar-Kochba revolt (AD 132-135) until the state of Israel was proclaimed by the Zionist National Council in Tel Aviv in 1948. Secondly, a diaspora population may retain its diaspora status *despite* the existence of a 'homeland'. The reasons for this might be complex and one could again use the Jewish diaspora as an example: the act of the establishment of the Israeli state did not mark the end of the existence of the Jewish diaspora. Clearly, the existence of the diaspora population is not dependent on the simple fact of deprivation of homeland.

As Sheffer (1986b, p. 1) put it, the research into "networks created by ethnic groups which transcend the territorial state" is a relatively new field of study. He criticises the existent definitions of diaspora because they define diasporas as a transitory phenomenon which is "destined to disappear through acculturation and assimilation" (Sheffer 1986a, p. 8). He argues instead that it is the other way around, as "diasporas and their trans-state relations will continue to exist even as diasporas acculturate" (ibid., p. 9).

More recent theorising (Safran 1991, Tölölyan 1991) considers the term diaspora as a metaphoric designation for different categories of individuals:

> ... expatriates, expellees, political refugees, alien residents, immigrants, and ethnic and racial minorities *tout court* – in much the same way that 'ghetto' has come to designate all kinds of crowded, constricted, and disprivileged urban environments, and 'holocaust' has come to be applied to all kinds of mass murder. (Safran 1991, p. 83)

Such a broad definition (as used in most contemporary writing) makes the distinction between diaspora and migrant settings superficial to a considerable extent. In a recent paper Tölölyan (1996, p. 8) expressed some reservations about such a broad use of the term diaspora, which is increasingly turned into a "promiscuously captious category that is taken to include all the adjacent phenomena to which it is linked but from which it actually differs in ways that are constitutive, that in fact make a viable definition of diaspora possible." Although Tölölyan's critique makes some well measured points, for the present purposes I have no difficulty in embracing Safran's definition cited above, which is commonly used in the contemporary literature. Conceptualising diaspora in this broader fashion reinforces the link between globalisation processes and rapid diaspora formation, and breaks with the past tradition which perceived diasporas as a consequence of necessarily traumatic and massive uprootings. The formation of modern diasporas is not necessarily linked to such developments but could be seen as a product of a combination of economic, cultural and/or political factors.

2   Long-distance nationalism

The present study builds on the assumption that the formation of new diasporas is an ongoing process, closely related to a combination of economic, cultural and/or political factors. Diasporas are not necessarily a consequence of social or political upheaval. One should consider the possibility that diasporas are a consequence of migrations induced by economic processes or even a consequence of a conscious and orchestrated effort by the homeland establishment. McDowell's (1996) study of Tamil asylum diaspora in Europe could be used to illustrate the latter possibility. He reveals how Switzerland has become the target country of Tamil asylum seekers and how Switzerland's Tamil community is vibrant, well organised and supportive of the homeland struggle by design rather than default. The long-distance orchestration between the Swiss-based Tamil diaspora and Tamil Tigers in Northern Sri Lanka is instrumental in keeping up the Tamil resistance against Sri Lankan military forces. Furthermore, this long-distance orchestration of political and nationalist passion and money donating is entirely necessary for the Tamil liberationist struggle to continue. The main purpose of the existence of diaspora in Switzerland is to fund the conflict.

The significance of fundraising was brought to the fore during the recent and current military struggles in Kosovo between the Serbian police and Albanian resistance fighters. It is a well-known fact that Albanian resistance has been made possible by the financial backing of well-organised Albanian diaspora in Western Europe. Their members not only contributed generous funds but many have also returned to Kosovo to fight.

The logic behind the highly publicised, religiously inspired terrorism also has a lot in common with what is here described as long-distance nationalism. In particular, they share the obliteration of the significance of distance and the appreciation of financial backing. The international hunt for Saudi multimillionaire Osama bin Laden is a case in point.

The enormous range of possibilities which long-distance interaction offers invites a researcher to reconsider its impact on modern nationalism. Nationalism is neither becoming obsolete, as some authors would like us to believe, nor is it becoming an overdetermining factor in world politics, as some others argue. Is long-distance nationalism a new form of nationalism or maybe just a modified version of something much older? Paradoxically, one could argue both. Long-distance nationalism is still a nationalism but one that is profoundly adapted to the conditions of a modern global system. I propose the following working definition of long-distance nationalism: it is that type of nationalism which crosses neighbouring states and/or continents.

Long-distance nationalism is an ideal-type and I do not postulate the existence of anything as absurd as 'short-distance' nationalism. Reference to long distances is simply used to indicate the focus on nationalist processes which transcend a relatively strictly limited locality. At best, one could argue that at the opposing pole of long-distance nationalism we can talk about 'easily localisable' nationalism – i.e. nationalism which emerges and subsequently seeks resolution in relatively well defined and compact territories without the considerable assistance of a co-ethnic population arriving from beyond the neighbouring states or other continents. Such 'easily localisable' nationalisms have never existed in pure form, but 19th century nationalisms come quite close to this ideal-type model.

The term long-distance nationalism derives from Benedict Anderson's writing (1992a, 1992b, 1994) in which he charts the way for further explorations into the intersections of migration studies and nationalism. He establishes a close link between the capitalist order, mass migrations and mass communications and argues, for example, that the survival of the Irish Republican Army (IRA) is possible "not only because of its nationalist appeal and its ruthless methods, but because it has gained political and financial support in the United States and inside England, weapons on the international arms market, and training and intelligence from Libya and in the Near East" (Anderson 1992a, p. 13). Furthermore, he asks whether we are witnessing the emergence of a new category of nationalist, the long-distance nationalist. He concludes (ibid.) by stating:

> For while technically a citizen of the state in which he comfortably lives, but to which he may feel little attachment, he finds it tempting to play identity politics by participating (via propaganda, money, weapons, any way but voting) in the conflicts of his imagined *Heimat* – now only fax-time away. But this citizenshipless participation is inevitably non-responsible – our hero will not have to answer for, or pay the price of, the long-distance politics he undertakes. He is also easy prey for shrewd political manipulators in his *Heimat*.

The problem of long-distance politics in Anderson's quotation delineates the interest and scope of this study. In most cases, Croatians and Slovenians in Australia who have been holders of dual citizenship have been encouraged to assume the role of long-distance participants at the elections taking place in Croatia and Slovenia. Homeland political establishments use them as players in their political games. While such long-distance ballot participation is nothing extraordinary (the British Prime Minister Tony Blair is one of the more recent politicians to learn about the usefulness of a diaspora vote) it nevertheless harbours the potential for large-scale political manipulation.

Long-distance voting should not be confused with long-distance nationalism, although the former can be used as a vehicle for the latter. Modern long-distance interactions can range from the most personal exchange to the most decisive political intervention and it would be wrong to reduce long-distance nationalism to such easily quantifiable phenomena. While the menacing potential of long-distance nationalism has seldom been realised, the question of accountability and quasi-responsibility deserves critical attention.

One does not need to go very far to find examples of such individual long-distance nationalists. For example, at the beginning of 1998, Valdas Adamkus of the United States was elected president of Lithuania, although he has no political experience. The long-time leader of the Greek political scene, Andreas Papandreou, conveniently changed from a Greek to an American citizen only to pledge his utmost loyalties to his Greekness when opportunities arose. A wealthy Serb, Milan Panić, the one-time Prime Minister of Serbia, underwent a similar transition.

In this context, the successful career of Gojko Šušak, a Croatian migrant to Canada, should be mentioned. He left Yugoslavia in 1968 and was heavily involved in Canadian-Croatian affairs and some smear campaigns against the communist regime in Yugoslavia, the most infamous one involving a piglet with the painted inscription 'Tito' (Graham 1997/98). After conducting a series of successful fund-raising campaigns to help the election victory of the Croatian Democratic Union (HDZ, *Hrvatska demokratska zajednica*) in his homeland in 1990, he returned to Croatia in the same year. Upon his return, he became a member of the Croatian government, and between 1990 and 1991 he was Minister of Emigration. In 1991 he became Minister of Defence and in 1993 the vice-president of the leading HDZ. He remained in the position of Defence Minister until his death in May 1998 (Anonymous 1998a). A recent issue of Canadian *Saturday Night* proclaimed Šušak to be one of Croatia's "ugliest strongmen" (Graham 1997/98, p. 56). He was often considered to be the Croatian president's right hand man with enormous influence among Croatians in Herzegovina, the province which is currently a constituent part of the Bosnia and Herzegovina federation, but is predominantly populated by Croats. Herzegovinian territory plays an ambiguous role in the relationship between Bosnia and Herzegovina and the Croatian political leadership. The Croatian government is often accused of undermining the territorial integrity of the Bosnian and Herzegovinian federation.

Šušak was one of the key players in the so-called informal Herzegovinian lobby in Croatia. In fact, during his maiden speech in the Croatian parliament in 1990, he blatantly exclaimed that he was born in "Široki Brijeg, Croatia", although to everyone's knowledge the place he was referring to was part of Bosnia and Herzegovina (Lovrić 1998, p. 3). The Croatian president Tudjman and Gojko Šušak were very close confidants, and Šušak was always held to be the second man in the country. Šušak's death in 1998 was used for official glorification of his supposed heroism. Critics of Tudjman's regime, however, used the example of Šušak's success as an indication of the corruption of the current political regime in Croatia, as well as to criticise the supposed existence of the right-wing Herzegovinian lobby in the Croatian government. Pro-government sources mythologised Šušak's contribution to Croatian independence. The following famous last words were even attributed to him: "I do not regret dying, because I have experienced something that I never dreamed of!", referring to Croatian independence (Ivanković 1998, p. 1). Indeed, these are the perfect words for a long-distance nationalist and they were accompanied with a compatible editorial comment: "These were the last words of Gojko Šušak, the Croatian Defence Minister. The last words of a patriot, proving that nothing should be expected from the Homeland, but that everything should be given to it. The Homeland is to be served!" (ibid.).

But, of course, not every career of long-distance nationalists is blessed with blissful success and crowned with a sense of immortality. There are stories of others who failed, such as Kim Kethavy, the United States millionaire who was a Cambodian presidential candidate, or Rein Taagepera who, although an American citizen, ran for the Estonian presidency, and the Canadian Pole, Stanislav Tyminski, who ran for the presidency of Poland (c.f. Anderson 1994, pp. 324-5). Jože Bernik, another American citizen, a resident of Chicago and an unsuccessful candidate in the late 1997 presidential elections in Slovenia, needs to be added to this list. Last but not least, the strategic omnipresence and importance of American Jewish advisers to the Israeli Netanyahu government are also paradigmatic of these developments (Colvin 1996).

Australia seems to provide no less fertile ground for nurturing long-distance nationalists. The best known player in this long-distance game is an Australian billionaire, Joe Gutnick, who is thought to have decided the 1996 Israeli election by mobilising the ultra-orthodox Jewish vote with his one million US dollar donation to support Netanyahu. By simultaneously supporting the main Australian political parties, he stirs up little dissent in Australia.[4] The Australian Prime Minister's office says that as a private citizen, Mr Gutnick has the right to decide how he spends his money (Yallop and Rabinovich 1997). All the above mentioned individuals have two things in common: political ambition and the financial capabilities to afford such long-distance extravaganza.

E.P. Thompson (1991, p. 8) once famously remarked that class is neither a structure nor a category but rather something which in fact happens in human relationships. I feel tempted to say something similar about the study of long-distance nationalism which must not be reduced to a study of well-known long-distance nationalists. The above examples of prominent political figures such as Adamkus, Papandreou, Šušak and others who drew their nationalist inspiration and political ambition from the comfortable distance of the exile and/or the diaspora are examples of long-distance nationalism at its extreme. Their examples are indicative of a much wider pattern of long-distance exchanges between diasporas and homelands, although specific contexts may vary considerably. But importantly, this is not the whole picture with which a student of long-distance nationalism should be concerned.

In this study I shall use a rather different approach, focusing instead on ordinary individuals and local diaspora organisations. This broader focus is useful as it reveals that long-distance nationalism is not something that happens and stubbornly persists in well-known individuals only. It is – and most often so – a group-based phenomenon which pervades both public and private spheres of life.

The objective of this book is not so much to prove the existence of long-distance nationalism, but rather to show some possible ways in which the genealogy and manifestations of the phenomenon of long-distance nationalism and nationalists could be looked at. One needs to consider the multifaceted nature of nationalisms and the sense in which they are always a part of a broader and heavily symbolic discursive field. Nowhere is this multifaceted nature of nationalism more obvious than in the study of nationalism among migrants and their children. In a migrant diaspora context, nationalism often assumes a variety of forms, but it is precisely this variation and multilayeredness – on a spectrum from public to private – that this book endeavours to analyse.

3   Methodology and research design

3.1   Historical note

The decision to analyse Croatians and Slovenians in Australia is as arbitrary as it is well suited to the task ahead. They are the two neighbouring ethnic groups, which were united under monarchic Serbian rule (1918-1941) and later shared the single, unified state of Yugoslavia (1945-91).[5] The period of the Second World War represented the disruption of this institutional continuity. During that time, the Slovenian territory was divided up by German, Italian and Hungarian occupying forces and Slovenians found themselves on different sides of the political and military spectrum: some joined the pro-fascist *Domobranci* (Home Guard) forces, others chose to join the communist-dominated partisans, while others still were forcibly conscripted into the German army. Croatia, on the other hand, was proclaimed an Independent State in 1941 under Ante Pavelić's Ustasha government which was supported by both Italy and Germany. Obviously, not all Croatians supported Pavelić's regime, and considerable numbers of Croatians joined Tito's partisans. Although I cannot provide the reader with an exhaustive and comprehensive overview of the Second World War situation, I shall return to these questions in the following chapters due to the significance of this period for the context of this study.

The ethnic composition of Croatia and Slovenia is worth noting at this point. In comparative terms, Slovenia is more ethnically homogeneous than Croatia, which has had a substantial Serbian minority. The ethnic composition of the latter has changed in favour of increased ethnic homogeneity since 1991. In 1953 the total population of Slovenia was

1,965,986 and 96.5 per cent of the population was Slovenian. The number of non-Slovenians had been increasing steadily up until 1991 and the measure of ethnic homogeneity of the nation fell from its height of 96.5 per cent in 1953 to 87.84 per cent in 1991 (Anonymous 1992, p. 7, Zavod Republike Slovenije za statistiko 1992, p. 7). Demographic multiculturalism in Slovenia is thus steadily on the increase. In Croatia meanwhile, the proportion of Croatians during the post-Second World War period has hovered at around 80 per cent, standing at 78.1 per cent at the 1991 census (Republički zavod za statistiku Republike Hrvatske 1991). The religious affiliation of residents of Slovenia has also become increasingly diverse. According to the 1991 census, the distribution of three major religious categories in the Republic of Slovenia was as follows: 71.3 per cent were Catholics, 2.38 per cent Christian Orthodox and 1.51 per cent followers of Islam (Zavod Republike Slovenije za statistiko 1992, p. 5). The Croatian 1991 census showed that of a population totalling 4,760,344, Catholics made up 76.5 per cent, Orthodox Christians 11.1 per cent and followers of Islam 1.2 per cent (Republički zavod za statistiku 1992).

3.2 Sample characteristics

I agree with the criticism which Herbert Gans (1979, p. 5) directed towards Catholic ethnic intellectuals in America, whose writings have been 'nostalgic' and devoted exclusively to the celebration of migrant cultures. A serious theoretical discourse has to move away from this celebratory practice.

This study utilises a considerable amount of ethnographic material and it weaves together narrative and analysis. The main goal is to elaborate on the dynamics which potentially leads to the construction of ethno-nationalist diasporic identities. As stated earlier, the question of long-distance nationalism is explored through an attempt to understand the micro-processes which may contribute towards the development of an explanatory model that identifies the conditions which create and sustain long-distance nationalism. Obviously, it is individuals as members of specific ethnic collectivities who play a central role in this respect.

Acknowledging the difficulties in defining the second generation (Vasta 1992), I employ the category 'second generation' as an umbrella term. It comprises both those individuals who were born in Australia to overseas-born parents and those born overseas but whose education was mainly acquired in Australia. Those who arrived in Australia as formed adult personalities are defined as first generation migrants. Ethnicity assigned to second generation subjects in this study is strictly self-ascribed, although they all have at least one parent born in the homeland.

The present study is based on ethnographic research, the core of which is based on semi-structured, confidential interviews with 31 second generation individuals of Croatian and 30 second generation individuals of Slovenian backgrounds living in Adelaide, South Australia. The Slovenian sample consisted of the same number of males and females while the Croatian sample consisted of 14 females and 17 males. The interviews with the second generation were conducted between 1991 and 1994. A snowballing technique was used in the selection of respondents. All respondents were children of post-Second World War migrants to Australia and their ages ranged from 20-43 (there was only one respondent who was under twenty years of age).

Information obtained from second generation respondents was supplemented by the inclusion of interviews with 50 individuals who played a significant role in the Australian-Croatian and Australian-Slovenian settings. These individuals, of whom a few were second generation, provided me with specific information and many of them have had (or still have) a say in decision-making processes: religious figures, presidents of the so-called ethnic clubs, and presidents of political organisations. These individuals were interviewed not only in Adelaide but also in Melbourne and Sydney.

There are some other characteristics of both samples which are of considerable relevance. In terms of place of birth, an overwhelming proportion (90 per cent) of second generation Slovenian respondents were born in Australia, whereas Croatian second generation respondents were almost equally likely to be born in Croatia as in Australia. This is also a reflection of substantial migratory movements from Croatia to Australia during the 1960s and early 1970s. A comparison of the marital status of Croatian and Slovenian respondents shows that Croatian respondents are more likely to be married. Statistically, 65 per cent of Croatian married respondents were married to fellow Croatians. Comparatively, none of the Slovenian respondents was married to fellow Slovenians at the time of the research. In terms of religious affiliation, the vast majority of both Croatian and Slovenian second generation respondents stated Catholicism as their religion. Croatian respondents were more likely to state that political reasons contributed to their parents' decision to emigrate.

In this book, every effort has been taken to disguise to the greatest possible extent the identity of respondents and/or informants. To achieve this I refrained from coding respondents in this study. Quotations which are prefaced solely by a statement revealing ethnic identity of Croatian or Slovenian respondents' are from second generation individuals. Depending on the context, I occasionally reveal their gender identity. When referring to individuals who played an active role in their respective communities but were not part of the second generation sample, their status is clarified.

3.3 The size and representativeness of the research setting

This research attempts to surmount the methodological difficulties which arise from treating ethnic groups as organic homogenous communities, rather than as groups stratified by power, and composed of individuals with different interests.

The fact that I was a 'native' of Slovenia and an 'outsider' (an overseas student) was something which impacted on my work in a positive sense. To second generation Slovenian respondents I was quite often 'the one whom they can tell' (because of my relatively young age) and the one who would not object to their criticisms of the state of affairs in what they mostly defined as an established 'Slovenian community'. Also, to many second generation Croatian respondents I was a 'natural ally': as a Slovenian I was not one of them (which meant I would have difficulties spreading the gossip) and yet I was perceived as 'a guy from the right side' (for my ethnicity was not defined as antagonistic to theirs). For these reasons I was also able to discuss their attitudes towards other ethnic groups which they considered to be the common enemies/antagonists of both Croatians and Slovenians.

But all of this does not mean that there was no distance between the research subjects and myself. The first generation Slovenians often perceived me as being somewhat distant. Because of the different periods in which we left Slovenia we did not share the same historical experiences and historically conditioned attitudes. For some, I was not perceived as equal because of my education. These factors meant there was a significant social and emotional distance between us, particularly at the very beginning. A glaring example of this distance was an event in the Slovenian Club, South Australia in February 1993. On one of my visits to the Club I was verbally offered physical assistance to immediately leave the Club's premises by a member who was soon afterwards – for apparently unrelated reasons – promoted to the highest echelons of the management of the Club. This verbal encounter was accompanied by comments referring to 'intruder' Slovenians who had recently arrived from Slovenia.

It is next to impossible to estimate the number of Croatians and Slovenians in Australia. The main reason for this is what statisticians call 'inclusion' and 'exclusion' errors in statistics. According to Lieberson and Santi (1985), the *inclusion error* on the one hand "occurs to the degree that the nativity category includes people who belong to an ethnic group other than the one presumably represented". Their example is Finland where the largest single ethnic group are Finns. Therefore, a naïve understanding that Finland is a country of Finns excludes other smaller ethnic groups, such as Swedes. The *exclusion error* on the other hand, "occurs when first- or second-generation members of a given ethnic group are not born in the surrogate country. Such people will therefore be missed when the nativity data are used to describe the ethnic group" (ibid., p. 37). Australian censuses have until the mid-1990s operated with the undifferentiated birthplace category, 'Yugoslavia'. They have managed systematically to conceal the numeric strength of ethnic groups represented by this hegemonic category and thus have contributed to the inclusion error.[6] I have attempted to produce a rough estimate of the numbers of both groups. By taking into account both official statistics (Australian Bureau of Statistics 1993a, 1993b, 1994a, 1994b, Bureau of Immigration Research 1990, Castles 1990, Hugo 1989) and estimations made by representatives of diaspora organisations in Australia, I would like to propose the following estimate:

Table 1.1
Australia and South Australia: estimation of the number of Croatians and Slovenians

	Croatians	Slovenians
South Australia*	7,000	2,000
Australia	100-110,000	25,000

*   The biggest settlement area in South Australia for both groups is Adelaide where most of the research was conducted.[7]

An ethnographic study of this format makes no claim to be representative of the overall situation among the members of Croatian and Slovenian diaspora in Australia. I would, however, like to suggest that responses by respondents in this study seem generally reflective of the overall attitudes among individuals of Croatian and Slovenian backgrounds in Australia.

3.4   Fieldwork update

While the fieldwork and interviews with Australian respondents was completed in mid-1994, I have continued to research the Croatian and Slovenian transition to democracy. While the reader of this text will find some very recent theoretical references in this work, it must be acknowledged that the fieldwork settings in Adelaide, Sydney and Melbourne have not been revisited and that the situation might have changed since. My recent (December 1997 – January 1998) fieldwork in Croatia and Slovenia was particularly instructive as it made me realise how quickly the processes described in this book – from a homeland perspective – are changing. This is particularly the case with my elaboration on right-wing diaspora party politics. It was comforting, however, to realise that my original fieldwork notes envisaged such developments.

The second generation Slovenians in Australia have almost no opportunity to become engaged in the politics of their ethnic homeland and comparatively much less opportunity to involve themselves with homeland-based political parties, compared with second generation Croatians. In fact, Slovenian political parties have no Australian branches. Only a few instances of political activity have occurred in the recent past, for example when providing financial and moral support to *Demos* (an anti-Communist political coalition) prior to the first free elections in Slovenia, held in 1990. This activity was to a great extent limited to first generation Slovenian migrants. In contrast, there are many Croatian political parties with branches in Australia.

The most significant Croatian political party is the HDZ which has been the leading party in Croatia since the first free elections in 1990. The HDZ party has also dominated the politics of the diaspora since approximately 1989. This is strongly enforced by the continuing dominance of the HDZ in the homeland. Two other notable and disputed Croatian political parties in Australia, active during the period of fieldwork (1991-1994), were the Croatian Liberation Movement (HOP, *Hrvatski oslobodilački pokret*) and the then-emerging Croatian Rights Party (HSP, *Hrvatska stranka prava*). While the HDZ assumes a boldly central position in the political spectrum, representing the centre-right political camp, the HOP and the HSP belong to the far right of the political spectrum.

The role which the above parties have played in diaspora politics since I embarked on fieldwork is clearly illustrative of the constant shift in power relations in the Australian-Croatian setting. The HOP is a party which has made its presence strongly felt through the three decades since the 1960s and even earlier. When I embarked on fieldwork I was often told that the HOP represents a kind of a 'paper tiger' which is vocal but marginal. I could not completely verify such claims at the time, although it was clear that the HOP was in demise both due to internal tension and the ageing of its membership as well as because the HDZ started to co-opt some of the HOP's political radicalism and ideological militancy. The HOP in present-day Croatia is a completely marginal political faction, headed by Ante Pavelić's son-in-law and supported by a few enthusiasts. In this study, the HOP represents the very prototype of right-wing Croatian political radicalism in the diaspora. It is now increasingly marginal in its impact on diaspora networks but was less so at the time when I embarked on fieldwork in the early 1990s.

The HSP's emergence coincided with the transition to a plural political system in Croatia. The idea was that at the moment of establishment of Croatian independence, the HOP would cease to exist as it was established to keep alive the idea of an independent Croatia while Croatia existed as a part of the Yugoslav federation. Ironically, with Croatian independence renewed in 1991, the HSP did emerge to continue the HOP's legacy but the HOP itself refused to disappear.

In direct contrast to the HOP, the HSP is a notable political faction in Croatia. It basically rallies the radical right-wing aspirations of Croatian voters and is nominally highly supportive of the Croatian diaspora and the aspirations of Croatians in Herzegovina. It is interesting that the HSP never made a significant impact in Australian-Croatian settings. The reason for this is to be sought in the HDZ's domination as well as in the fact that the HDZ in the diaspora is more right-wing than the HDZ in the homeland. This is how the HDZ manages to assimilate the right-wing vote.

Due to ties which link diasporas and homelands, it is impossible to understand the processes in the diaspora without taking into account developments in the homeland. At this stage I would like to mention some recent issues characterising Croatian and Slovenian homelands.

Croatia still tends to be associated with one of the Balkan's hot-spots. The unfavourable economic situation, the lack of success in the international political arena in terms of joining international associations are coupled with the general perception of political nepotism in the Croatian government and charges of quasi-democracy. Slovenia can be perceived as comparatively more successful and it certainly has a better position in international relations. It successfully lobbied and subsequently obtained a non-permanent seat in the UN Security Council, signed an associational agreement with the European Union and is a full member of the WTO and CEFTA. Slovenia is nevertheless to be seen as a so-called transitional democracy with some characteristic social, economic and political problems.

The past still looms large in contemporary Slovenian political debates and the society still seems to be polarised on the issue of Nazi collaborationism during the Second World War. But importantly, this does not seem to paralyse the actions of the state. Comparatively speaking, the Croatian past seems to have constant present-day political implications, including the question of Ustasha (1941-45) genocide against target groups of Serbs, Gypsies and Communists. During the completion of this manuscript, Dinko Šakić, the second in charge of the infamous Ustasha concentration camp, Jasenovac, was deported from Argentina to Croatia and has since been put on trial. The question of the past which haunts present-day Croatia is aggravated by the very ambiguous attitude towards the Ustasha movement of the Croatian president, Franjo Tudjman, a former Yugoslav communist general turned historian. In his major work (Tudjman 1989) he tried – among other things – to minimise the atrocities of the Ustasha regime. In a sense, contemporary Croatian politics and (varying interpretations of) Croatian history go firmly hand in hand. There are, for example, strong indications that Tudjman's traditionally rather soft position on the Ustasha movement represented the main hurdle in the process of the establishment of diplomatic ties between Israel and Croatia (Alborghetti 1998b). To all of this one should add the very ambiguous attitudes of the present-day political establishment in Croatia towards the question of the future of Bosnia and Herzegovina. Again, just before finalisation of this manuscript, president Tudjman made some comments pertaining to the future of Bosnia and Herzegovina which prompted the US administration to request further explanation of the matter (Alborghetti 1998a).

But equally burdening, detrimental and as ambiguous as the question of Croatia's past are the charges of political nepotism aimed at President Tudjman and his leadership of the HDZ. Tudjman's family successes coincided with his ascent to power. One of his sons had been chief of the Croatian Secret Service for several years up until April 1998. His daughter is the owner of a chain of shops, and his younger son is a successful businessman who allegedly has some lucrative business deals with the Croatian army. But the family's recent success is not limited to the generation of the president's children as one of his grandchildren is (despite being in his twenties) president of one of the strongest private banks in Croatia. [8]

The political relations between Croatia and neighbouring Slovenia are constructive, although there are numerous unresolved issues. These range from conflicts over responsibility for the Slovenia-based nuclear power station to the unfinalised maritime borders between the two independent states. However, the most significant difference between Croatia and Slovenia is the extent to which their respective present-day national affairs are embedded in discussions about the past. The occasional disputes in Slovenia about the supposed corrupt morals of those who favour the legacy of either pro-communist partisans or the pro-Nazi Home Guard seem to be highly topical, although an entirely internal matter. However, the process of reconciliation with the past in Croatia is a hotly contested matter which regularly transgresses the national framework and has numerous international implications. But apart from the question of the past, there is a whole variety of pragmatic issues which the Croatian state faces today and which have a direct external referent. One such issue is the return of Serbian refugees to Croatia and also the above mentioned ambiguity of the Croatian state in respect to the resolution of the question of Bosnia and Herzegovina.

4 The war and its impact on the outcome of this research

My embarking on the research for this study almost coincided with the outbreak of the military conflict in what was then Yugoslavia. Both Croatia and Slovenia went through an armed struggle to achieve their independent statehood in 1991, although the casualties in the case of Croatia were incomparably higher than in the case of Slovenia. It is estimated that the armed struggle in the territories of the former Yugoslavia between 1992-95 cost 200,000 lives. While the loss of human lives went into tens of thousands on the Croatian, Muslim and Serbian sides, there were only several dozen – several dozen too many, that is – casualties of war during the 10-day armed struggle in Slovenia in June and July 1991.

It is certainly true that the conflict heightened the sense of ethno-nationalism among the respondents. As the bulk of empirical research was undertaken between mid-1991 and mid-1994, the impact of the war was gradually but persistently and obviously receding. Consequently, I wish to argue that the war in the ethnic homeland is to be considered as a process which heightened certain types of actions and emotions in the research setting. It did not, however, create responses which would not be imaginable/possible before the outbreak of the war, albeit on a less intensive scale. For example, the Croatian diasporic construction of the Serbs has generally been negative – this negative construction was already in existence when the war started and was *not* invented anew because of the war. Similarly, before the outbreak of the war in 1991, people of Croatian descent who identified themselves as Yugoslav were perceived as 'traitors' of everything Croatian by a vast majority of Australian-Croatians. After the conflict began, one could continue to observe this antagonism between 'Yugoslavs' and those who called themselves 'Croatians'. At the same time, the question of Yugoslav identity, which will be discussed later in this book, has never been acutely problematic for Slovenians in Australia, neither before nor after the conflict.

There is very little doubt that any group of second generation individuals and their parents would be affected by such dramatic and tragic events in the homeland but it could be expected that the intensity of these feelings would vary between different groups. It should come as no surprise then that differences between Croatians and Slovenians were considerable. The differences are not to be attributed simply to the fact that the war in Slovenia was rather episodic, although time-span "is crucial in considering the effects of war on ethnic cohesion" (Smith 1981, p. 391). The very social and political infrastructure of Australian-Slovenian diaspora organisations as opposed to Australian-Croatian ones was different. Thus, in comparative terms, to mobilise the former, a far greater effort by its members (of the second generation in particular) would have been required.

The Slovenian first and second generation respondents were not affected by the recent war to the extent that their Croatian counterparts were. Nevertheless, as a result of the military conflict, the second generation respondents commonly referred to their pride in their Slovenian origin, which was "stronger than ever as the result of unfortunate aggression". As one second generation Slovenian respondent put it: "You become more proud of [your background]. Now I certainly don't call myself a Yugoslav but I am probably more inclined to say I am Slovenian. People now know where it is. I feel proud, I really do."

A Slovenian male whose father plays a rather important role in the Australian-Slovenian diaspora commented: "[The recent war] in Slovenia doesn't worry me that much. No, I don't get upset if things go wrong or excited if things go well. ... I don't feel any obligation to help". Another Slovenian respondent commented that she was concerned when the war broke out in Slovenia and that she rang her relatives after many years to see if they were safe and well. But she was surprised because: "When we talked they hardly mentioned the war. They said they are all right, healthy, that I shouldn't worry and then wanted to know when I am going to visit them." However, her workmates and friends in Australia expressed "sympathies for what was happening [in Slovenia]".

Around two-thirds of Slovenian second generation respondents did say they were emotionally affected by the war, although mostly as passive observers (see Table 1.2). The most striking feature which emerged from a comparison of the Croatian and Slovenian samples is that the majority of Slovenian respondents managed to distance themselves from the situation overseas. Whereas only 10 per cent of second generation Slovenians from the sample took active steps to support Slovenians overseas, over 80 per cent of Croatians were moved to some kind of action (typically fund-raising or lobbying).

Certainly, none of the Croatian respondents expressed anything similar to the following comment made by a Slovenian respondent in relation to the question: "Do you feel more Slovenian after the war?" The response was: "I am proud that they made a good show with the war, didn't they?" None of the Croatian respondents interviewed expressed the kind of insensitivity reflected in this quotation, although it would be wrong to say this was a prevalent opinion at the level of Slovenian diaspora organisations. Concrete deeds, action, aid as well as prayer became the most common responses to the war in Croatia. Respondents often referred to a dramatic intensification of the attitudes of Australian-Croatians: "This war in Croatia nevertheless positively affects our Croatian community here. For example, the atheist gets Christened – I can see this."

These feelings of support for those in the homeland were so intense that many respondents talked about their guilt at enjoying the freedom of life in Australia. A young Croatian woman explained:

> You just feel guilty if you have a good time because you know that your own people are suffering. There were a few functions that we had to go to. My husband just said that he really doesn't feel like it – he'd rather stay at home. One girl said to me: "If I go out and buy a special dress I feel guilty because I am spending on a luxury while the people back there go through hardship."

That the war had an impact on second generation individuals is undeniable as the following comments from different respondents indicate:

> [My brother] was always in political disharmony with my father. Since this trouble started in Croatia and everything, he is absolutely opposite from what he has been for his whole life. He is reading Croatian newspapers, taping the news to see what happened, visits my father and they talk about the war. I keep saying: "Bloody you, what happened to you?"

> When I watch the news I either end up angry or in tears as I watch those lying heathens in Belgrade and see what they are doing to my people and my country. The thought of my relatives and friends being in danger angers me.
> They are only out there acting like barbarians destroying and massacring people for their own blood-thirsty satisfaction. As the saying goes 'Justice wins in the end' and so I firmly believe the Croatian nation will be justified if there really is a God in Heaven. So as you can see yes I am affected by the events.

A.D. Smith (1981, p. 378) wrote in relation to Simmel's contribution to the study of the interrelationship between conflict and a group's cohesion: "Not only does conflict accentuate the cohesion of an existing unit; it also mobilises its members, bringing together persons who have otherwise nothing to do with each other." If anything, the recent war encouraged a sense of *Gemeinschaft* among Croatians. Central to this re-creation and re-affirmation of a sense of belonging was the visibility of suffering of the people of their own ethnic stock made possible by global telecommunication networks. Members of diaspora populations are absent witnesses of the tragedies taking place in their homelands (e.g. Constantinides 1977, Kolar-Panov 1996). However, it is important to resist the temptation to fetishise the importance of modern communication technologies and their impact on the identity formation of modern diaspora populations and therefore to slide into both technological and social determinism (Skrbiš 1998).

It is the individuals' awareness of the suffering of the members of their ethnic group in conjunction with their identification with that group which makes them overtly mobilisable. One respondent's comment touched exactly upon this problem:

> The war unified a lot of different Croatian groupings. It made me think: what should I do regarding this war? Rather than being helpless, watching the events on TV, it has made me become far more active within the community, more than I have been for a number of years. My cousin actually said he feels guilty that he is not fighting over there. I could say the same thing, except I know it takes more than just guns to fight the war.

Another Croatian respondent observed:

> I realised during my visit [to Croatia in 1991] what the fear of war is all about. I never felt it here before, the fear of oppression, this is a feeling I have never ever experienced; the kind of emotions you never ever have to call on in Australia. You know... your home is being attacked; it is easy to go on and kill someone whereas before I never thought about killing someone. I couldn't imagine it. But there I could. Ugly sort of feelings.

Not one single Slovenian respondent considered taking up arms to support the Slovenian independent nationhood. However, three out of 31 Croatian second generation respondents, male and female, reported they seriously considered the idea of either taking up arms to fight or of helping Croatia on humanitarian grounds. One of them joined the Croatian Army. It is impossible to estimate the numbers of those second generation Croatian individuals who really went to fight. Although this is not a taboo subject, no-one really wanted to talk about the numbers involved. The Croatian president Tudjman (Ministarstvo povratka i useljeništva 1997, p. 7) nevertheless openly acknowledged that "for many young Croatian women and Croatian men who were born abroad the first encounter with the Homeland was the departure to the battlefields stretching from Vukovar and Gospić to Dubrovnik."

As one first generation migrant and highly distinguished member of the Australian-Croatian diaspora commented:

A substantial number of youngsters wanted to go over there to fight. We said it would be better if they stay here, work and each month contribute 100 dollars for Croatia. With that money, they could feed one soldier. ... As far as I know there weren't many people who went to fight over there. But their decision to go has to be welcomed. It is their democratic right and I am sure they would have fought for Australia as well if it was attacked. ... You have to understand that some of them go there because of adventure.

How is such a difference between the samples possible? The short duration of Slovenia's involvement in hostilities compared with that of Croatia is only part of the answer. Although emotionally disturbing to some of them, the war made hardly any observable impact on the second generation Slovenians. The second generation respondents perceived Slovenia generally as their parents' country: "I don't feel a part of it. It is not my homeland, Australia is my homeland. But I feel for my parents". Or as another Slovenian respondent commented: "I paid some attention to the war in Slovenia because it was in the papers every day... but again that was not a huge change for me. I think that Slovenians became more aware of themselves here". And the final example: "I'd love to know a lot more about what is going on in Yugoslavia. I don't really get to find out much about what is going on. And plus, I have got two dogs, I am never home".

In complete contrast to Croatians, about one third of second generation Slovenian respondents perceived the war in their parents' homeland as nothing more than a World News bulletin. The degree of intensity of responses respondents showed to the war is elaborated in the following table:

Table 1.2
Reactions of second generation respondents to the war in their ethnic homelands

	CROATIANS	SLOVENIANS
Extreme concern – verbal commitment to go overseas and help/fight	3	0
Expressions of a high degree of concern and subsequently higher degree of community involvement	23	3
Emotionally disturbing	2	18
No specific interest – interest reduced to world news affair	3	9

The discrepancy between the both samples is obvious with Croatians appearing far more mobilisable and proactive in their commitment to their homeland. This reveals an important distinction between the two groups which will be further elaborated on in the next chapter. But at this point I wish to stress that this discrepancy is a reflection of already stronger homeland-centred political sentiments among Croatians in Australia before the recent war. If the war in Slovenia had been prolonged, this would probably have brought about a change of some attitudes among Slovenians. However, the lack of homeland-centered political sentiments among Slovenians in Australia prior to the 1991 war, means that the ground was far less fertile for subsequent war mobilisation in comparison with Croatians.

5 Plan of the book

In this study I dismissed the conventional idea of presenting the life of ethnic groups purely in terms of formal structures and organisations. My approach focuses more on the ethno-cultural identity perceptions and relationships entered into by second generation Croatians and Slovenians.

Because of the centrality of the narrative about the two diaspora groupings, little attention is given to the ever-evolving changes of the immigration policies in Australia and the overall change of attitudes towards immigrants. I have no intention of denying their significance and the important shifts which did take place in this respect. There is a great deal of history to be told about the post-Second World War immigration and settlement processes in Australia as well as specificities within this broader pattern. While failing to satisfy the historian, I wish to emphasise three important shifts in Australian post-Second War immigration and settlement practices which in one way or another affect the argument in this book.

The first shift took place in the immediate post-Second World War era which was still deeply immersed in the White Australia Policy and guided by Minister Arthur Calwell's (1972) idea of 'populate or perish'. This instigated a large, although strictly regulated, influx of migrants from European countries (with rather refined preferences for Northern over Southern Europeans). It is in this period of the late 1940s to the mid-1950s that migrants from Croatia and Slovenia, previously scattered around refugee camps in Europe, started to arrive. The grip of the White Australia Policy and the overt assimilationist rhetoric started to show signs of easing throughout the 1960s and the diversification of the demographic composition of the intake was revealing of this change.

It was not until 1973 that the second important shift emerged. This was marked by the official abolition of the White Australia Policy and the formal and bipartisan endorsement of the policy of multiculturalism (Viviani 1992, Jupp 1988a). These two closely interrelated events profoundly influenced the following two decades by providing support for and encouraging a range of processes aimed at a cohesive yet diverse society. Migrant groups largely benefited from this change in the political climate, and Croatians and Slovenians were no exception. The government provided a range of services which aimed at enabling migrant groups in Australia to nurture – however superficially at times – their ethno-cultural distinctiveness. Despite the sporadic dissent of the government's multicultural rhetoric (Blainey 1984, Rimmer 1991), it was not until 1996 that the political climate changed considerably and decisively.

It can now be argued that the 1996 Australian elections, which saw the transfer of powers from the Australian Labor Party to the coalition between the Liberal Party and the Australian National Party, signified the third shift in policies and political attitudes concerning migration and settlement. These changes to a large extent mark the abolition of policies endorsed during the multicultural period through the rather heavy-handed rhetoric of politicians of Pauline Hanson's ilk.[9] Although it is too early to predict future developments with any degree of certainty, it seems that Australia might experience a marked increase in anti-foreigner and anti-migrant rhetoric and political action.

It is not exactly clear in which way different migration policies have impacted upon the intensity of nationalism pertaining to homelands among migrants. Further research into this area is required, although it is possible that ethno-national feelings are not directly affected by a host country's migration policies. After all, long-distance nationalists are to be found in countries with very different migration policies – eg. *Gastarbeiter*-oriented Germany as opposed to permanent settlement-oriented Canada and Australia.

The above is a bare-boned sketch of historical and contemporary circumstances which have impacted upon Croatians and Slovenians in Australia. The significance of more specific historical factors will be further elaborated in *Chapter 2*. The chapter begins with an overview of the resettlement processes of the post-Second World War European refugees with particular reference to Croatians and Slovenians. It is argued that understanding these resettlement patterns can help us to explain the reasons for the current strength in ethno-national identification among Croatian and Slovenian populations in Australia. Specific attention is given to diasporic conceptualisations of the homeland and the way in which migrants' distance from the homeland in time and space impact on its construction. It is also shown that the links that exist between diaspora individuals and the homeland – regardless of the generation – can be revealing of many issues, including the intensity of ethno-national identification. I elaborate on such identification processes by revealing the extent to which the homeland is portrayed in a romantic fashion, abstracted from the complex political and economic realities. The question of return to the homeland turns out to be one of the central considerations in assessing the attraction of homeland to its diaspora populations. In this context the Croatian and Slovenian samples become highly differentiated, with Croatians espousing relatively strong links to the homeland and a desire to return. Representatives of the Slovenian sample revealed relatively limited and more-or-less symbolic links with the homeland. These differences between the samples are supported by an initial historical assessment of post-Second World War migration patterns.

Chapter 3 discusses the cohesion in diaspora settings. In Australia, the ethnic community is often – and to some extent misleadingly – applied when discussing ethnic groups of migrant origins. The idea of community in sociology commonly implies the promise which rarely manifests itself in reality and which raises a range of questions about the delineation of communal boundaries. Diaspora seems to be a more value-neutral term and therefore better suited to describing migrant settings. By making reference to Croatians and Slovenians, the chapter explores the prominence of tension (and conflict) which results from the generation gap, differing political beliefs, gossip and so on.

There is considerable evidence to suggest that historical and political developments, as well as responses to these developments, differ between diasporas and homelands. *Chapter 4* thus begins with a discussion of the mediation of information between the two settings and introduces the concepts of 'distant view' and 'sieve effect'. The distant view relates to the relatively static viewing of the homeland which encourages (often via diaspora elites) a selective receptivity in diaspora. It is shown how somewhat marginal developments in the homeland can be seen in diaspora as considerably magnified or as minimised. Diaspora settings are similarly more likely to allow and encourage the radical reinterpretation of history. The chapter later explores party politics in Croatian and Slovenian diaspora in Australia. Finally, the question of power and the utilisation of symbols in diaspora are discussed.

Chapter 5 discusses in detail the different ways in which respondents in this study perceive Others who are supposedly placed on opposing sides of the political and ethno-national divide. Some interesting differences between the two samples emerge again. Slovenians seem to be less preoccupied with the classification of the Other, whereas Croatians construct a variety of categories to serve this purpose.

The argument up to this point primarily focuses on those manifestations of ethno-nationalist politics that are easily noticeable. *Chapter 6*, however, takes this problem a little further and explores how ethno-national sentiments affect the intimacy of individuals. *Chapter 7* concludes the argument and makes some projective commentaries.

6   Notes

1   I define ethno-nationalism broadly as a form of ascriptive affiliation which may be associated with phenomena such as patriotism, chauvinism, ethno-centrism, linguistic nationalism, religious nationalism and xenophobia.

2   Gallipoli is a Turkish port where the British generals' attempt to lead the Allies through the Dardanelles (February 1915 – January 1916) failed miserably. The troops were composed mainly of Australian and New Zealand soldiers and the whole tragic episode is a cornerstone of the modern Australian republican movement.

3   For historical contextualisation of the concept of diaspora see also Gellner (1983, pp. 101-09), Smith, A.D. (1971, pp. 121-2) and Smith, A.D. (1986, pp. 114-19).

4   Mr Gutnick was a proud sponsor of the Liberal party until the second half of 1998. He made a much publicised switch in his preferences to the Australian Labor Party just before the federal election in October 1998.

5   There are very complex reasons leading towards the break-up of Yugoslavia in 1991, but it is not the aim of this book to discuss the underlying causes. For more information see Cohen (1993), Silber and Little (1995).

6   Inclusion error applied to the category Yugoslavia would mean that – strictly following its meaning – Yugoslavia is a country of Yugoslavs. This concept could possibly have been justified if this term had been used in a generic sense by most or all its inhabitants. In reality it was used as a means of positive ethnic self-ascription by a relatively small percentage of the population. The former Yugoslavia was a country where declared Yugoslavs lived, but they represented only a relatively small proportion of the total population – according to the 1981 Yugoslav census, only 5.76 per cent (Chamber of Economy of Slovenia 1988, p. 15, c.f. Sekulić, D. et al. 1994).

7   This is a relatively conservative estimate, although most probably more accurate than more generous estimations by some authors. Paric et al. (1997, p. 81), for example, claim that the overall number of Croatians in Australia is over 150,000 and most likely closer to 200,000.

8   The popularity of Tudjman in Croatia is relatively strong although some of his personal characteristics combined with the allegations of the corruptibility of his family tend to make headlines in the opposition press. His unadmitted fascination with the cult of Tito and his replication of some of his personality traits (attraction to Tito-style uniforms and life-style) makes him a popular target of satire (c.f. Letica 1998).

9   Pauline Hanson, the leader of the One Nation party, is 'famous' – among other things – for arguing against Aboriginal welfare provisions and continuous migrant intake.

2 History, homeland, nostalgia

In this chapter I explore the possibility that some collective characteristics of the groups migrating to Australia (e.g. migratory patterns, common experiences, etc.) had a significant effect on the nature of their settlement in the host society. All second generation participants in this study are descendants of migrants who arrived in Australia in the post-Second World War period. Many of these second generation respondents – in fact a majority – have links to the group of early post-Second World War Displaced Persons (DPs).

The category DP designated people who, rightly or wrongly, assumed that their return to their country of origin would result in their imprisonment and/or execution. It was not uncommon for DPs simply to want to get as far as possible from Europe. The resettlement of these DPs could provide an explanation for some crucial differences between the Croatian and Slovenian samples. Unfortunately, due to the absence of precise data it is very difficult to make fully substantiated statements on this topic.

One significant terminological clarification is in order. In this study I differentiate between DPs from the immediate post-Second World War period (from 1945 to approximately 1950) and other DPs who illegally crossed Yugoslav borders throughout the 1950s and up until the early 1960s and who claimed some political reason for their decision to escape. Numerous informants who escaped illegally in that latter period acknowledged that their motives were predominantly (but not necessary solely) economic. In short, they would face repatriation from the refugee camps in Austria and Italy if they failed to state political repression as the main contributing factor to their decision to flee the country. The illegal border crossings continued up until the early 1960s when Yugoslavia embarked on a series of economic reforms which resulted in a massive, controlled and legal emigration flow (Hoffman 1973, Schierup 1990, pp. 76-9, Woodward 1995). After the late 1960s most migrants to Australia can be roughly defined as economic migrants. The main exception is the migration of Croatians in the early 1970s as a result of the so-called Croatian Spring movement during which some liberal members of the Croatian Communist Party challenged the centralist policies of the Yugoslav government (Lendvai 1972, Bertsch 1973).

In any event, there is a considerable blurring of boundaries between economic and political reasons for migration. The existing literature tends to differentiate between *political* and *economic* migrants as if there was an unbridgeable gap between these two categories. Although I utilise the distinction between the 'political' and 'economic' migrants for explanatory reasons, I allow for the possibility that in many cases these two terms overlap to a considerable extent. In this chapter I will refer to DPs as those individuals whose refugee status was in some way related to the Second World War conflict. Other migrants will be defined as either economic or political, depending on the prevalent motivation for emigration.

1   The European post-Second World War refugee problem

The end of the Second World War, the victory over fascism and the attempts to re-establish the political order led to massive movements of the European population (Kay 1995). As Jean Martin (1965, p. 1) wrote, there were about twelve million DPs in Europe at the beginning of 1945. The overall shifts of the European population immediately after the war – mainly in East-Central Europe – involved more than 25 million individuals (Clouth and Salt 1976, p. 21). Post-Second World War refugees represented an extremely heterogeneous group made up of diverse ethnic backgrounds, political beliefs and individual fates: prisoners from concentration camps, political prisoners, civilian expellees, escapees from the East, and children born in camps. Among them were also defeated prisoners of war, known in American 'victorious' slang as '*kriegies*' (*Kriegsefangenen*) (c.f. Marrus 1985, p. 300). The vast majority of these people were resettled under various IRO (International Refugee Organisation) programs with the support of organisations such as UNRRA (United Nations Relief and Rehabilitation Organisation) and SHAEF (Supreme Headquarters Allied Expeditionary Force).

In the available statistics concerning refugees from the territory of Yugoslavia in the aftermath of the Second World War, the principle of nationality completely overrides the question of ethnic identity and gender. This relative statistical imprecision reflects the haste of the IRO and other administrators to proceed with the process of resettlement as quickly and as practically as possible.

At the end of the Second World War there were 229,000 people of so-called 'Yugoslav' origin who were cared for or repatriated by SHAEF in Germany, Austria and Czechoslovakia. There were also 160,000 'Yugoslavs' who were cared for or repatriated by the Soviet forces. 'Yugoslavs' were also the single largest group among the remaining DPs in Italy (17,558 at the time). There were also 248 'Yugoslavs' in Denmark, and 1,463 in Norway (Proudfoot 1957, pp. 159-61). In a short period of one year, the number of DPs fell substantially due to intensive resettlement programs which were designed to speed up the process of stabilisation in Europe. On the 30 September 1945 there were 124,618 'Yugoslavs' in European DPs camps (ibid., pp. 238-9). Holborn (1956, p. 197) reports that fifteen months later the number of individuals of 'Yugoslav nationality' in DP Camps in Germany, Austria and Italy had further dropped to 39,494.

It can be assumed that some DPs of so-called Yugoslav origin were forcibly mobilised men from Yugoslav territories within the German army.[1] The majority of these were later repatriated. IRO figures (ibid., pp. 361-2) show that during the period between 1 July 1942 – 31 December 1951, 6,870 refugees were repatriated to Yugoslavia from different IRO areas around the world, mostly Europe. It is impossible to estimate what proportion of DPs was made up of Croatian and Slovenian pro-axis defeated forces, such as Croatian Ustasha or Croatian and Slovenian Home Guard soldiers. What is certain, however, is that they comprised, along with natives of Estonia, Latvia, Lithuania, Poland, Czechoslovakia, Hungary and Soviet Ukraine, the group of *unrepatriables*, i.e. people who could not return to their home-countries due to the hostilities which they might encounter.[2] In fact, some sections of the pro-axis military formations which existed in Yugoslav territory in the intrawar period were forcibly repatriated by the British army and mercilessly massacred by the Yugoslav Army forces (Tolstoy 1986). According to official Croatian statistics, 111,000 Croatians were executed in the Austrian Bleiburg by the Yugoslav Army forces on 15 May 1945 (Anonymous, 1998c, p. 2). To put this in comparative terms, according to official statistics about 18,000 Slovenian DPs were generated in total following the collapse of Germany (Genorio 1993/94, p. 61).

Table 2.1 lists the major countries of destination for post-Second World War DPs whose last residence was Yugoslavia:

Table 2.1
The first four countries of destination for refugees with Yugoslav citizenship, 1 July 1947 – 31 December 1951

Country of destination	Number of people
Canada	9,828
Argentina	10,105
United States	17,213
Australia	23,350
TOTAL	60,496

Source: Extracted from Holborn L.W. (1956) *The International Refugee Organization*, Oxford University Press, London, p. 439.

As Table 2.1 shows, Australia, the United States, Argentina and Canada were the countries with the greatest intake of DPs, with Australia taking the largest number. The period from the late 1940s to the early 1950s in Australia coincided with the ambitious 'populate or perish' plan aimed at substantially increasing the population of the Australian continent (Calwell 1972, Jupp 1988a). The numbers of DPs accepted by the receiving countries varied as did the reasons for their acceptance which included the fear of unpopulated open and defenceless spaces (Australia), labour-market goals (United States, Canada) or a combination of these (Argentina). All receiving countries, however, implicitly or explicitly differentiated between 'desired' and 'undesired' migrants (Kay 1995, p. 156).

There is no doubt that Croatian DPs were much more numerous than Slovenian DPs. Their numbers were sufficient, their beliefs powerful enough and global organisation networks sufficiently effective to interconnect Croatian diasporas in different continents. Slovenian DPs, on the other hand, were fewer and directed mainly to a handful of countries, namely Argentina, the United States and Canada:

> In contrast to the general direction of Yugoslav political refugees, almost half of the Slovene political refugees emigrated to Argentina and other South American countries, followed by the US, Canada, Australia, and Western European countries. (Genorio 1993/94, p. 61)

Although the numbers might be subject to critical debate, understanding the direction and streaming of the flow of DPs is essential.

The differences in the numerical strength of the Croatian and Slovenian DP contingents had obvious implications for the resettlement process. Firstly, the resettlement process of the post-war Croatian DPs would have taken far longer than the resettlement of Slovenians; secondly, it is reasonable to expect that the greater number of Croatian DPs resulted in a more even distribution of the DP contingent across recipient countries; thirdly, the policy of mass immigration to the Australian continent began to unfold rather late in the 1940s and it was only then that Australia started to accept significant numbers of non-British migrants. All these factors help us to explain why more Croatian than Slovenian DPs arrived in Australia.

1.1   Slovenians in Argentina

Why such a massive migration of Slovenian DPs to Argentina instead of to some other recipient country? According to Corsellis (1997, p. 140), the strict US immigration laws provided little hope that all or most of the Slovenian DP contingent could settle there. South Africa, Canada and New Zealand, although willing to settle some DPs, were interested only in fit and preferably skilled migrants. Argentina had fewer such restrictions but the 'acceptability' of Slovenian migrants was also helped by the fact that the Argentinian government had given preference to those of Roman Catholic faith. According to Holborn (1956, p. 401), by "the end of June 1948 some 12,000 persons, mostly from Italy, had been moved by [the International Refugee] Organisation to the Argentine." Slovenians (and to a much lesser extent Croatians) comprised a large proportion of these.[3]

The migration of such a large group of Slovenians to Argentina is a consequence of a successful lobbying operation. Holborn (ibid.) makes a brief reference to the role played by the Slovenian Welfare Society, based in Buenos Aires, which 'lobbied' the Argentine government to issue landing permits to Slovenians. Some other sources (Urbanc 1993, Corsellis 1997) reveal the significant contribution of Monsignor Janez Hladnik, a Slovenian priest in Argentina, in this process. The Slovenian politician, Dr. Miha Krek, a former Deputy Prime Minister of the Yugoslav Government in exile, and a leader of the Slovenian Charitable Committee (*Slovenski dobrodelni odbor*) in Rome was also instrumental and pivotal in organising the emigration of DPs from Italy to Argentina.

In addition to the lobbying power of various individuals and organisations, there was considerable political will involved on the part of the Argentinian government as well. In November 1946 president Peron personally intervened in favour of the arrival of 10,000 Slovenian anti-communist refugees. He pledged to make their arrival "as easy as possible" (Jevnikar 1996, p. 98).

2   Memory...

The fact that Croatia existed as an independent political entity between 1941-45 ought to be seen as an important factor which influenced the formation of the political consciousness of the diaspora. The entire post-Second World War Croatian diaspora discourse was based on the transformation of this historical fact into a source of inspiration. The re-establishment of the Croatian state was considered an ultimate goal. But to make the myth functional, the possibly embarrassing historical facts, such as collaboration with Nazis and Fascists had to be dismissed as lies or 'explained' in terms of historical inevitability.

Slovenians did not form an independent state during the Second World War, nor did there exist a clear notion of it. The pro-communist partisans were espousing Slovenian nationalism to an extent but they were no less keen on the idea of Yugoslavism. The Slovenian Home Guard soldiers, on the other hand, always tried to portray themselves as genuine and concerned Slovenian nationalists. But on close examination, one finds surprisingly few signs of any propagation of Slovenian independence by the Home Guard during the Second World War. In fact, the wording of their military oath of allegiance (the equivalent of the Australian Army's blood oath) did not mention the word 'independent Slovenia' but only a rather undefined 'Slovenian homeland':

> I swear to almighty God to be faithful, brave and loyal to my seniors and that I will, in joint struggle with the German armed force which fights under the leadership of the leader of the Great Germany, SS-troops and police, conscientiously accomplish my duty towards the Slovenian homeland as part of a free Europe against the communist bandits and their allies. In this struggle I am prepared to sacrifice my life. So help me God! (Fink 1984, p. 6, translation, Z.S.)

Although the idea of a Slovenian nation and culture was undoubtedly the driving force of the Home Guard fighters, the lack of an unambiguous claim for Slovenian independence represents an important distinction between Croatians and Slovenians in the diaspora. The arguments for Slovenian independence started to dominate the diaspora discourse only in the 1980s (particularly in Argentina), although in a less intransigent and vengeful form than amongst diaspora Croatians.

3   Innocence...

More than 50 years on, the tragic fate of Croatian and Slovenian 'unrepatriables' who were massacred by the victorious Yugoslav Army forces is still strongly present in the minds of their surviving brothers-in-arms. Most of these soldiers were very young at the time of the massacres and it is not surprising that these people – now in their old age – maintain and still express an acute awareness of the political views they happened to believe in and/or fight for.

Let us first focus on the Slovenian example. The fact that they could not return to Slovenia suggests that most of them strongly embraced Slovenian cultural traditions, language and anti-communist political ideals. They transformed their political and military defeat into nationalism. This acute awareness of their banishment from the homeland also most definitely contributed to their nourishing of the 'innocent victim' mentality in the diaspora. This mentality was sustained by the belief that they were the victims of historical circumstances and that their sympathising with Fascist and Nazi ideologies was justifiable as it was the only way to protect Slovenian national interests. The very strong belief in their historical mission later served as a basis for the belief that they have a legitimate right and morally justifiable reason to be a part of the opposition against the socialist government in the homeland. Of all Slovenians around the world, it was the Slovenians in Argentina who most clearly nurtured their identity as innocent victims and who relatively successfully transmitted these ideas to the second and following generations. The reason these views are better preserved among Argentinian-Slovenians is that post-Second World War migrants – the core of which consisted of DPs – formed a relatively coherent (both in a political and an ideological sense) grouping based on shared memories and experiences.

Detailed descriptions of the post-Second World War massacres of the Slovenian Home Guard soldiers have often appeared in newspapers and magazines published in the diaspora. After the celebrated collapse of communism in the late 1980s and early 1990s, these stories have started to appear not only in diasporic but also in the homeland presses, and the mass graves of the massacred victims have been turned into symbolic sites of national reconciliation. The stories relating to the massacres obviously evoke powerful images and emotions and give the reader relatively little opportunity to establish an emotionless perspective on the topic. The propagated notion of the presumably innocent Slovenian *fantje* (boys) – as they are often referred to in these stories – who were massacred by Yugoslav partisans in a most ruthless way was/is utilised to reproduce the collective pain. The reproduction of the collective pain, in consequence, was a factor which helped in the construction of the Slovenian diaspora on the base of a common traumatic experience. The mobilisation of Argentina's Slovenians has been firmly rooted in a share in this collective trauma. These innocent victims, the peasant *fantje* (rather than soldiers), were definitely used as moral and ideological capital in the diaspora.[4]

It is precisely at this point that one needs to note an important difference between the Slovenian diasporas in Australia and Argentina. A highly articulate anticommunism combined with the frequent recalling of the inter-war years was never the core constituent element of Australian-Slovenian diaspora narratives as it was in Argentina. This does not mean that Australian-Slovenians have not held largely negative views on the post-war homeland political establishment and that they did not frequently recall negative homeland-related personal experiences. What I argue here is that the major differences between the Slovenians in Argentina and Australia include the fact that the migration of Slovenian post-Second World War DPs to Argentina preceded the migration of Slovenians to Australia and that the former were significantly more numerous, ideologically highly coherent and therefore the most radical opponents of communism.

4 Political migrants and their contribution to the formation of a distinct diaspora identity in Australia

Let me now return to the similarities and differences between Croatian and Slovenian diasporas in Australia. First, as already stated, the initial number of Croatian DPs was larger than that of Slovenian DPs. The numerical strength of Croatian DPs and their relatively coherent political and nationalist ideology represent the major factors contributing to the ethno-nationalist intensity found in the Australian-Croatian setting. The larger numbers of Croatian DPs mean that not all of them could be accommodated by one major recipient country. Trans-continental dispersion of DPs would also imply a related dispersion of ideology.

Second, as outlined above, it is well-documented that Slovenian DPs of the immediate post-Second World War period migrated to Argentina in an organised way and in a large group. Croatian migration to Argentina is not the result of such a successfully concerted effort, although a considerable number of Croatians from this category migrated to Argentina as well. My research further suggests that some Croatian post-Second World War DPs who initially went to Argentina later moved to Australia. It could also be argued that these processes to some extent reflected family reunion patterns. It is likely that in the second half of the 1950s, the Croatians in Argentina could have started to feel considerably insecure in the light of the assassination attempt on their exiled leader, Ante Pavelić (10 April 1957).

Third, the politically radical core of Croatian DPs already in Australia provided a context which allowed for the absorption and political re-education of economic migrants who followed later. While Slovenian economic/political migrants were also arriving in Australia they did not encounter diaspora organisations which were primarily politically defined. This meant that in the Australian-Slovenian case the arrival of these later migrants represented a further dilution of an already weak and largely non-politically defined core.

The so-called Australian-Slovenian political migrants – in sharp contrast with Australian-Croatian ones – lived their lives quite isolated from mainstream Australian-Slovenian organisations. Jean Martin (1965, p. 95) mentioned that it was her impression that DPs generally tend to live outside settlement concentrations of their own ethnic groups and that they "are influenced only marginally or superficially, if at all, by ethnic institutions". The following comment from a well-known Slovenian political migrant in Australia supports the view that they were not only relatively unnoticeable but also difficult to mobilise:

> There was very little [Slovenian] political migration to Australia. Perhaps around a hundred people. There were many attempts to unite political migrants in the whole of Australia. But there was very little support. I was one of the founding members of the 'Captive Nations' in Sydney. We held demonstrations every year and I always tried to arrange for a Slovenian flag to appear. Sometimes there were fifteen Slovenians present, at other times five. I even have a photo showing how I had to carry the flag myself. ... (translation, Z.S.)

Slovenian 'political' migrants in Australia never organised groups which had any real chance of gaining control over diaspora activities. The 'politically tainted' accusations were most commonly used in petty feuding between different segments of the diaspora setting. In contrast, Australian-Croatian diaspora organisations were heavily influenced by political factionalism.

An additional indication of this relative political disinterestedness among Australian-Slovenians is to be found in the view of the editors of two of the oldest Slovenian magazines in Australia, *Misli* and *Vestnik*. The *Vestnik* in its first issue published in September 1955 explicitly pledged to be non-political (Birsa 1994, pp. 41-2). The Catholic magazine *Misli*, published in Melbourne, whose long-standing editor was a former DP and a Home Guard soldier himself, was openly anti-communist. Yet, the magazine was never, according to its editor, intentionally used as a tool for political propaganda (ibid., p. 154).

To summarise, the presence or absence of strongly politically defined post-Second World War DPs is an essential determinant for the constitution and the nature, strength and orientation of organised Croatian and Slovenian diasporas in Australia. In the case of Croatians, this internally complex grouping of political migrants nurtured a specific kind of ideology, politics and world-view, centring on the re-establishment of the independent Croatian state and the question of Croatian ethno-national survival amid the perceived threat from Serbia. Comparatively speaking, Argentine-Slovenians could be seen as the equivalent of Australian-Croatians in terms of the intensity of their political and ethno-national mobilisation. The former group is often seen as an "unusual phenomenon: the Slovenian enclave in Argentina" (Jančar 1993, p. 103, Dular 1993, p. 26, Jenšterle 1995) characterised by a degree of ghetto mentality and intense Slovenianism explicitly discernible in second and subsequent generations. A comparatively high degree of Slovenian language maintenance among second generation individuals in Argentina and the frequent occurrence of inmarriage could serve as indicators of a considerable preservation of Slovenianism. Just as the un-political nature of Australian-Slovenians can be explained by the relative absence of political migrants, similarly their presence in the Argentine context can be explained by the significant role played by the high concentration of Slovenian post-Second World War DPs in Argentina (Švent 1995).[5]

It would be mistaken to assume that Slovenians in Australia completely lacked subversive ideas about the political establishment ruling their homeland. However, the developments in Croatian diaspora organisations in Australia in recent years, particularly those that occurred as a result of the war in the former Yugoslavia, proved that a politically-defined core (with certain modifications in its structure) remained what it was at the very beginning – a catalyst for the formation of ethno-national identity of the subsequent diaspora generations. The relative absence of a 'pure' political core in the Australian-Slovenian context produced developments in a slightly different direction. Paradoxically, in the absence of a politically oriented core, a flexible and politically heterogeneous 'core' was invented *ad hoc* during the war in Slovenia in 1991. It did not use the radical political arguments that were coming from Argentina from the political migrants *and* their children. Not surprisingly, this flexible core dissolved soon after the proclamation of Slovenian independence.

5 Homeland, nostalgia and the myth of return

5.1 The elusive concept of homeland

The relationship between ethnic homelands and their dispersed populations is in many ways crucial to our understanding of long-distance nationalism. Homelands are spatial representations which are influenced by political and cultural factors, rather than a simple fact of geography. It is important to view the homeland as a constructed and imagined *topos* rather than a clearly definable entity. Said (1991) addresses a very similar dilemma when demystifying various conceptualisations of the Orient. He says that there were different Orients, but "never has there been such a thing as a pure, or unconditional Orient" (ibid., pp. 22-3). This fluidity of meanings proves that constructs such as the Orient and/or homeland are more profoundly related to historical and political opinions than *hic et nunc* legal delineations of territories. The question of a territorial definition of homeland – as I will show later – proved to be of considerable importance in this research, particularly in the sense in which it impacts upon our understanding of Australian-Croatian settings.

Not only is the homeland not an easily definable entity, but it in fact appears to be particularly resistant to what Armstrong (1982) termed 'ethnic mapping'. There is a profound "lack of coincidence between borders of states and homelands" (Connor 1986, p. 20, Sheffer 1986b, pp. 1-15).

Where is homeland? How is homeland defined? Diana Forsythe (1989) tackles this problem by trying to locate Germany. As she argues, there are great difficulties involved in defining what and where Germany is. Before the fall of the Berlin Wall, there were three distinct usages of the term: it was used as a synonym for the then Western Germany (the Federal Republic of Germany) only, as a designation of the territories of both Germanies, and as a conglomerate of Western Germany, Eastern Germany (the German Democratic Republic) and what was labelled *Ostgebiete des Deutschen Reiches* (eastern areas of the German Reich) which included some territories in Poland and the Soviet Union. So how can one precisely define the German homeland?

Such definitional dilemmas are almost normal in a world in which ethnic boundaries do not coincide with the political boundaries of nation-states. It is easy to think of many examples which resemble the above German dilemma. Do we mean all Jews when we say Israel? Is Serbia really everywhere that a Serb puts his or her foot – as recent Serbian nationalism has tried to justify? Croatians are not spared these dilemmas. It is common knowledge that Croatians define the borders of their homeland in different ways. For many Croatians, the Croatian homeland is defined by the borders of the present-day Republic of Croatia. Some of them add Herzegovina, others Bosnia and Herzegovina. And then there is that small minority which still includes parts of the Serbian territory (including the very outskirts of Belgrade, the Serbian capital). Budak (1988, p. 342) accurately observed that the fact that "not all historically Croatian areas are within the borders of [the Croatian] republic" presents one of the main problems and preoccupations for post-war Croatian migrants. The maps of Croatia in its 'historical borders' is one of the typical decorations of Croatian diaspora organisations in Australia. Many Croatians – particularly in right-wing political circles in Croatia and the diaspora – see the question of homeland boundary delineation as still awaiting final resolution. The question of Herzegovina, which is at present a constitutive part of Bosnia and Herzegovina, is a key territory in this process. At present, the Croatian media often subtly reinforces the idea that the question of boundaries is yet to be finalised. During one interview with a group of Australian-Croatians, the expansion of Croatian state borders was said to be historically justifiable and necessary for the final resolution of the Croatian-Serbian conflict. While not all Croatians interviewed perceived this matter as being so crucial, it is true that relatively few interviewees were completely opposed to the idea. It should be noted that members and supporters of the radical right parties are more inclined to such extreme ideas. In addition, Croatians from Bosnia or Herzegovina are more likely to argue for such an expansionist position. The two elements – political beliefs and origin – are often (albeit far from exclusively) complementary.

In contrast to Croatia, the Slovenian homeland is generally defined with the borders of the present-day Republic of Slovenia and it is significant to note that – in stark contrast to Croatian Clubs – there are no maps of Slovenia in its 'historical borders' to be found in the Australian-Slovenian diaspora organisations. There is little doubt that for Slovenians, the desire for the change of state boundaries to be more reflective of a 'historical' *Lebensraum* for Slovenians is not a consideration at all.

5.2 The ethnic homeland: the questions of time and space

The very idea of homeland has the power to evoke memories, intense emotions and put into action more or less deeply learned attitudes. The intensity of attachment between diaspora individuals and their homelands varies and depends upon their temporal and spatial proximity to and/or distance from the homeland. The present emphasis on these two dimensions can help us to understand the present argument. The temporal aspect is not to be measured solely in terms of the years elapsed since the dislocation of the individual or a group from the homeland. Similarly, the spatial aspect is not to be measured solely in terms of physical distance from the homeland.

Spatial factors fluctuate around the temporal ones – they are in habitual and symbiotic relationship. The same spatial and temporal distance does not necessarily produce the same effects. It is also necessary to consider such factors as the historical conditions and migrant flows which contributed towards the constitution of these settings, the individual's psychological constitution, the individual's embededness and dependency on diaspora networks and other related issues.

The idea of homeland may therefore have different meanings to different individuals and could range from a romantically defined goal towards which almost every single aspect of an individual's life is directed, or as a simple geographical reference point. Homeland could serve as a mental shelter and – among political migrants – as a teleological concept (often expressed in the form: "One day, when our country is free, we shall all return"). Yearning for homeland becomes a teleological concept in the sense that *telos* is always an uncontested given (stage 1: 'when our homeland is liberated', stage 2: 'when the fighting stops... we will all return', stage 3: 'when our children grow up', etc.). Of course, the homeland can also represent a constraint and a burden which may cause individuals to turn their backs on their ethnic culture.

Political migrants tend to develop a very clearly defined position towards their spatial dislocation. As the Croatian émigré writer, Korsky (1983, p. 24), puts it:

> The essence of the political migrant is that he [sic] opposes the political structures or regime in the homeland. He only lives in his new environment by default. Spiritually, however, he is in a dynamic relationship with his old environment. He lives in and for this old place. (translation, Z.S.)

The predominance of either political or economic motives for emigration from the homeland are decisive in determining the intensity, power and persistence of various questions related to homelands. To a 'political migrant' and especially a DP, the homeland is not physically accessible. It plays the role of a forbidden fruit, an area impenetrable by any other means than the imagination. Consequently, the temporal and spatial distance become even greater and heighten the sense of loss.

The relationship between ethnic group members and their homeland and its political establishment (regardless of whether they are the first or subsequent generations) is one of the main indicators of their connectedness to their ethnic pasts. The relationship between people's loyalties to an ethnic homeland, and their integration into the new host society, is not necessarily a mutually exclusive one. Rather, it is contingent on circumstances. Or put another way, it is possible to retain a rootedness in the past with successful integration into a new society.

5.3 Nostalgia

Nostalgia is a term often used in discussions of homeland. In its original use it refers to a painful condition related to the homeland (Gr. *nostos* means 'to return home' and *algia*, 'a painful condition'). As Davis (1979, pp. 10-1) writes: "Whatever in our present situation evokes it, nostalgia *uses the past* - falsely, accurately, or [...] in specially reconstructed ways – but it is not the product thereof." He sees nostalgia as a "special optic on the world" and also as a "distinctive *form of consciousness*" (ibid., p. 74).

Any discussion of nostalgia and homelands in English hits the wall of semantic difficulties. The famous book on nationalism by the Royal Institute of International Affairs [1939](1963, p. 28) reveals the difficulties the authors encountered in translating the German expression *Heimatliebe* which has no English equivalent but is descriptively translated as 'love of one's native heath' rather than merely 'love of home' (c.f. Applegate 1990). Hobsbawm eliminates this dilemma by his persistent usage of German vocabulary. He differentiates between *Heim* and *Heimat*, terms which are hard to translate adequately. Summarising the distinction, he wrote: "*Heim, chez soi*, is essentially private. Home in a wider sense, *Heimat*, is essentially public" (Hobsbawm 1991, p. 67). Hobsbawm stresses that we are thus dealing with a double-sided phenomenon, a phenomenon which is both essentially public and essentially private and that neither of these two is to be underestimated. Obviously, the 'public' attitude towards *Heim* and *Heimat* could well be socially prescribed and culturally, situationally and politically conditioned. Public expressions of Palestinian *Heimatliebe* for the Occupied territories and Jewish public disclosures of their loyalty to a Jewish state meant two different things and were expressed with two entirely different contexts in mind. It is also useful to think of the idea of *Heimat* as being closely linked to the past. Morley and Robins (1993, pp. 7-8) make the following comments by referring to Marshall Berman: "Heimat is a mythical bond rooted in a lost past, a past that has already disintegrated: 'we yearn to grasp it, but it is baseless and elusive; we look back for something solid to lean on, only to find ourselves embracing ghosts'."

Although popular representations of exile and emigration often refer to disaster or despair (Jančar 1993, p. 96), it is worth emphasising that viewing one's homeland in a nostalgic and uncritical fashion is not a universal or inevitable characteristic of the migration process. Evidently, not all stories of emigration and exile tend to be uniformly long and tragic sagas. But the narratives of political exile are intrinsically heroic in nature and passionate in expression in order to legitimise the inherent political views.

What became strikingly apparent in my empirical research was the romantic portrayal and/or imagining of the one's ethnic homeland. Anderson's (1992a, p. 9) example of a Peloponnesian *Gastarbeiter* could be read as an illustration of the position of a migrant who is forced to imagine and romantically portray his Golden Country:

> We may recall the famous photograph of a Peloponnesian *Gastarbeiter* sitting mournfully in his tiny room in some anonymous German industrial town – Stuttgart perhaps? The pitiful little room is bare of any decoration except a travel poster of the Parthenon, produced en masse by Lufthansa, with a subscription, in German, encouraging the gazer to take a Holiday in Sunny Greece. The Lufthansa Parthenon is transparently not a real memory for the melancholy worker. He has put it on his wall because he can read it as sign for 'Greece', and – in his Stuttgart misery – for an 'ethnicity' that only Stuttgart has encouraged him to imagine.

This quotation gives more than a simple depiction of a particular type of sadness and misery. The migrant in question imagines a constructed substitute for home and re-invents his ethnicity with the help of graphical imagery. This very act of imagining is romantic and surreal in its nature. Romanticism in the sense used in this book is an expressive preoccupation located in idealised feelings about an object – the homeland. The objects of romantic aspirations assume qualities based on refined memories or mediated narratives.

In what follows, I will try to construct several categories based on empirical findings. These categories represent a variety of approaches to homeland construction. The homeland is not necessarily portrayed as a 'lost paradise' but it is certainly a reference point for one's thinking. It may not figure as a realistic option for one's place of living but it could serve as *the* place, a privileged location, towards which yearning is directed. After all, the devoted Zionist does not necessarily find the real Israel appealing.

6   Ideas about homeland

For second generation individuals a strong attachment to the homeland could well be a mediated process in which parental constructions of the past play a decisive role. I classified references made by second generation respondents in relation to their ethnic homeland into four major categories:

6.1 Romanticism – second generation respondents
6.2 Parents' romanticism through their children's eyes
6.3 The second generation's critical attitudes towards the ethnic homeland
6.4 The myth of return

Respondents' references to homeland were all made completely randomly and in relation to other issues during interviews. However, the bulk of these answers came in relation to my question: "Do you or your parents ever consider going back to your homeland for good?" Interestingly, none of the second generation respondents objected to the obvious suggestion in my question that homeland signifies a country overseas. All of them were able to relate this term to their (parents') ethnic homeland.

6.1 *Romanticism – second generation respondents*

Romanticism as used in this context tends to censor negativity: "My father wants to go back. To him, Croatia is an idyllic world where there is no crime, no unemployment, ... a land of opportunity." The romantic construction of homeland, as this example reveals, may contain many unrealistic beliefs, with very few, if any, negative characteristics. The homeland in this sense is often perceived as a place signified by a radical difference, as a place 'beyond conception'. A second generation Croatian female respondent said:

> The first time I went to Croatia I was 12 and I thought it was fantastic. I was living in a village for three months and there were a lot of children my age. You had *bunar* [a well] in the back yard, farm property, *guske* [geese] would pass in front of the windows and I was learning the language. I felt quite exotic because I was from Australia and I was different. I enjoyed that very much.

In the above example the respondent frequently used Croatian words during the interview to describe the reality which resembles her emotional attachment to the homeland: a well in the back yard, geese which freely wandered around... The use of the mother tongue to refer to what is perceived to symbolise the 'radical difference' was very common even among those who did not know the language very well. The speaker in the above example was not aware that she constantly slid into the Croatian language and the fact that she tended to reproduce positive rather than negative memories. A respondent who migrated to Australia as a child reminisces:

I remember my childhood. Maybe because I was so unhappy when I first got here. I really remember because I wanted to go back. I was unhappy for about 3 or 4 years. I think I was very romantic about the way it was. I used to suffer for my friends but that was probably because I didn't have that here.

When I went back I was a teenager and I think [my childhood friends] were nice to me. I felt closeness, but we were different people. I had changed and they had changed. I think that was the first time that I realised that I do belong here any more than I belong there. I always thought I didn't belong here, that I was different and so on.

The recent war and its destructive power provided an additional stimulus for the idealisation of the homeland. It reinforced the respondents' desire to return home to help with the post-war reconstruction of the homeland. A second generation Croatian respondent stated: "If this situation calms down I would like to go to my city: to re-build what has been demolished, to return the old beauty to the place." It should be noted that the respondent was born in Australia but nevertheless felt obliged to respond to the 'call' of the homeland. Despite the temporal and spatial distance which separated him from the homeland, his feeling of closeness to the homeland culminated in his feeling of responsibility towards it. Another respondent stated similarly: "I even feel I want to go [to Croatia] for Christmas [1991] just for two weeks. That's how strongly I feel about trying to repair the damage that's happening right now."

The homeland was commonly perceived as a romantic designation, an exemplar of almost mythical qualities. It seems that it is precisely this combination of the unreal, mythically beautiful and distant which manages to communicate through the silent demand for sacrifices. This can be illustrated by the case of a Slovenian respondent who relied entirely on mediated knowledge and messages about the homeland. The homeland of her imagining figured as a place which one cannot resist loving. For this respondent who had never visited the homeland, the homeland could not possibly fail to provide gifts of emotional fulfilment and is therefore to be seen as the legitimate object of one's desire:

> I have never been to Slovenia,... What you see in photos, in movies and stuff like that can all be covered up. From the papers and all that you know that there is a bit of fighting (interviewed in late 1991, Z.S.), but then, everyone is moving forward over there. Whereas, I think Australia is going backwards. Everything about it is pathetic. I know it seems stupid but I can't handle it any more. One friend of mine went to Slovenia to see my relatives that I've never seen. I'd like

to go to see my relatives, to have their place as my touring base. Because once over there, it's easy to travel and visit people. And from there I could pick – if I love it as I hope... People who have visited Slovenia from here are in a hurry to go back again. I know I'll love it, it's just finding the place where I'd like to stay and live.

It is interesting to note that this respondent had almost no knowledge about Slovenia, no knowledge of the Slovenian language and – due to her low socio-economic status – no realistic chance of making her hopes come true. Most importantly, she was the only second generation Slovenian respondent from my research sample who claimed to have plans and the desire to live in Slovenia. Almost seven years after the above interview was taken, she was still living in Australia. And yet, Slovenia still served as a substitute for her earthly Heaven. The case of this respondent clearly reveals the power of the nostalgic emotions directed towards the homeland and the relativity of time-space factors discussed above.

6.2 Parents' romanticism through their children's eyes

A factor which contributes considerably to second generation respondents' attitudes towards the homeland is the communication of parental messages. It should be noted that second generation respondents reported the contradictions in their parents' responses. They explained that their parents tended simultaneously to glorify the homeland's beauties as well as talk about their personal negative experiences in the homeland. Most of the reported positive comments were made in the statements coloured by nostalgia, homesickness and isolation in the new environment. One Slovenian female reported:

> My mother talked about her family in Slovenia quite a lot. Big family, fourteen children, a big house... My mother used to talk a lot because she was so homesick. She talked about it all the time. She would teach us songs, tell us stories about how they picked blueberries and mushrooms in the forest. Yes, she talked about it a lot and I remember a lot. In my mind it was very much alive: about the snow and about all the customs, about how much they all loved each other, how happy they were, how they slept on the top of the *krušna peč* [the bread oven, Z.S.].[6] Someone would play the accordion and others would dance.
>
> My mother didn't like it here. For a person used to the mountains and the farm, a big family and good people who help each other,

Adelaide was not the best place. She didn't like it here. She didn't like it. (translation, Z.S.)

The respondent accepted and internalised her mother's nostalgic memories. As in the former example, when talking about accordions being played and the bread oven, picking blueberries and mushrooms, she used the Slovenian language, her mother tongue. What is particularly interesting is the respondent's celebration of pre-constructed images and 'local' virtues which are attributed to a semi-mythical world of homeland in her own construction. The respondent's narrative evokes – to use Schama's (1991, p. 14) terminology – "the innocent, domestic parochialism." Her descriptions reveal a complete absence of independent thinking and, as her subsequent comments during the interview revealed, she accepted her mother's ideas about the homeland entirely. In mediated narratives like this, the 'positivity' of homeland images produces no residual 'negativity'.

Unlike the romanticised view of the second generation respondents categorised earlier, the first generation often uses the skill of persuasion to re-position the negative experiences into a source of strength and cross-generational aspiration. The stories which parents (first-generation migrants) tell their children are likely to contain and evoke negative images: the hard life on the farm, the backward attitudes of homeland settings, hunger and poverty (particularly after the Second World War). Even the above respondent's mother used these attributes regularly, but idealised them at the same time. During my fieldwork I was continuously provided with examples in which poverty was not necessarily directly associated with the negativity but in fact miraculously transformed into an inspiring positivity. A considerable number of Slovenian informants nevertheless conceded that stories with such negative content in fact encourage the indifference of second generation individuals towards their Slovenian heritage.

It is interesting to compare the impact of similarly negative parental narratives in the Croatian context. The explanation for the fact that second generation Croatians more numerously and actively participate in the life of their diaspora organisations is claimed to be because poverty, hunger, etc. are seen as consequences of a reality which is beyond the control of the Croatian homeland: i.e. because of the subordinate role of Croatia in the former Yugoslav federation, reflected in its economic exploitation and political repression. Consequently, the homeland figured as something separable from unfavourable (and what were always believed to be temporary) external conditions. Obviously, some of these claims rest comfortably on a political mythology, associated with a lost and then regained Croatian independence.

6.3 The second generation's critical attitudes towards the ethnic homeland

Explicit critical views of the ethnic homelands were rare. Analysis of interview material revealed that critical attitudes were often hidden behind economic arguments: "I earn too much money to leave [permanently for Croatia]." Family reasons were also put forward to explain the hesitant views on the homeland. Nevertheless, there were respondents who were openly critical about their parents' romantically constructed homeland and perceived their parents' romanticising as considerably misplaced. These criticisms in personal accounts of second generation respondents were – as a rule – based on individual experiences during visits in the homelands, although the very same experience produced the exact opposite effects with many other respondents:

> The second time [I visited Croatia] I was very disappointed by the country. Firstly, because I had a romantic illusion of what it looked like according to the stories which my parents told. When I saw it when I was twelve it did have that faraway look. When I went there as an adult, I was very disappointed. Everything was very neglected... That was the first time that struck me. [...]

The lower standard of living and the perception of ever-present bureaucracy in the homelands appeared to be the most unacceptable characteristics for second generation respondents: "... just coming in contact with bureaucracy... like my uncle who was told exactly how to build his house, what kind of windows and doors to have."

Some of the criticisms of parents' homelands were expressed either with a degree of prejudice or in a very subtle way. The following respondent, unsure of my views regarding the political situation in Croatia, criticised the politics of the ruling party and Croatian president Tudjman in the following way:

> I've become really frightened with the idea of the HDZ because I see [Croatia] as being a one-party state again. [People] are communists today and they are HDZ members next day. They haven't changed their opinion about anything and yet their vote counts.

The respondent's criticism of the ruling party was (as was made obvious to me later during the interview) a reflection of the respondent's critique of the nature of the functioning of contemporary Croatian society.

6.4 The myth of return

In relation to the question of return which represents the ultimate solution to nostalgic yearnings of individuals in diaspora, I tried to understand whether there are distinct patterns in responses between Croatian and Slovenian samples or not. Also, I wanted to ascertain whether there are any observable differences across the generations. Are Croatians (irrespective of generation) more inclined to consider returning to the homeland than Slovenians or is it the other way around? If this difference does occur, how can it be explained?

In regard to the question of return, differences between both groups and across generations were in fact vast. It seems that there has been an important and perpetual belief in the Australian-Croatian diaspora that Croatia was oppressed within Yugoslavia and that once this oppression ceases and Croatia is free again, the majority of Croatians would eventually return. The homeland was formally liberated from the Yugoslav state in 1991 but the belief in massive Croatian free-will repatriation is still being promoted, although with an increasing number of 'if' qualifiers.

A slight diversion in the argument is now required to fully understand this issue. A partial explanation for the ideological dominance of the myth of return is related to the stigma attached to being a Croatian in Australia. The public pressure exercised upon the Croatian community in Australia in the past was considerable and often referred to by respondents who participated in this study. Croatians have very often been presented and stigmatised by the Australian media as an ethnic group whose collective actions are politically driven. An analysis of a collection of 166 articles concerning Croatians which appeared in the *Sydney Morning Herald* between 1955 and 1988 clearly reveals the negative way in which Croatians have been presented to the Australian public (Kovacevic and Gladovic 1990). Not one of these articles takes a favourable stand towards Croatians. Most of them focus in some way either on acts of terrorism or demonstrations and protests. Even the more 'neutral' articles deal in some way with the existence of highly political feelings, emotions and actions among Croatians living in Australia. The police raids of Croatian homes in the early 1970s added to the feeling among members of the Australian-Croatian diaspora that they were being 'singled out'.

Viviani's (1984) study of Vietnamese in Australia offers an interesting comparison in this respect. She analyses the political divisions of the Australian political establishment over the issue of accepting Vietnamese refugees. During this debate, the Australian Labor Party (ALP) was in office for the first time in twenty-three years. The ALP's argument against Vietnamese refugees was based on an historical parallel with the post-Second World War period which was characterised by a large influx of anti-communist and anti-left oriented refugees. The ALP feared that the influx of right-wing oriented refugees from Vietnam would possibly tip the political balance of the 1950s and 1960s towards conservatism. However, ironically, as Viviani (ibid., p. 56) states:

> These considerations were reinforced by another: the fear that, like the Croatian migrants before them, the Vietnamese in Australia would seek to 'liberate their homeland', thus causing the problem of legal control, diplomatic headaches with the government in Vietnam, and a backlash among Australians. This was the origin of the pungent epithet for Vietnamese refugees, Yellow Croatians; in one phrase, the sum of all these fears.

'Yellow Croatians' – the sum of all Australian fears! Croatians were shown to be used as a scapegoat-type category of convenience which may be appropriately attached to the negative notion of 'yellowness'. Viviani makes a powerful comparison between the two most 'visible' and negatively portrayed ethnic groups in Australia. Comparatively, Slovenians in Australia never attracted such public attention.

The impact of a similar sort of societal pressure is examined in a study of Turkish migrants (*Die Gastarbeiter*) in Germany (Gitmez and Wilpert 1987). The authors state that because of the negative prejudices which the presence of the Turks evokes, and consequently due to "the stigma attached to being Turkish, the myth of return is reinforced for the majority of the first generation and many of their offspring" (ibid., p. 87). The talk and imagery of return amongst Croatians in Australia has clearly taken the form of what Sorel (1941) in *Reflections on Violence* calls a myth – a means of acting on the present. What was perceived in the Australian-Croatian context is entirely in accordance with Sorel's (ibid., p. 36) statement: "*It is the myth which is alone important*; its parts are only of interest in so far as they bring out the main idea." Indeed, such a myth has the power to orient the present action and to provide a guide for the future. Comparison of verbal commitment to return and its actual realisation was regularly revealed through respondents' statements.

The 'myth of return' is a phenomenon common to various migrant groups (e.g. Naficy 1991, Klausner 1991, Margolis 1995). However, different groups keep this myth alive for different reasons. If the reasons have to do with homeland politics, the myth is far more persistent than if it has no political connotation. The 'political' migrant or a refugee cannot simply 'go home'. I argue that the very nature of the concept of return in this context requires that it *functions* as a myth. The myth of return does not necessarily depend on realistic considerations pertaining to political or economic reality.

What amount of money guarantees the return? What degree of political freedom is required for return to be realistically considered? Most often, the return appears to be a goal in itself. Indeed, "... the exile must roam and pant to return but never actually achieve it" (Naficy 1991, p. 288).

The official statistics of the Croatian government has it that in the period between 1990 and 1997 precisely 39,177 Croatians returned to their homeland with the largest number of 14,279 arriving in 1992 (Anonymous 1998b, p. 10). As for the countries of origin of these returnees, most of them arrived from European countries (19,801 persons from Germany) and were followed by arrivals from Slovenia, Austria, Switzerland, Australia, Canada and the United States.

I would now like to turn to three subcategories which result from this discussion of the myth of return.

6.4.1 Second generation Croatian respondents' reflections on first generation Australian-Croatians: returning home The following examples are based on what second generation respondents believed is the attitude of their parents in relation to the question of return.

> When there were the first elections in Croatia many people considered going back but I think that's all changed now [1992] that Croatia is being destroyed. I think they feel lucky to be here, so far away from the fighting. That's really sad for those people who experienced the Second World War. How situations change! Six months ago there were a lot of people going back home, making old connections... I don't know, maybe things will change in six months time.

> Everyone in *Hrvatski dom* [i.e. the Croatian Club in Adelaide) talks about how they are going back when the war finishes. I know this is not too clever because Croatia has to improve its shaky economy.

> Oh yes, [my parents] still talk about going back. Yes. I think they will do it one day. Maybe in a year or two, when things start settling down over there. They really want to go back and retire over there with their family.

> My father was always by himself. [He] says: "As soon as this trouble stops, we'll go back". Sometimes, I think he means it. It's unpredictable: he wants to go back... Just a few months ago he said: "After all this trouble is over, I want to go back".

All these examples have one characteristic in common: they all reveal that the question of return figures in the form of perpetual suspension. The return itself is commonly suspended for external reasons which are beyond the influence of an individual. Personal dilemmas related to this are commonly not expressed publicly, particularly by first generation migrants. Their children, however, see these dilemmas most commonly as the main reason for their parents' postponing the return:

> I think [every first generation Croatian migrant] would go back there if they could take their kids with them. They would sell all the houses they have here and go back and then live in a one bedroom house. [Australia] is such a foreign country [to them]. Nothing can compensate for being in your country with your own people and your own language.

> My parents were homesick and I think if it wasn't for me and the kids, they would have gone back. Probably, as they get older, they need it more. Particularly, because they went back for a holiday, all that pain has renewed. I think they'd gladly go back. ...

It needs to be noted that return to the homeland is not necessarily to be understood as a permanent return.[7] In the case of people who believe they had strong political reasons for going into exile, a simple visit may function as a symbolic return. Once the notion of impossibility of return is overcome, the homeland boundary crossing becomes a symbol of victory and exercise of freedom. Most of the first generation Croatian 'political' migrants in Australia visited Croatia for the first time only relatively recently, after the proclamation of Croatian independence in 1991. A second generation Croatian respondent describes his father's dilemma about whether to pay a visit to Croatia in the following words:

> Until recently, dad hasn't been able to, or rather, he didn't want to go back home. He thought he would be assassinated, because his father was a part of Ustasha and my father himself was connected with many Croatian revolutionary movements. Dad would have liked to have gone back to Croatia with us in 1983. He would have liked to go but he was afraid of the conditions he would be put in, hiding from Serbians who would assassinate him. My father is rather fussy with Serbians.

The respondent continued by commenting on his father's political loyalties:

[My father] wants to go back and fight with the Croatians against the Serbs in the present conflict. He said that if things get completely out of hand in Croatia, he – as well as many of his friends and members of the Croatian Club – will stop everything and go back and help [their] comrades and all the other Croatians. I can understand him. That's his homeland. But if anything happened here in Australia, he wouldn't fight for it. He doesn't believe in fighting for Mother England. He believes in his own country.

The question of return has different meanings and plays different roles in distinct political contexts. At the beginning of this chapter I spoke about the disparities which occur in comparing the Croatian and Slovenian migrant settings in Australia in relation to specific historical factors. I particularly emphasised the significance of the presence or absence of early post-Second World War DPs in the shaping of the political, ideological and organisational profile of emerging diasporas. It is not possible to establish what proportion of Croatians in Australia believed they would be in danger if they returned (either permanently or to simply pay a visit) prior to 1991. However, five fathers (of the 31 Croatian second generation respondents), at least from the point of view of their children, believed they could not return. Comparatively, this was a relatively unimportant issue for Australian-Slovenians. Although 3 Slovenian respondents (out of 30) stated that their fathers believed they could not return to Slovenia prior to 1991 it should be noted that, according to one informant, there were only 5 such people in the whole of South Australia. It was impossible to establish the comparative overall figure for Croatians in South Australia but it would arguably go into dozens.

It has been argued that some specific discursive practices such as nostalgia and romanticism have the ability to keep the myth of return to the homeland alive. Furthermore, one can assume that a higher proportion of political migrants in Croatian diaspora organisations would enable a far easier transmission of those beliefs than would be the case in the Australian-Slovenian context, which is characterised by their relative absence. More than half of the second generation Croatian respondents reported their parents' desire to 'return'. Comparatively, as I will show in the section below, only one second generation Slovenian respondent reported a similar parental desire.

6.4.2 Second generation Slovenian respondents' reflections on first generation Slovenians: returning home Only one Slovenian respondent reported her parents' desire to return to their homeland. But even in this case it was later revealed through my acquaintance with this respondent's parents that they did not seriously contemplate returning home. The second generation respondent stated:

> [My parents] were saying to me they are thinking about going back for good. They might go next year to see the place. But I'd say that if dad went back and he really, really liked it, he'd go back.

Although the respondent's father went back and liked it very much, he explained to me that his wife is totally opposed to the idea of return. Ultimately, he has given up the idea of return. A couple of other examples reveal a complete absence of the desire to return: "I think my parents miss the family, not the place. They miss their brothers and sister. Just as I would if I moved interstate." Or, as stated by another respondent:

> My parents are homesick. But not to live there. I think dad wants to go back for another visit. They wouldn't go there to live. There is only one family that I can recall that's gone back. Apart from them I don't know any other Slovenians in Adelaide that have gone back to live. It says a lot for Adelaide and for Australia.

Clearly, political considerations were almost completely absent from this reasoning. Slovenians also have no immediate and threatening external factor which could serve the purpose of teleological suspension. The belief that there will eventually be a massive free-will repatriation once the homeland is liberated played no role whatsoever.

A closer analysis of those migrants who came out to Australia for political reasons leads to a somewhat surprising result if compared with Croatians in the same category. Slovenian political migrants have never publicly promoted the myth of return. None of those people whom I have met was contemplating returning home. One of the Australian-Slovenian political migrants (Ahlin 1993, p. 44) used language which is a mixture of religious devotion and nostalgic memory (yet distancing himself from the images of the past):

> It would be a lie if I said I do not miss the forests, green hills and glorious, crystal clean creek which flows down the valley. Here [in Adelaide, Australia] I have comfort and peace which neither the [government] minister nor a hero [in Slovenia] could afford. The fact that I neither allowed the communists to pull my leg, nor let them seduce or scare me will always be my great satisfaction. I will wait here [in Australia] to be called by the eternally wise Judge. (translation, Z.S.)

It is only through an understanding of the patterns of re-settlement of political migrants after the Second World War that one can comprehend why the idea of return so prominently featured among Slovenians in Argentina (Žigon 1996, p. 85) but not among Slovenians in Australia.

6.4.3 Second generation Croatians and Slovenians – returning home

What is the significance and symbolic status of the ethnic homeland among second generation individuals? How intense are the feelings of the second generation towards the homeland? What are the elements which impact upon the intensity of these feelings? Obviously, the second generation individuals who took part in this research have been moulded by social institutions such as the family, school, church and/or ethnic clubs. Various diaspora organisations play a very significant role as the parents often use them to socialise their children. They also play – by default just as much as by design – an important public relations role. It could be argued that both parents and the host society use diaspora organisations as: first, a symbolic representation of a lost or left behind homeland; second, as the embodiment and transmitter of values (that may even be perceived as lost in their ethnic homelands) deemed to be desired universals for an ethnic group; and third, as the institution whose main task is the perpetuation of the above-mentioned functions.

The results obtained in relation to the question of return to the homeland of second generation Croatians and Slovenians reveal exactly the same pattern as the comparison between their respective parents' generations. In other words, first generation Croatians are more likely to contemplate return to the homeland than first generation Slovenians. The very same pattern is repeated in the second generation context. This suggests a significant correlation between these attitudes and the transmission of values and ideas across generations, whether these processes take place in the families or in diaspora organisations. By saying this I do not wish to imply that there is a mechanical correlation in cross-generational transmission of beliefs and ideas, although such links are often readily discernible (Miller and Miller 1991).

When one of the second generation Croatian respondents was asked: "Do you think it is realistic for you to talk about going back to Croatia?", the answer was:

> It is. Yes. Because my wife has been back three or four times. I've never been. Last time when she was there, she worked there for three months and when she came back she said she really wants to go back and live there. It was hard for me because I have never been there

before. But there is a person [another second generation Australian-Croatian] that I was going to marry (I wasn't married then) forcing me basically to get out of this Australian life-style to go back there. Well, I said to her, I'd like to go there for six months just to stay there, work there on a holiday-type work and then we'll see. But the more I think about it: what has Australia to offer me to stay? I got work here and I got work there. As long as these problems in Croatia are over.

Later his wife, who was also a respondent, unaware of her husband's opinion, independently stated: "I don't think I'd go back permanently. Now, I sort of realise: I have a good life in Australia. (...) If you go there it wouldn't be a holiday all the time..."

A Croatian second generation female respondent who wanted to settle permanently in Croatia stated:

I had the intention of going to Croatia permanently this year [1991]. I'd already bought a plane ticket and I was ready to go up until three weeks before departure. And then the war broke out and that's what I was afraid of. I'd just be another woman there and I would be an additional obstacle. Because men fight, not women. (translation, Z.S.)

According to another informant, this respondent joined the Croatian Army forces later in the course of the war. Although rare, this is not an isolated story. In early 1998 a monthly magazine, sponsored by the Croatian government, featured a story of another young Australian-Croatian female who departed for Croatia in 1991 and joined the ranks of the Croatian National Guard (Miličević 1998, p. 17).

It is important to note that second generation individuals allowed themselves comparatively more negotiation space when making statements about return than their parents. Probabilistic rather than deterministic language was used in the explanations of second generation respondents. The widening of the negotiation space is illustrated in the following examples:

My wife knows that if things settle down in Croatia and it becomes a Westernised economy (you can do what you can), then I certainly want to go back. If not permanently, I want to go back regularly and spend most of the time over there and visit Australia occasionally. That's sort of the way I am thinking but of course, nobody knows what the future holds.

> I'd like to go back to see if I can live there forever. It would be nice to have a job, a house or flat or whatever and live there. I think I'd like to do that, yes.
>
> I would go to Croatia on a trial basis, not to sell everything here. Even if we had decided to live there permanently, I'd have to have something here to come back to.

There were, indeed, some dissenting voices to be heard. A second generation contributor to a popular Australian-Croatian magazine wrote: "It is time to stop harbouring fantasies and illusions about all of us returning – these are the dreams of romantics fuelled by a sense of loss" (Dusevic 1993, p. 15).

Slovenian respondents generally did not place as much attention and importance on my questions concerning the homeland as Croatian respondents did. As mentioned earlier, there was only one female second generation Slovenian respondent who suggested that she considers going 'back' to Slovenia and her statement later turned out to be less than plausible. Second generation Slovenian respondents (with this one 'odd' exception) used a range of arguments to justify why Slovenia is far from being a realistic place for them to live. They all reduced the homeland to a relatively nice, pleasant and distant object. Although this argument will be further substantiated in the following chapters, so far I have provided a conceptualisation of the difference between Croatian and Slovenian samples.

This chapter has shown that the political profile of individuals who formed the backbone of the Australian-Croatian setting determined its ideological framework to a very considerable extent. A part of the world-view which these individuals have tended to promote – an important part of it – was a wishful, and in essence a prophetic, belief that returning home would one day be possible. The absence of a similar belief in the Australian-Slovenian context results from the less articulate ideological and political profile of the politically-oriented core of post-Second World War political refugees. This basic distinction and the reasons for the discrepancy developed and elaborated on in this chapter are central to understanding differences in responses and attitudes of the second generation respondents which will be further elaborated in the chapters which follow.

7   Notes

1   A large number of men from the South-Eastern part of Slovenia were subject to such forcible conscription.

2   These unrepatriables were often seen simply as remnants of the "pre-war regimes that reflect Nazi and Fascist concepts", as described by the UNRRA director for the American occupation zone in Germany (in Kuropas 1991, p. 391).

3   The role of the Catholic Church in Argentine politics is examined by Rein (1993). Žigon (1996) claims that in the period between 1947-48, about 7,000 Slovenians arrived in South America.

4   The distinction between the 'soldier' and an innocent 'peasant boy' is a distinction between the symbolic power of the terms. *Fant* (a boy) in the context of a massacre evokes the idea of an innocent, defenceless victim.

5   The following interpretation from the programmatic statement entitled 'Politics for Slovenians in Australia' (*Zveza slovenske akcije*, not dated, p. 2) is interesting as it utilises typical political language: "Some people think that Slovenianism in Argentina is strong because of the high number of intellectuals that went there. The number of Slovenian intellectuals in Germany is far greater and yet they are barren as far as Slovenianism is concerned. They completely assimilated in the space of a few years. The important difference is that those in Argentina are political refugees while those in Germany are migrants educated in the communist schools" (translation, Z.S.).

6   *Krušna peč* was an integral part of Slovenian architecture in Slovenian rural areas. Due to its characteristic construction, a part of the bread oven always expanded into another room. If being used, the top of the oven was the warmest place in the house during the winter. Therefore, the bread oven is traditionally associated with warmth and domesticity.

7   The phenomenon of return visits has recently been addressed in the context of the theorisation of transnationalism (e.g. Ang 1994, Basch et al. 1994, Baldassar 1997).

3 Diasporas and community sentiments

In migration literature migrant populations are commonly referred to as ethnic communities. It is easy to understand that this term is used rather habitually but in reality these so-called communities radically depart from the sociological ideal-typical constructions of community. The main characteristics of community in both its classical (Tönnies 1988) and its modern (Etzioni 1995) version is the assumption about the possibility of holism, closeness and unity. The obsession with identification and search for communities should be juxtaposed with Benedict Anderson's (1993 rev.ed., p. 6) classical statement that "all communities larger than primordial villages of face-to-face contact (and perhaps even these) are imagined." Indeed, it seems that the notion of community obliterates the richness of empirical heterogeneity from the field of vision.

The organisational structures of 'ethnic communities' (e.g. clubs and churches) provide a common ground for the association of their 'members'. However, the human bond which forms the substance of the community ethos is – and this is precisely the point I wish to emphasise – rather prone to antagonisms (c.f. Dench 1975, p. 34). It is important to move beyond the trappings of such communitarian discourse. I suggest that the broadly defined term diaspora delineates the reality of modern migrant settings more appropriately. Most importantly, they make no value claims and do not implicate any – except organisational – judgements.

There is no reason to make authoritative statements against the use of ethnic communities. In fact I shall use this term in this chapter as it was regularly used by respondents and it is also commonly used in the academic discourse. My preference for the term diaspora is based purely on the grounds of value-neutralisation. Instead of talking about ethnic communities and ethnic community organisations, I prefer to talk about diasporas which are defined by ethno-national criteria. Diasporas are further internally differentiated into diaspora organisations which can be based on religious, social, interest or other criteria.

This chapter addresses the influence of diaspora organisations on the second generation's identities and the extent to which – if at all – they serve as sources and mediators of ethno-national identification. I do not intend to bombard readers with facts and specificities pertaining to various Croatian and Slovenian diaspora organisations in Australia. There are very many such organisations and the loyalties and alliances between different factions are changing fairly rapidly. To avoid the excess of organisational detail, the material in this chapter relates strictly to South Australian-Croatians and Slovenians. The institutional set-up between the two groups was very similar during the time of this research. The Croatian diaspora organisations comprised a Club, the priest who led the Croatian congregation, and the associated soccer club. The Slovenian diaspora organisations on the other hand comprised a social club, as well as a priest and a church.

All Croatian respondents and all except two Slovenian respondents were at some stage in their lives associated with what *they* called ethnic communities – institutionalised meeting places of people who share things in common. Even those few respondents who were not involved with their activities still talked about such communities as truly existent entities, usually incorporating various ethnic clubs and religious congregations.

In a sense, my intention in this chapter is to provide an insight into this constantly fluctuating environment of what is normally perceived as ethnic communities. I viewed these environments as being characterised by tension and internal factional fighting just as much as by overarching ethno-political commitments concerning homeland politics. In other words, I saw various diaspora organisations as being united predominantly through both common ethnic affiliation and mutual boundary maintenance.

Soon after I had begun my empirical research I was surprised by the extent of disunity as well as discord which was an important characteristic of the diasporas I had chosen to analyse. I was conscious, however, of the fact that one should be careful neither to under- nor over-estimate the occurrence of the conflict. Paradoxically, I was also surprised by the extent of the relatively cohesive collective response to problems arising from the war in the homelands.

1 Some limitations of the prevalent discourses on ethnic communities

What is the social boundary which demarcates the inner and outer world of what in popular jargon is called an ethnic community? Most importantly, who sets this boundary up? In other words, what is meant by phrases such as 'Croatian ethnic community' or 'Slovenian ethnic community'? Is this just a type of administrative labelling? Do we mean people of one particular background who identify with and participate in ethnic group organisations such as clubs, churches, retirement homes, sport clubs, and so on? Or, do we mean the entire population of one particular ethnic background (e.g. all people of Croatian, or Slovenian ancestry) living in a particular geographical area? First, if the term community is used to refer to those who participate in the organised life of diaspora organisations, one automatically excludes a substantial part of the population of a particular ethnic background which does not take part in organised activities. This definition of community entails what I call *the paradox of exclusion*. Second, if we have in mind the entire population of one particular ethnic background, we do not take into consideration the fact that many of these people – maybe even a majority of them – may have little in common. This practice is characteristic of the way in which the broader society constructs ethnicities, regardless of the intensity of commitment to ethnicity by people who are constructed as 'belonging'. The latter type of situation, which is a reflection of popular jargon, may be called *the paradox of abstract inclusion* and can be illustrated as shown in Figure 3.1:

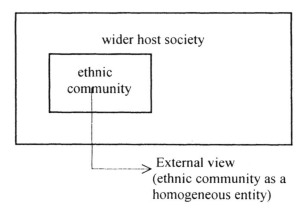

Figure 3.1 **External view of ethnic community: paradox of abstract inclusion**

This brings us to the question of arbitrary *ad hoc* labelling of different ethnic groups. Constructing general ethnic categories (e.g. for statistical and policy purposes) amounts to an artificial setting up of boundaries. Categories such as 'Yugoslav' (along with other multi-ethnic states) in the Australian Bureau of Statistics Censuses of Population and Housing are cases in point. What hermeneutical value – if any – is hidden behind the general census category 'Yugoslavia'? These broad terms are nothing but 'categories of convenience', as Pettman (1988, p. 4) said for the term 'Aboriginal', and they often resemble a paternalistic stance towards ethnic groups, which attempts to make the otherwise complex social reality categorisable and apparently suitable to policy initiatives. Politicians seem to be particularly inclined to refer to ethnic communities in a non-problematic fashion, carefully avoiding anything which could unearth the existent tensions and divisions within these.

Ethnic communities in migrant societies are commonly perceived in terms of ethnic, ethno-national and kinship criteria. This view seems to promote a belief that an ethnic group member in Australia recognises his/her fellow ethnic group members metaphorically as a brother/sister-in-blood. However, the use of blood and kinship determined metaphors of ethnic group membership have their own difficulties. They completely ignore the interest group, gender, class, social status or even regional elements which all determine one's position within a particular ethnic group or community. They see an ethnic community as a relatively coherent group based on primordial ethnic criteria with social, religious and other criteria being almost mechanically attached to ethnic classification. Anwar's (1979, p. 12) definition of the Pakistani ethnic community in Britain is illustrative. According to Anwar, Pakistanis in Britain form a community because: "they share a common background, have common interests, some form of social structure, hold a common religious belief and a value system and also have a territorial nucleus in parts of Rochdale and in other areas in Britain." The weakness of this definition is quite apparent as it is easy to imagine an atheist Pakistani who does not share 'common' interests with his/her compatriots, who lives miles away from Rochdale and whose value system could potentially be perceived by his/her fellow Pakistanis as very much atypical and therefore unacceptable. Is this person any less Pakistani than those who observe 'common' religious beliefs, live in a particular area and possess a particular value system? The logic behind Anwar's definition is one that helps in the construction of stereotypes. These may be positive, as in Anwar's case, but they are often negative; 'lazy' Mediterraneans, 'stingy' Scots or 'primitive' and/or 'drunken' Aboriginals are but a few examples.

As a result of this conflation between ethnic identity and the existence of ethnic communities as representations of these identities, researchers ask questions about 'patterns', 'core values' and the 'typicality' of ethnic traits and groups. What these approaches actually presume is that all individuals of particular ethnic backgrounds participate in ethnic cultures which are, by and large, defined through 'ethnic' clubs, 'ethnic' congregations, 'ethnic' schools, and other similar institutions. For example, Smolicz (1979, 1981), the main proponent of the theory of core values, argues that each ethnic group has certain core values (such as language and/or family structure). These core values are understood as fundamental features of an individual's or group's ethnic identity. One of the difficulties with this approach is that it presupposes the *existence* and consequently the *transmission* of these core values. The process of the transmission of these core values would only be possible if an ethnic group is understood as a well-functioning community, where values and ideas are transmitted with certainty. Unless one takes for granted the existence of a community, founded on its 'core' values, the theory becomes meaningless.

It appears that many authors frame social reality into a clustered entity called a community for reasons of expediency, trying to avoid the confusion which would occur if the segmentation and factual divisions in the ethnic community space were acknowledged. It is very naïve to believe that these communities show anything approaching cultural, political or ideological homogeneity.

1.1   Ethnic community boundaries and the segmentation of ethnic community space

For a short time during the period I was conducting my research a note with the following message was pinned just above the bar of the Slovenian Club in Adelaide in 1993:

> WARNING!
> Any quarrel and discussion of politics between the members of the Club and the Club's visitors on the premises of the Slovenian Club Adelaide is forbidden. (translation, Z.S.)

A member of the Club, who believed I was the 'intruder-type' of Slovenian as I was a recent arrival, offered to escort me off the premises after my research curiosity precipitated what the note referred to as a discussion, but which I experienced as an attack.[1] The person concerned was simply irritated by my research curiosity. The warning note was promptly removed when the Club's committee changed soon afterwards.

Similarly, when I was visiting the Croatian Club in Adelaide one Friday night my presence was immediately detected and I was politely asked to sign the Visitors' Book. When I asked for the reason for such a precaution, I was told it was a preventive measure taken because of the so-called 'former Yugoslavs' who now come to the Croatian Club and "cause trouble" (see the next section below).

There are common features in these two incidents. In both examples I was perceived as 'an Unknown', an inquisitive person who was not perceived as 'belonging'. In the first case I was 'a familiar visitor', a familiar stranger, and in the second one the 'unfamiliar face'. The reason for caution or warning in both cases was related to the particular political norms and criteria relevant to the ethnic group/organisation or individuals who voiced their opinions believing themselves to be the executors and best possible representatives of the wishes of the members of the ethnic organisation. Interestingly, this indicates that members of an ethnic group may perceive themselves as *the* community, particularly if there is a need to reinforce the boundary between those believed to be its in-members and those held to be the out-members. This boundary is more or less symbolic, but potentially capable of forming an unbridgeable gap between the insiders and the outside world if need be.

In a sense there is a paradox hidden in this perception and representation of community. I argued earlier how community is often a result of thinking which seeks a common denominator (e.g. ethnic identity) and then constructs the community on its basis. One could argue that such a view creates a community where it actually does not exist. But the previous paragraph indicates that a different process can also be at work, for the community is not created from without but from within – it is enlarged not because of the external construction but because of the presumptuous imagining of its insiders.

Allowing the outsider to take part in commonalities shared by the in-group is not always a matter of course. Ethnic communities often try to keep outsiders as far away as possible. The 'us' feeling is in itself very contradictory. At some level, it contributes to keeping outsiders away from the group. Yet at the same time it contributes to including those who do not necessarily perceive themselves as members of that group, although they may satisfy certain external criteria (e.g. ethnic, racial). The extent to which ethnic organisations are flexible and willing to tolerate and accommodate those who do not belong to the group because of different ethnic background, colour, political views or religion is something that is very context specific.

According to the model I propose, the boundaries of ethnic communities are neither totally fixed nor completely loose but subject to ever-changing situational factors. Such a model takes into consideration the constant boundary definition and redefinition processes which take place within ethnic groups. The membership space is apt to change. This model, however, does not propose that outer realities are the sole factor in defining ethnicity, for the existence of inner boundaries and inner segmentation should not be neglected. These inner boundaries may be as solid as those demarcating the outer boundaries: the space between the in-group (the ethnic community) and the out-group (the host society).

2   Politics, otherness and diasporas

The dynamism of boundary delineation within the diaspora was particularly clearly discernible at the beginning of the conflict in the former Yugoslavia. At that time, the Croatian diaspora organisations across Australia were rapidly gaining new membership and there was a high degree of tension between established membership and the newcomers. It is in this context that I wish to address some of the issues related to these processes.

As a matter of clarification, I would like to emphasise that ethnic identification and its intensity in particular are not to be seen as unchanging. This allows us to conceptualise the idea of multiple identities and to understand the changes in intensity of ethnic identification through the lifespan. In practical terms, such allowance of flexibility in terms of ethnic identification clearly leads to tolerance and acceptance of difference. It is useful to differentiate between individuals who, for whatever reason, opted to call themselves Yugoslav in Australia and those who accepted Yugoslavism as an exclusive form of ethnic and national identity. In regard to the latter, Sekulić and his colleagues (1994) successfully show how Yugoslav identity was not forcefully and ruthlessly promoted by the Yugoslav communist leadership but was in fact the result of a combination of factors and motives. The former Yugoslavia was not a country of Yugoslavs in the same sense that contemporary Italy is a country of Italians. At the time of the break-up of Yugoslavia less than 10 per cent of the population declared Yugoslav identity as opposed to other particularistic identities, such as Croatian, Serbian, Slovenian. Generally speaking, "urban residents, the young, those from nationally-mixed parentage, Communist Party members, and persons from minority nationalities in their republic were among those most likely to identify as Yugoslavs" (ibid., p. 93).

In Australia, the question of Yugoslavism was interpreted through the prism of predominant political standards in diaspora organisations. As the very word Yugoslavism espouses tolerance of the idea of Yugoslavia, people who defined themselves in this way were often suspected of being active supporters of the former communist Yugoslav government. Considering the reader's familiarity with the previous chapter, it is easy to imagine how the idea of Yugoslavism could have been perceived in the diaspora context, and particularly so in the Australian-Croatian context.[2]

As will be discussed in more detail in Chapter 5, throughout the post-Second World War period in Australia, it was the Yugoslavs rather than the Serbs who were constructed in the mainstream Australian-Croatian opinion as enemies of (literally) everything Croatian. The Croatian respondents often suggested that many of those who called themselves Yugoslavs have 'the little red books' which supposedly proved their membership of the Yugoslav Communist Party. My acquaintance with some of these 'Yugoslavs' who frequented Yugoslav clubs, showed that Yugoslavia to them was a broad and non-specific homeland concept rather than necessarily the personification of their political aspirations.

Who are these Yugoslavs? The most straightforward answer would be that this identity label refers to individuals who refer to themselves as Yugoslavs regardless of their parents' ancestry. However, my concern with Yugoslavs concerns people who were *constructed as* Yugoslavs in the Australian-Croatian organisations and who have not necessarily identified as such. The Yugoslavs I am concerned with in this chapter are individuals who started to appear in Australian-Croatian community organisations around the start of the conflict in the former Yugoslavia and who had Croatian ethnic ancestries. Because they were 'newcomers' to well established Croatian organisations, they were almost automatically suspected and labelled as being Yugoslavs, although most of them probably had never visited any Yugoslav Clubs and although only some of them formerly called themselves Yugoslav. Their sudden appearance was generally the result of their genuine concerns for the well-being of their family, friends or relatives in the war-torn ethnic homeland.

Regardless of the reasons behind the intolerance of members of Croatian diaspora organisations, what was at work here was the setting up of a boundary which permitted the differentiation between the old and the new incoming members. The incoming members have generated enormous scepticism and suspicion among the established members of diaspora organisations. They were labelled by many different derogatory terms, such as: newborn Croatians, parachutists, former reds or New Year Croatians. These labels were also regularly used to stigmatise those symbolically representing the Other in the internal power-struggles, such as, for example, with younger, more liberal members. The feelings of suspicion are the result of a widespread belief that the ambition of these incoming members is to try to take leadership roles and gain command over the 'community'. In anthropological terms this approximates a fear of symbolic pollution. Their influx therefore caused a degree of siege-mentality among the established members. It is impossible to quantify the influx but it could amount to up to 30 per cent of the existent membership at the time. It needs to be emphasised that the majority of these were individuals who previously had felt no need to join diaspora organisations rather than being actively involved in pro-Yugoslav associations. Their presence in Australian-Croatian diaspora organisations dropped after the military and political tension in the Balkans subsided.

Despite the negative sentiments, these incoming members were tolerated as they could contribute considerably to the support of the Croatian cause in the homeland. The newcomers – although generally not trusted – have been, for example, specifically targeted by the HDZ in both diaspora and the homeland. In the words of one of the leading HDZ representatives in Australia: "We [in the HDZ] try to get these Yugoslavs involved as well. We want to mobilise them". However, this formal 'openness' towards the people they labelled as Yugoslavs encouraged criticisms by more right-wing political factions. These factions complained that the HDZ leadership lacks dignity because it did not refuse to cooperate with the former 'enemies'. Such objections made by right-wingers were further coupled with assertions that many committed members of the HDZ may have questionable political pasts themselves in the sense that their enthusiasm for Croatian independence is of very recent origin and might in fact mask people's past pro-Yugoslav orientation.

Politics plays an important part in the constitution of diaspora organisations. It may involve the overt politics of the homeland, or, at the other end of the spectrum, it may have to do with the day-to-day negotiation of power relations, including the power to determine how these diaspora organisations represent themselves to others. While the former sense of politics is stronger amongst Croatians, the latter sense is found in both Australian-Croatian and Australian-Slovenian contexts. There was a strong tendency towards the politicisation of a wide range of issues: e.g. politically characterising the 'outsider', interpreting generational conflict as a conflict in political values, and interpreting the representation of the diaspora organisations as a political act. The level of politicisation varied widely and comprised a spectrum between the declared 'apolitical' status of the diaspora group to strongly emphasising its political nature.

Even the declared 'apolitical' acts often prove to be highly politically motivated. For instance, the Slovenian Club in Adelaide, South Australia did not accept the visit of a Slovenian Minister of Defence, Janez Janša, in 1992. They justified their position by stating that the Minister represented a *homo politicus* who could not be allowed to enter the politics-free zone of the Slovenian Club. In this case, even if the decision of the Club representatives was not overtly political, the very decision-making process which led to the ban on the Minister's visit was a highly political act.

In their explanations for various politically disputed issues, the 'leaders' of Slovenian diaspora organisations often contradict themselves when legitimising their decisions. When I asked one such Slovenian 'leader', who entertained a belief that 'his' ethnic organisation is free of politics, if the support of the Slovenian *Demos* (anti-communist) opposition bloc prior to the first free elections in 1990 was an expression of political support or not, he said: "At that time, we did not think politically. We had only one goal to follow: all Slovenians for free and independent Slovenia". Politics here was defined as party politics, not nationalist politics.

Many informants and respondents from both ethnic groups mentioned the role of politics in tensions and conflict in diaspora organisations. Diaspora associations are sometimes seen by second generation respondents as a place where people do nothing but discuss politics and "things which happened in 1941". Considerable political tensions occur both *between* and also *within* different political factions and waves of migrants. The political motives for migration of the first wave of post-Second World War Croatian migrants have been discussed in the previous chapter. It is very clear that Croatian political migrants used their political identity to strengthen their position of power in the diaspora organisations. A typical objection to this attitude is well expressed in the words of a young Croatian second generation respondent:

> They will have to accept that they are no longer a Croatian government in exile. That's what their thinking was for many years. They will finally have to give up this idea that they will have a say in a new Croatia.

Matters pertaining to the prestige of political migrants were of very marginal significance in the Australian-Slovenian context.

3 Conforming to norms and standards in diaspora organisations

Despite internal divisions, conflicts, ever-changing alliances and levels of co-operation in diaspora organisations, they nevertheless manage to promote the desired socio-cultural norms. Respondents often explained that they were aware not only of their parents' expectations, but also of standards and norms with which they would either have to conform or conflict.

Obviously, the norms, standards and opinions that are referred to here are not a set of written rules and regulations but the *perception of what people believe* is the right thing to do by an individual identifying with diaspora organisations. Different ethnic groups have different codes related to ethnic honour. These codes are expressed in statements like: "A real Slovenian doesn't do this" or he/she "is a real, honest Croatian". Such statements are to be found in various forms and they are all meant to appeal to the presumed characteristic traits of a given culture.

The notion of ethnic honour is very important in this context. The degree of attention given to questions of honour varies considerably between different groups. Greeks express their concern about 'what will other people say' by *ti tha pei o cosmos* (Bottomley 1979, p. 123) while Italians do so by *che dirà la gente* (c.f. Bertelli 1985). Diaspora organisations pay considerable attention to what other people say and how they are portrayed in public. Preoccupation with their public image and attempts to hide controversial issues as far away from 'outsiders' as possible are not uncommon practice. The censoring of a favourable image has its counterpart in the way in which the host society's state propagates the image of social cohesion through public displays of diversity. The folklorist celebration of ethnic cultures sponsored by the state under the banner of multiculturalism is a good manifestation of this.

The "everpresent gossip network is an important source of information because honor and prestige are generated and evaluated by gossip" (Bottomley 1992, p. 96). The importance of a gossip network within diaspora organisations should not be underestimated. It is one of the most powerful factors which reinforces group cohesion. Its significance was perceptively analysed by Gluckman (1963, p. 313) who argued that "gossiping is a duty of membership of the group" which strengthens the feeling of belonging to the group.

If the responses of the Slovenian respondents in this study are representative of all Slovenian organisations in Australia then it has to be said that gossip is one of the major reasons for the second generation individuals steering away from various diaspora associations. Every little detail of life is believed to be a potential excuse for gossip. Examples include fulfilment of gender-related behaviours and duties, political beliefs, social class and status, alternative life-styles, non-conventional appearance, and many others. Gossip can also be seen as a reason for one's voluntary exclusion from the 'community'.

My awareness of the role and regular occurrence of gossip stems from countless encounters with gossip before, during, and after interviews as well as during my socialising with different respondents. Gossiping was believed to be "a part of Slovenian culture", as one respondent put it. The belief in a permanent gossip network creates a sense of paranoia that makes people believe that they are a constantly vulnerable target. People even stop coming to functions organised by ethnic associations to avoid the possibility of being an object of gossip: "Maybe my father acts a bit paranoid. There is a lot of talking behind the back and he feels he doesn't want to be a part of this".

When in 1992 a young Slovenian sports journalist, MiranAlišič, came to visit Australia to report on a sporting event, he also paid a visit to Slovenian clubs in Melbourne and Adelaide. Upon his return to Slovenia he wrote three articles which were published in a Slovenian tabloid, *Slovenske Novice* (Ališič 1992a, 1992b, 1992c). The articles focused on divisions among Slovenians in Australia and their institutions. The titles of the articles were rather telling: 'Only holidays keep them together', 'Divided Slovenians', 'In Adelaide – like dogs and cats'. When copies of these articles leaked to Slovenians in Adelaide there was a collective outrage (*a là* 'we welcomed him, we gave him free drinks... and he publishes these sort of things'). The journalist returned the following year and again decided to visit the Slovenian Club in Adelaide, unaware of the outrage he had caused a year before. The person who was the president of the Club at the time of his first visit immediately lost emotional control and verbally and physically 'attacked' him. Leaving 'objectivity' aside,[3] within a few days, the gossip about the incident produced three rather different stories: first, "she (the former president, Z.S.) attacked him"; second, "she attacked him and hit him"; third, "she hit him badly and his lip bled". This example is very illustrative of the power of gossip which may ultimately lead to exclusion.

Gossip is, of course, far from used as a neutral tool. It is used to marginalise, stigmatise, exclude or ostracise people who do not conform. One young Croatian couple complained of being ostracised by the Club members for no reason at all when they got married and they went to visit friends living in the country: "We got back and they said we went over there so that [my wife] could have an abortion". Another respondent talked about his experiences as a child when his father switched from one political party to another. Although he was a child, he was ignored by his father's political rivals. The Australian-Croatian settings appear to be particularly sensitive about the political issues and norms which are seen as befitting Croatian ethno-national ideals. In the past, considerable pressure could be used to force a person to conform in a political sense. Gossip could be seen as the first step in this process. However, there are certain practices which were used to warn people about their need to conform, as for example, making harassing calls at night: "[...] we would ring them at two or three o'clock in the morning and then stop. They never tortured us like this but some people would be called like that for months". All of this because people were perceived as not conforming to the desired norms or because their loyalty to the Croatian cause was questioned.

Some of the conflicts among the second generation individuals – this topic will be further elaborated upon later in this chapter – are directly related to political values which are being promoted by a particular group. One respondent reported that in a disco he attended in the Croatian Club, they played the Croatian national anthem and he did not stand still. He was beaten up by his Croatian peers as a consequence of not showing deference and his behaviour was considered a symbolic gesture of disobedience. None of his friends who witnessed the quarrel would intervene to stop the fight. In addition to this, he received no support from his father whose only comment later was: "Well, you deserved it. [...] In the future you should stand up straight during the anthem and don't move until it's finished".

Despite the fact that 'communities' might be wrongly perceived as homogeneous from the outside, there are considerable pressures on their members to comply. The fear of being rejected is well illustrated in the following statement of one respondent:

> Unfortunately, [stereotyping] still exists among Croatians. I disapprove of it, but I never express my disapproval. I fear being rejected again: "*Ti si Jugosloven* (You are a Yugoslav, Z.S.) if you think like that." I just don't want to be confronted. I hope [the interview is] confidential...

Fund-raising was one of the most 'public' activities during my fieldwork in Australian-Croatian settings. It put a lot of pressure on people to publicly acknowledge their support for the Croatian independence struggle and – in a way – to affirm their Croatianess. In fact, one of the most important parts of the Sunday Croatian Radio Program (Adelaide, 5EBI FM) was the acknowledgment of the names and the amounts of money donated by particular persons. This practice was not favoured by a vast majority of the second generation. It was often the parents who donated money on behalf of their children so that the family name did not fall into disrepute:

> **Q:** Did you donate any money?
> **A:** My mum gave and put my name on the radio so that people wouldn't think I had forgotten.

Respondents also suggested that there was a very low tolerance for alternative appearances, therefore people with ear-rings or people wearing Doc Martin's boots would be ostracised. One of the respondents mentioned that a Bon Jovi-type haircut was fashionable among the Croatian youth who were gathering around the Club at the time: "They believe that if you want to be a real Croatian, you need to be like one of these so-called rock groups".

All this is part of a collective preoccupation with setting the boundaries of honour and shame. Peristiany (1974, p. 9) rightly discussed honour and shame as social conditions: "All societies sanction their rules of conduct, rewarding those who conform and punishing those who disobey. ... Honour and shame are two poles of [social] evaluation." The following example is particularly interesting because it reveals not only the pressure to conform to a stereotypical image of a 'good looking Croatian' but also because it clearly hows the gap between the cultural values in the host environment as opposed to those in the ethnic homeland:

> Take the example of ear-rings. In the Croatian community (in Adelaide, Z.S.) it was considered very bad; you were, you know, a lost person. I went to the Croatian club and was being harassed by the older generation. [...] "Nothing, there is nothing you can do unless you are like we want you to be – otherwise you are not with us." There have been comments around the bar: "Here is a hundred dollars to take your ear-rings out and never put them back." He put a hundred dollars in front of me, you know, like: "Get rid of them." Every time. That's why I didn't want to be actively involved in the community – because of this kind of attitude.
> And when I went overseas I thought: "Jesus, what are they going to say, my family [in Croatia]? If that happened to me here, what are they going to do to me over there? I thought: Should I take them out, or... I don't want to offend anyone, you know, I want to live with these people. I want to make friends with them. And I decided: look, they're gonna take me for what I am, I don't want to give them any false impressions. When I got to my uncle's... I was wearing a jacket, looking quite rough, with short hair. We sat down and our first conversation, you know... about country and our family and then, later on he said: "Oh, you have got ear rings!" I thought: Here we go! And he said: "Do you know that your great grandfather used to have one?" "Yes," I said, "my mum told me" (because she was good, she understood). He said, it's a sign of easygoingness and I was very, very surprised. You know, here is a man, 65 years old and from a village, no education,... and he understood exactly what it was. So, this community [here in Adelaide] has perhaps a very isolated perception.

The regulation of gender relations certainly represents an important aspect of normative structure in Croatian and Slovenian diaspora organisations. Gender stereotypes are presented in a more or less subtle way. On a Croatian radio program (5EBI, Adelaide, 15 August 1993), the radio announcer said: "I prompt fathers to remind mothers, they have to bake the biscuits." This example clearly uses the father as a sanction and authority enforcer and females as executors of their orders. It is interesting to note that the leadership positions in diaspora organisations are usually taken up by males. For example, no female has ever been the president of the Croatian Club in Adelaide and only one female has ever been the president of the Slovenian Club. All Croatian and Slovenian Clubs I visited in Melbourne and Sydney during my fieldwork also had male presidents. It needs to be emphasised, however, that the only woman in a top leadership position that I found during my fieldwork was almost totally dependent, in everybody's judgement, on directions received from a male person in a position second to hers. Nevertheless, women play crucial roles the workings at all levels of diaspora organisations.

The division of duties in ethnic organisations often resemble the patriarchal structures of their traditional cultures. Migrant environments are particularly prone to maintaining these structures to prevent the erosion of tradition in a host environment. This contributes to the development of a 'ghetto mentality'. Tradition in this context could be defined as a shelter offering protection from the intrusion of the alien. But, of course, traditions are often reinforced by multicultural policies as well. Consistent with traditional views, second generation women are often not expected to be as good achievers as second-generation men: "Later, when I started with my studies, the whole of Adelaide, all Croatians said: 'She is just a woman, she'll get married and she'll have a baby...'"

4 From antagonism to schism

Diasporas are commonly known to be prone to antagonisms and divisiveness. Italian communities in Australia, for example, are characterised by "stubborn regionalism" (Pascoe 1992, p. 94) which finds its expression in clubs attracting regional-specific membership. Australian-Italians are also known to successfully replicate the supposed superiority of Northerners over Southerners. Diaspora Serbs are similarly divided. In 1965, one segment of the Australian-Serbian diaspora decided to deny legitimacy to the Belgrade Patriarch who was believed to be under the influence of the communist regime. They opted to be governed by the Free Serbian Orthodox Bishop Dionisije in the United States (Kazich 1989, pp. 112-20, c.f. Shevill 1975). Two new and separate diaspora organisations emerged from this conflict, also in Adelaide, South Australia. It was only in 1992 at the synod in Belgrade, the Serbian capital, that the two sparring factions made formal attempts to overcome these divisions (Klemenčič 1993, p. 334).

Obviously, one needs to differentiate between various types and intensities of divisions. The divisions among diaspora Serbs along political lines are probably – although not necessarily – more radical and serious than the one-upmanship between Northern and Southern Italians. It is widely held that Slovenian migrant settings around the globe do not exist in harmony. An expert on Slovenian migrations, the late Peter Klinar (1993, p. 14), was quoted as saying that Slovenians are "world famous for political divisions, mutual arguments and intolerance". This may be illustrated for South Australia with a quote from a first generation respondent who said:

> When the Bishop from Ljubljana arrived in Adelaide in 1983 we pulled down the fence separating the Club and the Church to show him we belong to the same family. It never was that way and it never will be even if we live for a million years. When the visitor left, the fence was again in its place and the stones started to fly over it from both the left and from the right side. There are some 'hot-headed' individuals on both sides: on ours as well as theirs. (translation, Z.S.)

In South Australia, the Slovenian diaspora institutions are divided and have two loosely defined centres, the Church and the Club. I was offered different interpretations of the reasons for the division. Both 'sides' agree, however, that the core of the conflict lies in different approaches to the question about the role the clergy should play in the migrant setting. Some people believed the profane and sacred should be strictly separated, others believed that the Church should play a more traditional and prominent role. This tension reached its height when in 1973 the new rules of the Slovenian Club were endorsed which said that any person who "holds office" in a "religious denomination" should not be allowed also to be a full member of the Club.[4]

Since new rules have been adopted, communication between the conflicting sides has been reduced to a minimum. Any attempts at bridging the divide between the two have traditionally ended in a misunderstanding or have developed into a new conflict. While conducting my fieldwork, I was told by individuals from 'both sides' that 'their' particular arguments were the right ones. There were two kinds of attempts at bridging the gap between the Church and the Club in the past. The first ones were a consequence of genuine efforts to bring together the two sides by individuals who were regular attenders in both the Club and the Church. The second ones were simulated efforts designed to impress outsiders.

Comparing responses from first generation respondents from both sides of the conflict divide, one notices a common logic underlying their responses:

> So long as I am opposed to the Club, nothing can change,... I did not begin the conflict and I cannot finish it.

> While we old members are around, the Rules of the Club will not be altered.

Although the main initiators and protagonists of the conflict are no longer active in the politics of the Club, the problematic relations between the

Church and the Club have not significantly changed. Very similar problems have been encountered in other Slovenian organisations around Australia, although the conflict has never centred around the disputes between the Church (there are Slovenian Churches in Melbourne and Sydney) and the Clubs. Rather, the tensions – predominantly related to the question of profit making – were prominent between different clubs.

If the schism in the South Australian-Slovenian setting relates to the interpretation of the profane/sacred dichotomy, the reasons for divisions in the South Australian-Croatian context depended on the interpretation of political allegiances. Although the South Australian-Croatian diaspora was free of schismatic tensions, divisions were clearly to be felt in, for example, Melbourne "where this club doesn't go with that club, that club doesn't go with that club,...". A case in point is the history of the establishment of the Australian-Croatian Association in Melbourne which was the consequence of a disagreement between the founding members of the Association in 1951. Some of these members wanted to maintain firm contacts with Ante Pavelić's political leadership in Argentina, while others desired an association independent of any external political influence (c.f. Tkalčević 1992, p. 76).

It has been shown so far that politics plays a central role in the initiation of schismatic tendencies and that even disputes between the religious and the profane draw their legitimacy from political platforms. What remains to be explored is the extent to which intergenerational and intragenerational relationships influence the cohesiveness of diaspora settings.

5   Diaspora cohesion and the question of generations

An analysis of the interaction between different generations is crucial to an understanding of the internal dynamics of diasporas. To the second generation individual, the host society is not the direct result of a voluntary or involuntary migration. Essentially, second generation individuals are deprived of the experience of choice (or the experience which is the cause of displacement). For this reason, their whole perception of social reality is very different from that of the first generation migrants.

Israel's kibbutzim provide an interesting comparison as their first generation members joined the community out of free will and for personal reasons. However, as kibbutzim mature, they have increasing numbers of second generation individuals in their midst. The views of the second generation are necessarily different as their perspective is "from inside to without" and they accept the kibbutz's "way of life as unproblematically given, and not as a field of adventure" (Cohen 1982, p. 131). This difference conditions the angle of vision, and to analyse its role is crucial for an understanding of the generation gap which sooner or later gains prominence.

Inter- and intra-generational relations may have a considerable impact on the level of tensions in the diaspora organisations and indirectly determine their future. Peric (1993, p. 1) mentions the continuous regurgitation of the following statement in the Croatian community: "The youth do not know anything." The members of a young generation sometimes feel that the older generation will never recognise the fact that they have in a sense 'grown up'. Instead, they remain patronised: "We graduated from the Universities a long time ago, but we are still *studenti* [students, Z.S.], big kids... to them. We'll just always be kids. [...] Whenever I helped to organise something, the comment was always: 'Good, isn't that cute?'" [5]

The younger generation often feel frustrated with their lack of opportunity to change things and they often believe that it is worthless to try to challenge the first generation's patronising pose. Moreover, the dying out of the older generation members is portrayed by the second generation as either the beginning of the end or as the very last opportunity for diaspora renaissance. Interestingly, there was very little mention of constructive cooperation between different generations. Nevertheless, in the interviews the first generation migrants placed an enormous amount of emphasis on the attention they and 'their' organisations apparently pay to bridging the gap between the generations. Without a single exception, the members of the first generation were all in favour of an increased inclusion of the younger generation into the leadership positions. However, these assurances were normally highly declarative, such as: "Our first task is to involve the younger generation in the leadership positions"; or "Youth is our future!". Even more interestingly, many first generation participants in this study expressed self-criticism in relation to this question or at least held their generation responsible for these problems. Slovenians in particular emphasised the negative effects of the divisions between different segments of the diaspora organisations on the lack of participation of second generation individuals.

Let us take a look at the situation in both Croatian and Slovenian clubs in Adelaide in the second half of 1994. The Slovenian Club had no second generation individuals on the management committee, despite the ever-present rhetoric about the inclusion of the younger generation into leadership structures. Interestingly, in exactly the same period, the second generation South Australian-Slovenians attempted to organise themselves for the first time. Related to this was the production of an informative *Slovenian Second Generation Survey* (1994). The survey was initiated and commissioned by some Slovenians who decided to test the enthusiasm of fellow second generation individuals in becoming engaged in the affairs of the Slovenian Club. For the purpose of the survey, 64 questionnaires were mailed to

Slovenian households and 31 were returned. The survey asked a variety of questions ranging from Club activities to a question on what should happen to the Club in the future. The survey revealed that respondents seldom visit the present Club and that they are not prepared to sacrifice much of their spare time to become engaged in voluntary work for the Club. Nevertheless, the survey clearly revealed the second generation's desire for more involvement of their generation (88.5 per cent of respondents surveyed). This may be understood as a critique of both the past and the present exclusion of second generation individuals from the committee of the Club. One participant in the survey who had served as a committee member a while before stated that he/she was "not taken seriously" and was constantly controlled by the older generation (ibid., p. 8). However, the meeting of second generation individuals related to initiation and production of this particular survey in the Club's premises stimulated the following comment by a first generation female: "They will take over the Club and not allow us [the older members, Z.S.] to have any influence. They will forget about us" (translation, Z.S.).

The issue of the second generation's participation in the leadership is far less of a problem in the Croatian-Australian context. For example, in 1994, the committee of the Croatian Club in Adelaide had about 20 members and six of these were second generation individuals. While Australian-Slovenian settings suffer from inter-generational conflict and tension, the Australian-Croatian settings seem to be even more prone to them. This could be summarised by quoting the Croatian emigrè writer, Korsky (1983, p. 229), who interestingly explains the generation conflict in Croatian diaspora by mixing his narrative with elements of nationalist discourse:

> In the eyes of the old ones, the rising generation figures as a group of iconoclasts: breaking the established forms and attacking old dogmas. For this reason, the older ones relate to the younger ones mistrustfully, not giving them credit for being the young sprouts of the millennia old Croatian national trunk. They believe the breaking down of old forms is blasphemy and something which "good Croatians" have to oppose. (translation, Z.S.)

There was noticeable intragenerational tension in Australian-Croatian settings. The Croatian second generation presence in ethnic organisations indirectly reflected the distribution of political power within different organisations as most influential political parties had youth branches and their members sought representation in the overall running of the social clubs. The most interesting example of intragenerational tension was that between the influential right wing HOP youth and their Croatian peers. The latter negatively portrayed the former as "oriented towards the Ustasha movement and Ante Pavelić". Members of the HOP Youth obviously welcomed this accusation. Also, the young HOP members were seen by their opponents as: "the first of those you don't argue with. It serves no purpose. You don't talk about historical things. It's black and white [for them] without real arguments for a discussion. They believe they are more Croatian [than we are]." The intensity and nature of hostile sentiments towards the HOP Youth by their peers was revealed by the following statement which corresponds to what was mentioned to me by several other Croatian respondents: "The members of the HOP are young, good looking and stupid. They are too radical and they don't think with their heads but with their fists."

There are no similarities with the Slovenian second generation representation in this respect. The Slovenian Clubs were perceived and promoted as relatively apolitical institutions, and the political parties which would encourage second generation individuals to proliferate through the internal hierarchies of diaspora organisations are non-existent. The relative absence of second generation individuals from Australian-Slovenian organisations also reduces the possibility of intragenerational conflict.

6   Concerns about the future of diaspora organisations

The question of concern for the future of diaspora organisations is paramount in the rhetoric of members of the diaspora elite. This rhetoric, however, also indicates a genuine underlying anxiety among first generation migrants about the non-existence of ethno-specific institutional support in their old age.

There were important variations in opinion about the future of ethnic organisations between Croatians and Slovenians. Although Croatian respondents were just as concerned about the future as Slovenians, the majority believed that Croatian culture in Australia, as well as various formal associations, would survive for decades to come. The war in Croatia caused a considerable influx of new members and this gave an impression of particular communal virility and contained a promise of longevity of ethno-national strength. The war encouraged cohesiveness in the diaspora setting. In the words of a second generation respondent: "Today our community is harmonious and united as it never was before."

Second generation respondents found value in the existence of the 'community' – identified with the Club and the Church – although they did not necessarily see advantages in "being a part of this organisation". Quite a few second generation Croatian respondents appeared to be uncritically accepting of the status quo:

> I consider the Croatian Club as my second home. I can go there and it is just like a big family. Everybody gets along with each other. Big Croatian house, I think.
>
> I think that the Croatian community in Adelaide will continue to survive into the future. We have a beautiful new and modern club, and hundreds of members.

The majority of Slovenian respondents could not envisage a positive future for the Slovenian organisations in Australia. This finding is consistent with Birsa's (1994, p. 201) comment on the failure of the Slovenian youth radio program in Melbourne in 1981, namely that "the second generation are not interested in affirming their Slovenian ethnicity...". Although second generation respondents generally value the existence of ethnic associations as such, there was a considerable degree of dissatisfaction about their current state of affairs. A Slovenian respondent listed the following disadvantages of being involved with the Slovenian Club: "... frequent encounters with narrow minded views, encroachment on privacy; a drain on the purse; disillusionment with any illusion of preserving authenticity in the next generation." This quotation summarises succinctly the general thoughts and considerations of Slovenian second generation respondents. The majority of second generation Slovenians expressed highly critical statements about Slovenian associations: "I doubt there will be any change. Then perhaps there could be, but only if new people come from Slovenia. Slovenians here are always the same – from day to day. They do the best they can. But I can't see the emergence of change." Obviously, one feature which distinguishes both Croatian and Slovenian settings is the importance placed by the respondents on the intake of new migrants. There is very little migration from Slovenia to Australia while a significant number of Croatians have been arriving over the past years as refugees.

7 The problem of representation in ethnic communities

Bearing in mind that the most common diaspora institutions are the Clubs/Associations and the Churches or well-defined congregations, persons fitting the role of representatives who immediately come to mind include the president or spokesperson of a club and religious persons serving the people of a particular background. The president of a club (or its spokesperson) can hardly be seen as representative of the opinion of an entire 'community' because the club is just an institution with a limited membership.[6] There are similar problems with the religious leader as representative. Even if certain ethnic groups are seemingly homogeneous through a common religious affiliation, it cannot be assumed that all their members are religious, let alone active church members. More commonly, members of a single ethnic group may be affiliated with different religions. One could likewise dispute the position of the ethnic community spokesperson since it remains unclear who/what they really represent. Besides, they are usually individuals who have not been democratically elected to represent the community but have the capability and skills (language of the host society immediately comes to mind) to confront the public and the media. Second generation individuals could be used not only to represent but also to provide the link with host society institutions. Lack of knowledge of host society institutions, dominant political discourses such as multiculturalism, and lack of skills for effective representation effectively provide a fertile ground for the idea that migrants cannot represent themselves but must be represented.

The responsibility of diaspora organisation representatives is huge as they face an impossible task, namely to respond to the *felt* solidarity of diaspora members which is often contradictory in itself. They also have to act (or at least parade) as the defenders of 'tradition'. The need for ethnic groups to be represented is of the utmost importance to their membership in the host society.

In Adelaide's Croatian setting there were different aspirants for leadership. Different political segments of the community had characteristics of 'alternative elites' although their representatives were already incorporated into the existent leadership and management structures. An example of this was the competition and rivalry between the HDZ and HOP, although the former strongly dominated both in terms of the numerical strength of its members and its political influence. The religious congregation was also well integrated. An interesting example of an emerging alternative elite was the establishment of the Croatian Lobby Group which was attracting exclusively second generation membership at the beginning of the war in Croatia (1991). The members of this group introduce many alternative ideas and this started to challenge some of the actions of the established organisations. Its members strongly aspired to greater representation. However, with the recognition of the Republic of Croatia its power started to diminish and by the end of 1992 it had lost its appeal.

While Adelaide's Croatian organisations have integrated their constituent parts relatively well in the sense of providing an overarching institutional solidarity, this was not the case with Adelaide's Slovenian setting:

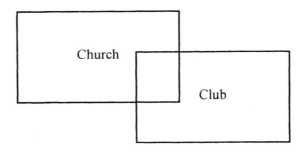

Figure 3.2   Schematic representation of Slovenian diaspora institutional framework in Adelaide, South Australia

Figure 3.2 shows that the members of the Australian-Slovenian diaspora gather around two different institutions. Although the split between them is in fact a schism, the overlapping of both institutions in the figure above illustrates that that schism can hardly ever be complete and that some individuals do cross the boundaries. Yet it has to be acknowledged that even those who cross the boundaries recognise the existence of a schism.

There is an important difference between these schismatic institutions. The Church functions differently to the Club, for in the Church there was very little internal differentiation and in terms of institutional power relations it is only the priest who matters. There are obviously no popular aspirants to his position. The Club is different in this sense and its civic structure encourages competition. Powerful and ambitious individuals with like-minded supporters function as 'alternative elites'.

The question of representation is apt to create conflicting situations and can be perceived as a general problem of ethnic organisation in diaspora environments. Who is chosen to represent and by whom? As one respondent analysed the situation in the Croatian community in Sydney: "There are certain bodies that try to bring together various groups. There are three of them. They would all consider themselves as an elite. They try to subvert each other".

7.1   Whither community

This chapter has explained the strategic prominence of tension, conflict and division in the diaspora context. While overarching values and interests are definitely observable, the communitarian implications of the term ethnic community seem rather inadequate. It was suggested that a broadly defined concept of diaspora is far better suited to this task as it implies no value bias.

Some interesting comparative differences between Croatian and Slovenian communities again emerged. It was found that in the Australian-Croatian context party politics and the question of ethno-national loyalty are significant factors in understanding the functioning of Australian-Croatian diaspora associations. Despite considerable tension in these associations, the feeling of significant communal strength is notably present. All of this was quite the opposite in Australian-Slovenian associations which are concerned with homeland-related politics to a very limited extent although heavily consumed with petty feuding. Also, Australian-Slovenian associations are characterised by the declining numbers of second generation individuals willing to take part in organisational activities. These generalised findings are supported by the discussion in the previous chapter wherein we established the underlying historical factors which determine the nature of Australian-Croatian and Australian-Slovenian infrastructure. Again, the prevalence of nationalist ideas pertaining to homeland politics in the Croatian setting can be seen as playing an important part in all this. Strong nationalist sentiments have proven to provide a fertile ground for overall diaspora strength.

The next chapter takes the argument further. The idea of a 'distant view' implies the lag which appears in relationships between homelands and diasporas. This lag relates to the question of a differential evaluation of phenomena and processes which are deemed to be of significance to an ethno-national collectivity. The chapter then assesses the importance of invented nationalist interpretations of history, the differential significance of political parties in the homeland and diaspora, the power of symbols, and so on.

8   Notes

1   This incident was also discussed in Chapter 1, section 3.3, 'The size and representativeness of the research setting'.
2   Further elaboration on this issue is to be found in Chapter 5, section 3, 'Croatians on the 'practical identity' of Yugoslavs'.
3   According to MrAlišič himself, the attacker actually missed him.
4   This disputed alteration to the *Rules of the Slovenian Club Incorporated* (Slovenian Club Incorporated 1973), is still firmly in place and reads: "Any member who holds office in any political organisation, or religious denomination shall not be eligible to serve on the committee of the club."
5   This issue was often discussed in the monthly journal *Klokan*, published by second generation Croatian youth.

6. The Club's committees could be seen as collective leadership bodies. While leaders of Croatian diaspora organisations usually act assertively, the presidents of Slovenian clubs all too often find themselves in a stalemate position. A representative account of this is the following quotation from an interview with one such president: "I have no mandate to talk on the behalf of the Club. I can tell you only generally how we think and how we see things. I wouldn't like to discuss the details about the Club. In fact, I have no right to do so as we have our committee and this is where we have to discuss things first".

4 The distant view

1 Mediation of information about the homeland

An analysis of the information flow and interaction processes between homelands and diasporas is of central importance to the understanding of contemporary migratory processes. The technology which enables long-distance communication and travel contributes to as well as encourages long-distance interaction on a massive scale (Margolis 1995, Naficy 1991). While it is becoming increasingly easier for people to transgress the constraints of time and space, this transgression is never complete.

It seems that quite often the imagining of a homeland becomes an exercise in manipulation with political symbolism. Schierup and Ålund (1986) give an interesting example of how the intensity of symbolic imagining is amplified by migrant experience and overall distance from the homeland. In their description of the experience of a Wallachian[1] labour migrant named Milorad in Denmark they mention an old Wallachian belief that dead people with whom one was in conflict during their life-time cannot find peace in the grave and therefore haunt the living – they turn into *vampires* (*moroj* in Wallachian). Milorad, an educated man, believed his dead mother was haunting him because he had chosen to marry a woman she disapproved of. As a consequence, he was prone to see his deceased mother "hovering outside the window in her white burial attire, muttering with a distant voice: 'Why have you left me?'" (ibid., p. 33).

Milorad's example is rather specifically Wallachian and fully conditioned by Wallachian tradition. Nevertheless, Schierup and Ålund make an interesting observation in relation to this resurgence of 'vampirism' in the Danish immigrant context:

> Thus, the strategic importance of "vampires" tends to increase as integration in Scandinavian society grows. *Vampires not only survive,*

but are even invoked more often in migrant communities, than in the premigratory rural situation. (ibid., p. 54, emphasis added, Z.S.)

The reasoning behind this argument resembles my experience in Australian-Croatian and Australian-Slovenian settings (short, that is, of specific mention of vampires). One interesting and very apparent characteristic of these settings was their *amplified receptivity* to ethno-national myths and propaganda. Just as Milorad was more prone to see his mother turned into a vampire in Sweden than he would have been back home, so are ethno-national myths more likely to be favourably perceived in the diaspora than in the homelands. This may not be a universal pattern but is definitely a valid point when discussing Croatian and Slovenian diasporas. Of course, it would be ridiculous to suggest that such myths do not appear in homelands or that diasporas are their exclusive producers and disseminators. What I wish to argue is that diasporas represent ideal targets for such ethno-national myths and propaganda. In addition, Australian policies of multiculturalism with their encouragement of folkloristic celebrations of culture, seem to act as their catalysts.

Diaspora settings tend to be very selective receptors of information concerning the homeland. Obviously, they do not function as passive receptors and they also selectively generate and transmit ideas. This generative function varies between diasporas, but as a rule, the more organised the diasporas, the greater the chance of generative success. Also, the greater the disparities between homelands and diasporas (whether because of political differences or because of the length of diaspora existence) the greater the likelihood of an emphasised generative function of the diaspora. This differential selectivity between the two settings is what I call the 'distant view'. As this chapter will reveal, the distant view is also related to a series of issues which will be discussed in this chapter, such as the manipulation of the past, the power of religious symbolism and so on, all of which seem to be at a *different level of intensity* and/or significance to similar processes in the homeland.

It needs to be emphasised again that distance is not defined in terms of miles but in terms of the cultural and symbolic detachment of the migrant setting from the homeland. This detachment appears to cause a tendency to amplify certain aspects of the homeland reality and to minimise or discard the significance of others. The 'distant view' is crucial for an understanding of nationalism in diaspora settings. It produces a *sieve-effect* which encourages the selective flow of information. It is precisely this sieve-effect logic which has a capacity in the diaspora to put a different spin on the nationalist politics which dominates the homeland setting. The diaspora may, for instance, nurture political conservatism (e.g. specific political ideals) where such conservatism is absent in the homelands. Naficy (1991, p. 297) illustrates this point in his analysis of Iranian exile television in the United States:

> The physical distance between Iran and the United States creates not only a difference of time zones [...] but also a feeling that Islamicized Iran is living (or even reliving) a different historical epoch. Exile television bridges these dual gaps: the exiles – distanced spatially – are made synchronous temporally.

I wish to express a degree of scepticism regarding the success of such purported 'bridging'. From my observations (which admittedly do not relate to exile TV but to a whole array of interactions between homelands and diasporas), such interaction can be used specifically for asynchronisations. In other words, differences may well be artificially stimulated. Naficy (ibid.) gets to this point when he further explains that the synchronisation is created by making "the pre-Islamic past, in whose fetishes are encoded the values of Iranian antiquity, historicity, national chauvinism, patriotism, and superiority" the main reference point.

The simplest version of a 'distant view' situation is lucidly captured in the words of a female respondent who was the first person from a family of 'political' migrants to visit Croatia in the mid-1970s:

> I think Croatian people here in Adelaide wanted to believe that the life they had here was so much better than what they had in Croatia. Because they left at a very bad time they wanted to believe it was still like that. They wanted to justify why they were living here. When I was there in 1975 ... I found that my generation was living very well – everybody was working, everybody was living comfortably, they ate well, in my opinion they had a better life than we did back here.
>
> When I came back [to Australia] I mentioned that to a lot of people and I was an outcast: "What are you talking about?" Because at that time people weren't travelling backwards and forwards as they do now. They told me that I was stupid, even though I had a movie camera and I produced film after film. ... When I said to people: "Look, it's not like you think it is", they didn't want to listen, they didn't want to hear that they had a good life there. My parents didn't want to believe that.

It is important to acknowledge that the first generation migrants can less easily entertain such a comparatively positive view of the homeland, as recognition of the progress or positive change in the homeland might challenge the appropriateness of their decision to emigrate. The distant view holds comfort.

It is not only the physical distance and detachment that matter. Benedict Anderson (1992b, p. 11) captures this point in his story of a Canadian Sikh who is a fanatical supporter of the movement for Khalistan:

> His political participation is directed towards an imagined heimat in which he does not intend to live, where he pays no taxes, where he will not be brought before the courts – and where he does not vote: in effect, a politics without responsibility or accountability. Yet, it is this kind of politics, with its ersatz aura of drama, sacrifice, violence, speed, secrecy, heroism and conspiracy that contributes substantially to making 'being Sikh' in Toronto a serious affair.

Perhaps it is the safety offered by the detachment from direct involvement and direct experience which makes diaspora populations potentially more stubbornly and passionately nationalistic than their homeland counterparts.

In analysing the flow of information both between Croatian and Slovenian diasporas and their respective homelands it became clear that certain kinds of information were more likely to reach the Australian diaspora than others. This selective process depended just as much on the desire of the homeland establishment to target its diaspora with particular information as it did on the willingness of diaspora settings to accept and disseminate this information, possibly even amplifying and further channelling its content. The nature and frequency of contact between the diasporas and homelands strongly affects the information flow and its selectiveness. In fact, the relative absence of contact between the two settings may cause an increased selectivity in the information flow.

This can most clearly be illustrated with reference to the highly selective flow of information from Croatia (which then formed a constitutive part of Yugoslavia) to the Australian-Croatian diaspora. Such sieve-effect interaction lasted from the early post-Second World War period until approximately the late 1980s. During most of this period (with political liberalisation in the homeland starting to take place around mid-1980s) all information from the homeland was perceived with mistrust as it could always be tainted with the ideas of Yugoslavism and 'brotherhood and unity'. It was for this reason that most information was *a priori* screened for what diaspora organisational elites perceived as ideological and political propaganda. The screening process did not take place in a formalised and institutional fashion but rather consisted of informal questioning of sources and messages. The final product of this selectivity was nevertheless very much according to expectations of what was believed to be the *communis opinio*. The selection of information was largely dependent on the norms promoted and deemed acceptable to the powerful elites in diaspora organisations. Where the diaspora discourse is determined by political migrants, the information which is acceptable, and indeed required, for the maintenance of the diaspora power structure will inevitably and almost invariably be coloured with 'suitable' political bias. The discouragement of alternative political views is another side of this process. The control of the information flow was perceived as enabling the maintenance of – what was believed to be – the purest form of Croatianism, a task impossible to achieve in the context of an ideologically corrupt homeland. As for the interaction between the Slovenian diaspora and homeland, the question of the selective flow of information was slightly less obvious, partly because of its relatively apolitical nature.

It should be noted that what I choose to call the 'distant view' is not sufficient for an understanding of information flows in migrant settings. One has to look at the related consequences of the phenomenon to understand this process fully. This is precisely what the next section attempts to do. It will explore how the research settings acted selectively in adopting, generating and transmitting information.

2 'Tabloid' political culture as mainstream culture

A second generation Croatian proudly exclaimed:

> I am very pleased to have been born into a Croatian family and feel rather lucky to be part of such a unique, beautiful nationality. I would never have wished to be a part of any other nationality. I believe Croatia and Croatians are unique, beautiful and special (the Virgin Mary[2] appears there) and know one day we will be free and independent. Croatians have a sense of belonging to one another as we are on the same road, the road to a free Croatia.

Selective and positive self-praising was very commonly encountered in the fieldwork. A Croatian male from Croatia who traveled around the world on a bicycle "to tell the world the real [sic!] truth about Croatia" wrote in the Australian-Croatian youth magazine *Klokan*: "I have passed many moments with Croatians [in Australia] and I can say that we Croats are a unique people: we are so good, honourable and benevolent, it is unbelievable. I am proud that I am a Croat and that my homeland is Croatia" (Tokic 1992, p. 11).

Similarly, the Slovenian Research Center of America (Ohio) devotes much effort to proving what Slovenians have contributed to the world. Its enumeration of Slovenian achievements is rather idiosyncratic. However, Slovenian diasporas around the globe get enormously excited about the whole project, as it promises to change the stereotype about 'a small nation and its people'. According to the Slovenian Research Center of America Newsletter:

> [Slovenia gave] the United States at least nine bishops... Vatican diplomats to Rome, Switzerland, Austria, Scandinavia, and Asia... the present archbishop of the biggest Catholic diocese in Canada... Tom Harkin, whose mother was born in Škofja Loka [Slovenia]... even became a candidate for the president [of the United States]. A Slovenian was the first to capture and interrogate Hitler's personal driver... (Slovenian Research Center of America 1993, pp. 1-2)

The reader might think that this information is irrelevant to Slovenians in Australia but in fact it quickly prompted the idea of a project to "list all people of Slovenian background in Australia who have at least tertiary education" (Gregorič 1994, p. 7). The argument behind this idea was as follows: The wider society believes Slovenians are a small and unimportant group, but 'we' also have our own culture, our own educated people, our own rich heritage... Such enthusiasm may hardly be warranted in a society in which tertiary educated people are not a rarity. It could hardly make a particularly breathtaking impression. In any case, among the first five listings which were part of this project were an astrophysicist with a PhD and a person who was awarded the "'Apprentice of the Year' in 1984 as the best fitter and turner apprentice in Queensland while attending the Eagle Farm Trade College" (ibid.). There are, of course, parallels with similar projects by other groups. In the United States ethnic groups' celebratory self-projections are commonplace, while in Australia the promotion of multiculturalism also invites them. When the Director of the Slovenian Research Center Inc. visited Australia in 1998, the Catholic monthly *Misli* was again quick to call: "If you know of any Slovenian or a person of Slovenian descent who succeeded in life in whichever way, please send information to..." (Ceferin 1998, p. 138).

Diaspora groups, with backgrounds in post-communist societies, are inclined to be very sensitive to any changes on the left side of the political spectrum in their homelands. For example, in 1993 six Slovenian politicians in Slovenia demonstratively returned decorations of honour awarded to them by the president of the Slovenian Republic. In their 'Open Letter to the Public' they criticised the fact that in Slovenia an alleged group of influential people is active who are "in favour of the revival" of Yugoslavia (Bavčar et al. 1993, p. 3). Although the Slovenian mainstream press interpreted this affair almost purely as a public gesture which should earn these politicians a few badly needed political points, the Australian-Slovenian press promptly interpreted this affair in highly alarmist language as if this action represented the reaction to a significant left-wing conspiracy. The Editorial to the Australian *Glas Slovenije/Voice of Slovenia* advised the reader to read the 'Open Letter to the Public' reprinted in the current issue:

> ... to get the real [sic!] image of what is happening at home; and there are sad things happening back there. Almost unbelievable! It seems suicidal that some Slovenian politicians, entrepreneurs, youth and journalists urge a return to some sort of confederative Yugoslav 'babble'. (Gregorič 1993a, p. 2, translation, Z.S.)

The alarmist tone present in the above message has an assured circulation. Maria Tenezakis (1984, p. 216) in her study of Arab and Greek newspapers and their readers in Sydney makes a comment which is quite appropriate to the present discussion as well:

> In looking for factors affecting content [of the 'ethnic' press], it is obviously important to pay attention to characteristics of the individuals involved in the production of ethnic newspapers as well as characteristics of the population groups to which these papers are targeted.

The 'ethnic' press is highly influenced by the diaspora intellectual elite. These elites are commonly guided by the belief that the spreading and propagating of particular ideas and information serve the interests of the cultural survival of their ethnic group outside the homeland. These concerns are most often genuine but the logic behind them and the procedures which follow from them often show an important difference between the migrant and homeland environments. The difference could be summarised by proposing that in many cases what is understood to be the *tabloid* political culture in the homeland is perceived and judged as the *mainstream* political culture in the diaspora setting. 'Tabloid' culture in this context mostly refers to three sources of information: first, alarmist information generally to be found in the right-wing oriented media; second, other media inclined towards sensationalism and *a priori* bias; and third, the purportedly scientific discourses which go against established scientific knowledge (see this chapter below). Furthermore, as many incidents reveal, the homeland's political establishment actually often 'sells' its tabloid political culture to diaspora populations as mainstream culture. The deployment and utilisation of tabloid political culture is a significant mode of homeland interaction with the diaspora, but obviously not the only one.

Let me try to explain the nature of homeland-diaspora interaction by referring to the above-mentioned case of the homeland sports journalist,Ališič.[3] He was 'attacked' in the Slovenian Club in Adelaide after publishing an article in a Slovenian tabloid magazine that portrayed Australian-Slovenians as consumed by petty feuding. While this was not in any way a mainstream characterisation of Australian-Slovenian migrant settings, his articles were considered by a substantial segment of the migrants as extremely serious and typical of the inaccurate portrayal of Slovenian emigrants in the homeland.

The process of selling political tabloid culture became obvious at several meetings between distinguished politicians from Croatia and Australian-Croatians. The most outstanding examples are two statements made by the high-ranking Croatian politician, Stipe Mesić (the last president of the collective presidency of the former Yugoslavia), at his meeting with the Croatians of Adelaide in early 1993. During that meeting he commented on Slovenian-Croatian relations: "[Slovenians] would like access to the open sea – well, they won't get it!" In relation to Croatian military advances on the Southern battle-fields, he commented: "Croatia will launch a counter-attack and we'll go as far as need be – to the Drina river and even further!" (applause). These two statements might appear unremarkable. Their contextualisation, however, sheds a different light on them. The comment about Slovenian-Croatian relations was made at a time when Croatian politicians in Croatia were talking extremely diplomatically about that same issue. At the time, this statement was at odds with the official Croatian policy which Stipe Mesić helped formulate. Australian-Croatians were not surprised by the references to 'crossing the border at the river Drina' as this particular hegemonic rhetorical formula has always been firmly present in diaspora circles: The Drina river flows on the border between Bosnia and Herzegovina and Serbia and has always been used as a symbolic frontier of Croatia within its purportedly 'historical' boundaries. The second statement was also at odds with the official line of the HDZ Government (the party and the government which he was representing), but obviously considered *suitable* for an Australian-Croatian setting. The effect of his verbal radicalism was to achieve the desired greater mobilisation of diaspora support without having to take any political risks. Similarly, the HDZ, as many of its representatives confirmed in discussions with me, uses a more heavy-handed rhetoric when communicating with diasporas than in the homeland.

Similarly, one of the main informal tasks of Australian-Croatian Radio programs was to try to keep up the nationalist sentiment of Croatians abroad. At the time of the military activity in Croatia and Bosnia and Herzegovina, the radio news always portrayed Croatians as the main victims of the military aggression. The formula for the news from the battle-front was 'Chetnic (or

Muslim) forces attacked the positions of Croatian defenders' rendering Croatians as innocent victims having the right to counter the aggression. One might have suspected that Croatian forces provoked the attack when the commentator used an impersonal expression and said that 'fighting occurred between' Croatian forces and Serbian or Muslim soldiers. The mortality rate among the Croatian-soldiers in these news bulletins was always unusually low compared to the numbers of the enemy casualties. At the beginning of the military conflict in 1991 and early to mid-1992 there was an emphasis on presenting the Serbs as the main aggressors in the conflict. The more the alliance between Croatians and Muslims deteriorated later in the conflict, the more Bosnian Muslims began to be presented as traitors. While the Serbian soldiers were almost always called the Chetnics, Muslims gradually began to be identified with 'Muslim fundamentalists', implying that the alliance started to deteriorate because of the territorial pretensions of Bosnian Muslims rather than the other way around. In the later part of 1994 when the alliance between Croatians and Muslims again grew stronger, the terminology of radio commentators adapted to the new situation and the language they used began to be more and more neutral.

A similar process of oscillatory assessment of Muslims was taking place in the Croatian homeland press. When Muslims were no longer seen as 'natural' Croatian allies, they started to be named "wild Muslim fanatics, Mujahedins, Islamic fundamentalists, Osmanlians" in the central Croatian daily Vjestnik (Malešević and Uzelac 1997, p. 294). But although the homeland media often acted in a similar fashion to those in the diaspora by distorting the truthfulness of information or emphasising the successes rather than the losses, the main difference relates to the greater media diversification in the homeland and the much higher likelihood of critical commentary.

3 Invention, manipulation and legitimation

3.1 The maps

Under the influence of the 'distant view', a simple speculation easily takes on the form of a truth. Prpic (1971, p. 399) imaginatively observes that "(t)here are some American towns with names which originated from Croatian lands and names. There are Dalmatia and Salona in Pennsylvania; Balkan in Kentucky; Zora in Montana; Bosnia in Kansas; and Tesla in West Virginia. Yet surprisingly, these places do not hold a Croatian population." What is interesting is a provocatively misleading use of some names. For example, 'Bosnia' *hic et nunc* is not a 'Croatian land' and 'Balkan' can hardly be equated with the 'Croatian land'.

Manipulative statements of the above type are particularly likely to be exploited in arguing for a nation's identity and heroic past. Why is it that diaspora settings are particularly susceptible to the perpetuation of such glorificatory information? It would be too simple to explain this in terms of political manipulation. If anything, this type of information is utilitarian as it gives a supposedly firm base for identity and a sense of historical continuity. Some diaspora settings mount little opposition to manipulatory information which parades as scientific fact. I was recently told by an Australian that Slovenians are lucky and blessed people as Mary took Jesus to Slovenia and raised him there. He learned about this information from first generation Australian-Slovenians. The point is this: if there is an assured public for such information, then it is to be found in the diaspora.

Manipulative propaganda was particularly exploited during the height of the military conflict in Croatia and Bosnia and Herzegovina. Semi-qualified arguments are handy and easy for readers to understand. For example, *Klokan*, the Australian-Croatian youth magazine published an article by a contemporary Croatian writer, Horvatic (1994a, p. 3), in which one can find quoted the following statement made by a Croatian politician in 1916: "... the Turks could never ever advance on Zagreb, never break Croatian resistance!... Croatia has never been defeated... Croatia is one of the oldest, if not the oldest, state in Europe, dating back to the seventh century." Horvatic added:

> ... and between the fifteenth and the eighteenth centuries the state of Croatia, although reduced to 'reliquiae reliquiarum olim magni et inclyti regni Croatiae' (the relics of the relics of the formerly great and glorious Kingdom of Croatia), nevertheless stood as the 'antemurale christianitatis', the shield of Christianity, that is, Western civilization. (ibid.)

This writing, published without critical or editorial commentary has all the qualities of nationalist mythology which tends to mix historical events with dramatic narrative interpretations. Horvatic's writing is a pure example of such mythologising which is made possible only by the 'selective amnesia' of the author in order to construct a suitable historical milieu for his narrative (c.f. Smith 1990, p. 180). Whether Horvatic's article was published to be read in Croatia or in the diaspora seems irrelevant; his is exactly the style profoundly characteristic of and suited to Australian-Croatian political culture. Horvatic's argument reveals that the mythical past has an enormous attraction to ethno-nationalist ideology (c.f. Armstrong 1982, p. 9, Djilas 1991, p. 105, Connor 1992). His use of *reliquiae reliquiarum olim magni et inclyti regni Croatiae* implies the unspeakable and not-very-precisely definable past and the notion of *antemurale christianitatis* suggests strong affinities with religious imagining. The relativity of Horvatic's claims becomes obvious when one discovers that Slovenian and Hungarian nationalists have also been known to pride themselves with *antemurale christianitatis* as one of the cornerstones of their ethno-national history. Fascination with the glorious past and the nation's past greatness is an essential element of every nationalist discourse. It should thus come as no surprise that the Croatian president Tudjman acted as a distinguished sponsor of the exhibition of 'Borders of Croatia on Maps from 12th to 20th Century' and wrote a Prologue to the Exhibition's Catalogue (Tudjman 1992). Some of his words read similarly to Horvatic's: "Torn apart and decimated, Croatia once became the *reliquire reliquiarum* i.e. the remains of the remains. Yet, it has never vanished or been destroyed without traces...".

Many Croatian Clubs in Australia have a map of Croatia in its 'historical borders' on their walls. According to these maps, Croatia comprises the present-day Croatia including Bosnia and Herzegovina and a large section of Serbia. Interestingly, my questions about these maps always caused a degree of uneasiness and it was usually mentioned that such depictions of an enlarged Croatia represent the historical fact rather than being suggestive of any expansionist ambitions. Only members and sympathisers of right-wing political parties felt comfortable explaining that the border on the river Drina is Croatian (i.e. their) 'minimal demand' for the enlargement of the present-day Croatian state. In my discussions with Serbian and Muslim individuals in Australia I was also enthusiastically invited to view maps of Bosnia and Serbia – both within their 'historical' borders. I have not, however, come across such a Slovenian map. Needless to say, when Croatian, Muslim and Serbian 'historical' maps are compared, there is a predictable territorial overlap and they all cover a substantial proportion of the Balkan peninsula.

3.2 The 'Tesla case'

A similar type of historical distortion and manipulation is noticed when one considers the highly ambiguous usage of the name and identity of the world-famous innovator in the field of electricity research, Nikola Tesla. Croatian nationalists commonly refer to him as a 'famous Croatian'. On the Croatian youth radio program in Adelaide (5 UV, 9 February 1992) he was simply referred to under the rubric 'important Croatians'. He is also referred to as "the son of a Croatian Orthodox priest" (Prpic 1971, p. 346) without actually explaining whether 'Croatian' refers to territoriality or ethnicity. The above-mentioned Horvatic (1994b, p. 14) wrote simply that Tesla was "the native son of his country". The manipulation of Tesla's identity stems from the purposeful neglect of the difference between place of birth and ethnic self-ascription. To reassert Tesla's alleged Croatianness it is often added (e.g. 5

UV Adelaide, 9 February 1992) that 'Serbian propaganda' is responsible for the fact that his Croatian background is not known about. Kesic (1996, p.15) went as far as to write in an Australian-Croatian magazine that the Serbs are "trying to use his genius as a means of bolstering their own sagging personal and public image."

In the representative *Dictionary of Scientific Biography*, Swezey (1976, p. 286) wrote:

> TESLA, NIKOLA (b. Smiljan, Croatia [now Yugoslavia], 10 July 1856; d. New York, N.Y., 7 January 1943. Tesla was born to Serbian parents in a mountain village that was then part of Austria-Hungary.

Tesla himself is quoted as saying that he is "equally proud of his Serbian family as of his Croatian homeland" (Sitar 1992, p. 97). In his famous biography on Tesla, O'Neill (1980, p. 289) writes that he was born in Croatia, but Tesla is also quoted as referring to "the heroes of *our* national Serbian poetry" (emphasis added, Z.S.).

It is interesting to mention that nationalist Croatian sources assert Tesla's Croatianness despite the well-documented fact that his mother's ancestors for generations served, with very few exceptions, as priests of the Serbian Orthodox church. Furthermore, Tesla's own father was a priest of the Serbian Orthodox church (O'Neill 1980, pp. 15-6). The above mentioned Prpic's claim that Tesla was a Croatian and the "son of a Croatian Orthodox priest", refers without hesitation to O'Neill as a source of information despite the fact that O'Neill explicitly refers to Tesla's Serbian parenthood.

The Croatian claim on Tesla is not simply related to a difference between ethnic self-ascription and place of birth.[4] It additionally reveals the claim, highly popular in diaspora circles, that the Serbian population of Croatia derives from the religious conversion of Croatians to the Serbian Orthodox religion. The Croatian diaspora writer, Korsky (1983, p. 94), thus writes about "one of the most tragic failures of Croatian politics which is rarely mentioned," which is, that the Croatian Orthodox population was nationally nonaligned until the period between 1861-1896, but then it became 'Serbianised'. Croatians in Australia are generally familiar with this theory of the Croatian 'essence' of the Serbian Orthodox population in Croatia. It is not my aim to challenge the validity of different competing theories. However, the fascinating thing about the theory, which argues that the present-day Serbians in Croatia were in fact Croatians of Orthodox faith, encourages the thinking that the Serbian problem in Croatia can be rectified either by re-education or re-Christianisation.

An examination of the post-Second World War Croatian diaspora reveals an interesting 'distant view' effect: that it was in the diaspora rather than the homeland where such ethno-national inventions were stored, reinvented and reproduced. The evidence clearly suggests that the susceptibility as well as exposure to this information was greater in Croatian diaspora circles for almost the entire post-Second World War period. It was only in the late 1980s that such invented narratives became rather happily embraced in the homeland context as well. Thompson (1993, p. 10), for instance, makes the following observation in his discussion of the television programs in the newly independent Croatia: "A prestige series called *Croats Who Made the World* began with Pope Sixtus V. who wasn't, so far as anyone knows, a Croat." This is obviously a part of the industrious efforts of some contemporary Croatian intellectuals who – as Hobsbawm (1993, p. 63) ironically remarked – "try to turn Zvonimir the Great into the ancestor of Franjo Tudjman".

3.3 Myths of origin

History is always the most convenient legitimator of theories of national origins. Myths of descent bear an important expressive dimension for an ethno-national collectivity. A.D. Smith (1986, pp. 24-5) introduced the concept of *mythomoteur* to explain their importance:

> The fused and elaborated myths provide an overall framework of meaning for the ethnic community, a *mythomoteur*, which 'makes sense' of its experiences and defines its 'essence'. Without a *mythomoteur* a group cannot define itself to itself or to others, and cannot inspire or guide collective action.

Myths of descent are undoubtedly important and inspiring although they only make sense when considered through the prism of contemporary political needs. Anderson (1993 rev.ed., p. 11) writes that "(t)he late President Sukarno always spoke with complete sincerity of the 350 years of colonialism that his 'Indonesia' had endured, although the very concept 'Indonesia' is a twentieth-century invention, and most of today's Indonesia was only conquered by the Dutch between 1850 and 1910." Hobsbawm (1993, p. 63) similarly refers to "a study of the ancient civilization of the cities of the Indus Valley with the title *5000 Years of Pakistan*. Pakistan was not even thought of before 1932-1933, when the name was invented by some student militants." Following a similar logic, recent times have witnessed the revival of the thesis that Croatians are actually not Slavs, but indeed the descendants of an ancient state, Harauhvatis (mentioned by Zarathustra), which existed between 630-553 B.C. between Iran and Afghanistan (c.f. Vitez 1970, pp. 13-21). Interestingly, while the theory was considered somewhat alchemistic in intellectual circles in post-Second World War Yugoslavia, it was well nurtured and kept alive in diaspora circles.

In the 1980s in Slovenia there appeared the thesis that Slovenians are not really what they always believed themselves to be – Slavs – but in fact Venets (Tomažič 1990) and therefore "autochthonous in their homeland between the Alps and Adriatic" (ibid., p. 5, translation, Z.S.). The theory also suggests that old Slovenian was once spoken in the territory of the present Switzerland. Furthermore, "the Venets did not leave their settlements but acquired new areas in a totally peaceful way by their 'missionary' enthusiasm" (ibid., p. 9). Even when military force was used, it was never done to "... enslave other peoples, but to bring them the new faith and firm social organisation..." (ibid., translation, Z.S.). The stereotypical belief in Slovenian peacefulness is the cornerstone of ethno-national myths which they themselves have built up over the decades. Slovenians who believe in this Venetological theory see themselves – no less than the nationalist Basques – as "a distinct national group, unrelated to all those around them" (Connor 1992, p. 49, c.f. Connor 1991). It should come as no surprise to the reader that the book espousing Venetological theory was a hit-read in diaspora circles. Australia, needless to say, was no exception.

This Venetological explanation shows some of the classical attributes of national myths such as unrelatedness, separateness from surrounding groups, and autochthonous existence from ancient times. Such attributes very clearly serve the purpose of accentuating the distinctiveness and uniqueness of a chosen group of people. These explanations, like Hobsbawm's 'invented traditions', "attempt to establish continuity with a suitable historic past" (Hobsbawm 1984, p. 1). Nationalist discourses link the past with the future and laboriously strive to establish continuity between the two:

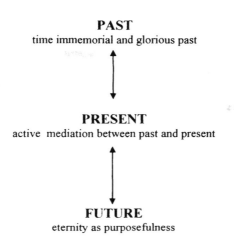

Figure 4.1 Nationalist discourse: mediation between past and present

Despite its frequent uses of history, nationalism is distinctly concerned with the future of nations. In essence, nationalism does not only operate through manipulation of the past but also through projecting the real and imagined characteristics of an ethno-national group into the future.

4 Diaspora and party politics: the case of Australian-Croatians

Politics in its multiple forms has always played a highly prominent role in the life of the Australian-Croatian diaspora.[5] Political diversity is one of the main reasons for the organisational diversification of diaspora life. According to the Croatian ethnic radio station 5EBI FM (19 June 1994), the Croatian Club in Adelaide, South Australia at the time hosted 28 different organised 'sections', many of them in fact political parties and/or politically motivated associations. Politics – which almost always happened to be nationalist politics – left a profound mark on second generation respondents' lives. The intergenerational transmission of right-wing political beliefs and values is a process which does not follow any clearly recognisable pattern and may elicit in children rebellion no less than approval:

> People considered me as a product of Croatian nationalism. It's true. My uncle died in [the Croatian] *domobrani* (Home Guard, Z.S) and according to my mum my father was in the *domobrani* as well. Although my father is a fascist. For some strange reason, he is a part

of the minority of Croatians during the war who picked up the German ideology of the time. ... Unfortunate fact, I suppose.

Basically, I rejected Croatian culture because of my upbringing. I was an altar-boy for the Croatian church for years and I sensed that right-wing fascism had become equated with religion and Croatian culture. I was into anti-authoritarianism, if you like, and I viewed Croatian culture, too, as being somehow authoritarian. But I think a lot of that was confused because of the Vietnam war. I had strong anti-war roots. So, I just rejected Croatian culture basically as a result of that.

... But some of my Croatian friends... they have a really deep hatred [of Serbs]. Their fathers are probably very active against Serbians or whatever, and they push this sort of ideology upon them. Even now, some of them feel proud of Ustasha. And I don't.

[F]ather's political past determined our lives. For my parents it was all politics, politics.

I remember once my father and I talked and I tried to explain to him how dangerous nationalism is and that nationalism is the reason for wars. I immediately added: "But because other people are nationalists, we can be nationalists, too," just to stay alive after expressing my views. I thought I'd covered it nicely but he was so angry with me that he wouldn't talk to me for about a week. I heard him screaming at my mum: "We send them to a private school and they turn into communists!"

Towards the end of the 1980s, the first non-communist political parties emerged in Yugoslavia. This was an important development which signalled that Yugoslavia had begun to exit from its one-party political system. The process of political diversification on the anti-communist platform was initiated in Slovenia and soon after replicated in other republics as well.

When during that period the HDZ was established in Croatia, the diaspora political establishment enthusiastically welcomed its appearance. The Australian-based Croatian National Council in 1990 organised the visit of a well-known Croatian dissident politician, Vladimir Šeks. The purpose of the visit was the establishment of HDZ branches in Australia. One of the organisers of that visit commented: "Everything was organised in the deepest secrecy because UDBA [Yugoslav Secret Police] knew what was going on. But what Šeks was saying was hair-raising even for us here [in the diaspora]" (translation, Z.S.). This visit probably represents the single most crucial development in the history of post-Second World War relationships between the Croatian homeland and the Australian-Croatian diaspora. As already mentioned, up until the late 1980s there were no formal relationships between the two. The homeland political establishment accused Croatian diaspora of being dominated by the Ustasha and interested in the dissolution of Yugoslavia. Most Croatian diaspora organisations indeed wanted just that. In fact, even travel by Australian-Croatians from Australia to the homeland was perceived as unacceptable in some segments of the Australian-Croatian diaspora.

Šeks' political radicalism made Croatian diaspora representatives realise that they were no longer to be considered as exclusive repositories of Croatian nationalist radicalism. The realisation that homeland politics is becoming more radical than their own reflects a complete reversal of the relationship between the diaspora and the homeland in two ways. First, the homeland political forces for the first time since the Second World War came to be seen as an accountable *and* legitimate force; the homeland was thus quite unexpectedly elevated from a passive to an interactive agent. Second, this statement also marks a complete reversal of roles in terms of nationalist and political radicalism.

What determined the nature of the Australian-Croatian political infrastructure before the 'arrival' of the first political party from post-Second World War Croatia in 1990? Although Croatians in Australia formed numerous political organisations and groupings throughout the post-Second World War period, for the purposes of the present discussion, I will single out the already mentioned HOP. There are two issues which need to be emphasised. The first one relates to the controversial status of the HOP in Australian-Croatian diaspora organisations and the portrayal of its members as right-wing zealots. The second relates to the impact which the HOP has made on the psyche of the Australian-Croatian population and its impact on the functioning of Croatian émigré organisations.

The HOP was established in 1956 by exiled Ante Pavelić, the leader of the Independent State of Croatia (1941-1945) and his political followers, with the aim of helping to re-establish the Independent State. Tkalčević (1992, p. 222) defined the profile of the HOP as "a determined adversary of communism, atheism and Yugoslavism in any possible form". The membership and ideological core of this political grouping was initially made up of individuals who defended the Independent State of Croatia during the Second World War: "Croatian Ustasha and [Croatian] Homeguard soldiers did not fight for fascism, not even for Dr. Ante Pavelić. They fought for a Croatian state with its historical border on the Drina [river] and in Zemun" (ibid., p. 223, translation, Z.S.).[6] Nowadays, the HOP in Australia increasingly draws its membership from the Australian born, although membership numbers remain confidential and my informants claim that any numbers released are usually an exaggeration.

As mentioned earlier, by focusing on the HOP I have left out numerous other political parties and groupings. I outlined the change (i.e. a decrease) in the HOP's significance in the diaspora in the Introduction. Most other parties bear much less weight on the topic of this inquiry and some of them were never referred to by respondents. The HDZ is a modern-day rival (and a very successful one) of the HOP and its membership actually greatly outnumbered that of the HOP soon after its inception. HDZ membership was extremely high in the early 1990s but formal membership has decreased since then. Despite this decrease in active membership, the role of the powerful HDZ networks still have to be accounted for. As mentioned in the introductory chapter, each of these two parties was distinguished by its approach. The HOP liked to surround itself with a wall of secrecy while the HDZ promoted itself as a popular movement rather than a classical political party. In fact, the more the HDZ in Croatia reveals its particularistic party ambitions, the less support it attracts. As the HDZ is still the governing party in Croatia, by appropriating and asserting its grip on power, it manages to present itself as a party which most strongly represents the interests of the Croatian population in Croatia as well as abroad.

The secrecy of the HOP and its political goals was very real and its members represented a highly organised close-knit grouping. This was further emphasised in the past, particularly in the 1960s, when the HOP had the upper hand in managing the Club. The following comments are revealing of the atmosphere which existed in the various Croatian associations in Australia:

> Straight [after our arrival in Australia] we tried to get ourselves attached to the Croatian Club. We felt we'd make some new friends there but a lot of people were suspicious of us. It took a while to make friends.
>
> [When my parents came to Adelaide] someone took [my father] to the Croatian Club. At that stage, he used to say, they asked a lot of questions. That was the time of a lot of friction. He really got interrogated, before he started going regularly. He lives for that club now.

Both these stories relate to the 1960s and 1970s, a time when the HOP still possessed considerable power in many Croatian clubs all around Australia. At that time, control over incoming members was exercised because of concerns that they might be agents of the Yugoslav secret police. Allowing oneself to be subjected to such control was the test of one's dedication to diasporic Croatianism. Although it will never be known to what extent the Yugoslav secret police really infiltrated various organisations – if at all – this possibility has always been taken into account. This was one of the reasons for the secrecy. Another reason was the belief, widespread among HOP members, that they represented the only true and possible way for the liberation of the supposedly enslaved Croatian people in the homeland.

It was not only the presence of outsiders but also deviation from the HOP political line which could cause suspicion:

> When the Croatian National Council was established [my father] changed from HOP to Croatian National Council membership. Not many people did. Until that year (1971-72) we had a circle of friends and overnight we had none.

As HOP politics were generally considered to be essentially 'old world' politics, the HDZ leadership in Croatia in the early 1990s reportedly advised HDZ branches in Australia "not to stir them up" and "to let them do what they want", suggesting that they had no serious political impact. This argument that the HOP actually embodies the old world reality was accurate. Since its inception, the HOP remained loyal to its initial political-national platform, based on a Cold War mentality and radical right political activism.

Respondents were rarely in agreement about issues related to the HOP:

> People from the HOP are usually great Croatians and there is nothing wrong with that. But their leadership are fossilised people from 1945... Their starting point was always that there is no other reality to theirs and that if something new appears it's for them to lead.

In the view of a first generation migrant:

> The HOP will always be the last to believe in change. They still don't want to get seriously involved with the politics in Croatia because they don't believe that anything will be achieved until Croatia is united with Bosnia and Herzegovina.

Members of the HOP Youth group attracted many negative comments. It was not only once that they were called 'right wing fascists':

> ... I call them fascists – HOP *mladež* [youth]. They are a bit more aggressive, right-wing, they are more into Ante Pavelić... They are

young and stupid, anyway. But that initially stopped me from going to the club. They were just too different from me. A lot of Croatian kids [stopped going there for the same reason] actually.

The following example by a second generation Croatian female is illustrative of the militancy of HOP youth:

> Among youth there is less friction [than among the first generation]. I'll tell you. I'll be honest. There is friction with the HOP *mladež* [youth]. People always oppose them but they are always there, you see? On the individual level [HOP youth members] are great people. It's just the leaders... It's pretty bad. A lot of people oppose them.
> Even [X], he wasn't a part of HOP but a lot of the guys that he grew up with were. They would call you to HOP and there would be secrecy, they stick together. It did worry him because he grew up with those guys. He doesn't believe in their political views but it's more than a political view.
> ... [HOP Youth members] have good hearts. Their hearts are in the right place but... They wanted, for example, I don't know how much money for arms, arms for living in Australia.
> **Q:** Why arms?
> **A:** They just got this idea in their heads. This is what it's like: a lot of them can't walk through Rundle Mall [in Adelaide] by themselves.
> **Q:** Why?
> **A:** Because they were in fights [with the Serbs] before. If [the Serbs] see a familiar face on the street they ask you whether you are Croatian. If you say 'yes' you just forget about it. It's as simple as that. [X] was walking with his girlfriend on the street and ended up in hospital.

The representatives of some Australian-Croatian organisations also spoke very negatively about HOP Youth members. They were described as "low class people" or "people with low intelligence who were fairly influenced by the family environment"; also people who are "naïve as this could be the only explanation for their behaviour".

While I was conducting fieldwork, there seemed to be a mysterious discrepancy between the HOP's negative reputation yet their persistent existence and their degree of influence in the Croatian club in Adelaide as well as in some other clubs in Australia. The HOP, their opponents said, possessed a negligible amount of lobbying power within diaspora organisations, while the HOP representatives claimed exactly the opposite, nearly the power of Bentham's Panopticon. Each side accused the other of the attempted domination of the diaspora. At the time of the research, the HOP still clearly represented one of the strongholds of 'old values' and political views. Some informants from Sydney and Melbourne referred to the Adelaide Croatian Club as an example of a club which was under HOP control. Interestingly, this was strongly, and to my opinion quite rightly, disputed by some Adelaide respondents who could be identified as 'high-ranking' members of the Croatian Club. Nevertheless, the HOP managed to have 'their people' as members of all important committees in the Club. One HOP representative argued assertively: "We can run the Club. The Club can't do anything without us. We can make them do something. We have a lot of influence". HOP members were confident that they still possess the power of influence and often make others wonder 'how will HOP members react' to suggested changes.

During my fieldwork the Australian HOP branches appeared to be maintaining their partial autonomy in the sense that they ran their own fund-raising. This was confirmed by HOP members and it was also implied that the focus of their interest were the Croatians of Herzegovina. Some respondents have given me subtle suggestions that the Croatian militia in Bosnia (HVO), established in 1992, was the main receipient of these funds.

On the occasion of a visit of a Croatian politician from Herzegovina, a Croatian respondent from Sydney commented:

> [Mr X] who is visiting Australia right now collected a lot of money particularly from among the extreme right. First of all, he is from Herzegovina and he is also, I believe, a member of the HOP. ... They still believe in the dream of a Greater Croatia with its border on the Drina river.

In an increasingly inter-dependent world, long-distance travel and communication are real blessings for long-distance nationalist endeavours. Fund-raising, a common phenomenon among diaspora populations, assumes an important place among these activities. Gans (1979, p. 10), for instance, mentions the role which Jewish financial support to Israel played in staving off Israel's destruction. Activities of Croatian politicians in the world arms market have been observed more than once, likewise the fact that they "draw substantial resources from emigrant Croat communities around the world" (Anderson 1992a, p. 13). Glenny (1992, p. 63) discloses that the victory of the HDZ required and received substantial financial backing from the *émigré* community. One of the leading figures of the HDZ in Australia said:

> The money [HDZ in Croatia] received from Australia, Germany, Canada and America enabled them to run a western-type pre-election campaign. When I visited Croatia in July 1990, you could see Tudjman's picture on every telephone pole.

Despite the massive support and following which the HDZ attracted in the early 1990s some critical comments about its functioning in Australia could also be heard:

> I am scared because the HDZ has such a big following. I am very worried about how important one party has become – there are no opposing views.

> Well, I'd support the HDZ. Not from a political point of view. President Tudjman started a movement and everyone sort of followed him. You just wonder: if all this is over and there is still a big following then it'll be just like communism, really. Like in communism you've got one party and you are not allowed to believe in anything else.

A liberal critique of the HDZ is exemplified in the following words of a second generation individual. The interview was conducted in late 1992 and it describes a hierarchical, manipulative and orchestrated relationship between the HDZ in Croatia and its branches in Australia:

> HDZ [members] think they are the same as the community. People from the HDZ think that Zagreb has the last say about what's going on here in the community. HDZ people here say: you can't do anything if you are not told by Zagreb. What they do is, they'd say that they talked to some functionary in Zagreb. Then the letter will come, stamped: *Ministarstvo* [The Ministry] or whatever. And then they'd say: look, we have a letter from Croatia which says this is what we should do.
> The HDZ acts like a Croatian Embassy in Australia. People expect from them answers which you normally get from the Embassy, like: where can I get my passport, I have got land there, I want to sell something, I have a declaration that needs to be completed...

This long-distance orchestration between the HDZ in Australia and Croatia was confirmed by one of the leaders of the HDZ in Australia:

We do not formulate any politics of our own and we are nothing but executors of orders from Zagreb. Only those orders, of course, which do not counter Australian laws (translation, Z.S.).

The HDZ has gradually been losing its symbolic prestige in the Australian-Croatian diaspora over the past six years. Despite this, however, it still remains a dominant political force both in the diaspora and in the homeland. Fund-raising, one of its main activities since its inception, had – by the mid 1990s – slowly turned into a routine quest for money. This was a bothersome activity and even towards the end of 1991 respondents were already commenting that Croatians throughout Australia were simply financially squeezed dry. This is not surprising. One prominent Croatian from Adelaide claimed that at the beginning of 1993 they had collected A$ 7 million in material goods and money. The result of the weakening of the HDZ support base encourages parties on the right side of the political spectrum to consolidate their positions, although it appears that these parties have had relatively moderate success in doing so.

This brings us back to the question of the changing nature of interaction processes between the Croatian diaspora and homeland. In Chapter 2 I argued that throughout the post-Second World War period the Australian-Croatian diaspora nurtured a highly romantic and sentimentalised – albeit politically critical and negative – view of the homeland. This was done autonomously, without the homeland's active participation. It was precisely the *passivity* of the homeland establishment which – from 1945 until the 1980s – compounded the effect of the 'distant view'; it made it possible for the diaspora to construct the homeland as tragically enslaved by the political apparatus of the Yugoslav regime. The shift from this notion of a tragically enslaved nation emerged with the beginning of the formation of the anti-Communist opposition in Croatia in the late 1980s and particularly and most radically with the formalisation of the multi-party political competition in Croatia in 1990. The then emerging opposition embodied in the HDZ *actively* approached Croatian diaspora communities all around the world and subsequently received substantial financial backing which facilitated their electoral victory. Suddenly, the seemingly unbridgable gap between the Croatians in diaspora and those in the homeland had suddenly appeared to have vanished – communism was dead and Yugoslavia was nearing its end. The re-establishment of contact with the homeland became openly encouraged.

There are some important implications of these newly formed links between the homeland and the diaspora for Croatian diaspora construction of the homeland. Since 1989/1990, Croatian migrant organisations have actively participated in providing very substantial financial and material support for the homeland establishment. There has also been a substantial increase in the movement of individuals between the diaspora and the homeland. At least at an imaginary level, the Croatian diaspora became integrated into the rudimentary homeland political project. This recent and active global inter-connection between the two settings resulted in the homeland being considerably de-mythologised. Despite this, romantic portrayals still characterise most diasporic perceptions of the homeland. The modification of the homeland's status from a passive to an interactive agent might have changed the intensity of the diasporic-homeland relationship but not its substantive nature. It is due to present-day troublesome (and recently tragic) circumstances in the Balkans that the previous diasporic perception of Croatia as an 'enslaved' homeland has been successfully replaced by the notion of the 'bleeding' homeland (see Figure 4.2) and/or the homeland which can succeed with post-war reconstruction and democracy building only with the ideologically constructed 'unfailing support' of the Croatian diaspora. This helps to perpetuate the feeling of the homeland's victimisation and therefore continues to promote it as a place which asks for and deserves the ideological, political and financial commitment of its dispersed population.

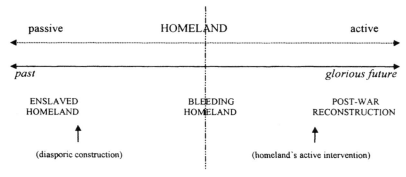

Figure 4.2   Homeland: from passive to an interactive agent

It is difficult to predict the long-term effects of this shift in homeland-diaspora relationships. The widespread feeling among Croatians that they were the innocent victims of foreign aggression in the recent conflict successfully provides the basis for further sentimentalisation practices to develop. This has already led to an upgrade of the notion of the 'bleeding homeland'. The notion of 'bleeding homeland' has recently been supplemented by the call for 'post-war reconstruction'. The practical success of this latest catch-cry has not only been linked to, but also directly related to and dependent upon, the perpetuation of the experience of victimisation in the past. Most importantly, this use of the idea of 'post-war reconstruction' as a rallying point for both homeland and diaspora has not been autochthonously constructed in the diaspora as was the case in the past, but subtly proposed by the homeland after the recognition of its utilisable potential.

5   The contrast: the case of Australian-Slovenians

It is difficult to draw any parallels between Slovenians and Croatians in the context of the present discussion. Two significant differences responsible for this need to be re-emphasised. The first is the absence of independent Slovenian statehood during the Second World War. The Croatian experience of state-formation and the subsequent loss of national independence represented a strong case for the nurturing of the idea of its re-establishment. Second, Slovenian 'political' migrants did not form any political parties in Australia and, as individuals, they had a limited influence on the overall processes in the Australian-Slovenian diaspora.

Paradoxically, there were still divisions within the Slovenian-Australian diaspora which sought legitimation on political grounds. Most clubs were vaguely referred to as either pro- or anti-Yugoslav. This label was usually applied according to the extent of co-operation with the homeland. The fact is that all Slovenian Clubs in Australia to some extent co-operated with *Slovenska izseljenska matica*, an institution which was to foster cultural ties between Slovenia and Slovenians living abroad and which, according to some informants, represented one of the channels for the Yugoslav secret police to operate in Australia.

It has to be stressed that Slovenians (with few exceptions) did not take as strong a stand against the institutions of a Yugoslav state in Australia (i.e. Embassies, Consulates, even the national air-carrier JAT) as did Croatians. Slovenians did use Yugoslav Consulates in Australia, although not in an organised way. The representative of a prominent Sydney-based Slovenian association which was widely recognised as anti-Communist stated rather proudly, albeit sarcastically, how he attended the official 29 November celebration (the day of the establishment of the Socialist Federative Republic of Yugoslavia) organised by the Yugoslav Consulate. By way of contrast, this date was always reserved for hostile and coordinated demonstrations of Croatians around Australia in front of the Yugoslav Embassy and Consulates. One such demonstration in late November 1988 ended tragically when a security guard of the Yugoslav consulate shot a 16-year old Australian-Croatian demonstrator.

As already mentioned, the *Demos* anti-Communist Slovenian coalition of political forces was given symbolic financial support by the Slovenian-

Australian diaspora at the onset of democratisation processes in Slovenia in the late 1980s. Similarly, financial support for post-war reconstruction was collected in 1991 through the only influential and articulate political body among Slovenians, the Australian-Slovenian Conference, which was a representative organisation for the Slovenian National Councils throughout Australia (c.f. Anonymous 1991, pp. 26-7). The final sum sent to the Slovenian government was $AU 250,000. Slovenia did not and could not rely as heavily on the financial support of the Slovenian diaspora (Slovenians in Argentina are again an exception) as the Croatian government did on support from the Croatian diaspora. The much more numerous American-Slovenian diaspora collected about $US2 million (Klemenčič 1993, p. 335). It is interesting to add that funds collected in the United States were only used to support two out of five members of the *Demos* coalition in the first free elections in the spring of 1990 in Slovenia: the Slovenian Christian Democrats and the Slovenian Peasant Union (ibid., p. 334). These two parties (the Christian Democrats in particular) enjoyed most of the tacit support of Australian-Slovenians. They were anti-Communist as well as popularly acceptable because of the reference to the Catholic religion which was (or so it was widely believed in Australia) threatened within Yugoslavia. In late 1991, however, the Slovenian Social Democrats, associated with Janez Janša (a person popularly held to be the key player in the defence of Slovenia during the short war) became the most popular Slovenian party in the eyes of Australian-Slovenians.

6   The power of symbols

6.1   Religious...

Diasporas are prone to encourage constructions of narratives and symbolisms highly charged with expressive connotations. Such narratives were used in the Australian-Croatian diaspora to illustrate the threat of Yugoslavism to Croatian identity. Belief in the complete destruction of Croatian identity within Yugoslavia together with religion was promoted in the Australian-Croatian diaspora. By the same token, the Slovenian church in Australia regularly reinforced the alleged fact that Catholic believers in Slovenia are harassed and oppressed.

To substantiate this observation, I point to the comments often heard at Sunday Slovenian church services in Adelaide where a belief in the harassment of churchgoers was attested to even in newly independent Slovenia. Although it is hard to find evidence of this in Slovenia itself (although the representatives of the Church regularly complain about their supposed marginalisation), the ideological appeal of such statements is very important, as "loyalty to the faith is also loyalty to the nation and homeland" (Interview with the Slovenian Franciscan Provincial, 5EBI FM Adelaide, 20 October 1993). Needless to say, this type of statement also legitimises the increasingly visible role of the Church in the political and public life of Slovenia.

In the Australian-Croatian context the belief in the inseparable link between Catholic religion and Croatian national identity is commonly believed to be the historical guarantor of national survival. I was told that the prayer-book and rosary beads are the two most recognisable Croatian symbols. This (as it is believed) indispensable link is well expressed in the Croatian slogan, very popular among Australian-Croatians: 'God and the Croatians'. Such a slogan presupposes a unitary and non-differentiated category: faithful Croatians. In a rather authoritative way, it subsumes a national category under the umbrella of one particular religious affiliation. This presumptive slogan leads to grave difficulties when one has to justify the existence of Croatian Muslims.[7] The exclusionist slogan 'God and the Croatians' also reinforces the belief held by diaspora group members that *they* have privileged access to God. It is appropriate to note in this context that the 'God and the Croatians' slogan was never popularised in post-Second World War Croatia but was commonly used in diaspora. The transition in plural democracy in Croatia, however, brought some changes in this respect. Since the beginning of 1993, radio news from Croatia produced specifically for South Australian listeners occasionally ended with a 'God and the Croatians' salutation. This salutation was commonly used in the diaspora but not in the homeland. Yet another interesting salutation was the one included in the HOP's radio advertisement which ended with "Hrvatska iznad svega" (5 EBI FM, Adelaide, 5 December 1993). This is nothing but a translation of the German Nazi refrain "[Deutschland] über alles" (Germany above everything, Z.S.).

Excessive Catholic enthusiasm is not unique to Croatian and Slovenian diasporas, however. Just to give one example, Polish exiles associate Polish national values with Catholicism in a similar manner. When the 'Virgin Mary' is called 'Our Lady, Queen of Poland', the logic behind the conceptualisation is analogous. Mickiewicz even believed that Poland represents the embodiment of Christ's suffering and that both are inseparably linked. According to Petersen (1987, p. 232), Polish parishes in the Polish diaspora "continued to function as a strong factor reinforcing social control and Polish culture, language and traditions".

Indeed, religion and the Catholic Church play an important role in the lives of Croatian as well as Slovenian diasporas. This is related both to the strong religious affiliation of most first generation Croatians and Slovenians as well as the (passive or, much less often, oppositional) role of the religious institutions in the former Yugoslavia. The very institution of their 'ethnic' church in Australia therefore always embodied the notion of countering the assumed religious, national and linguistic oppressions in the homeland.

The link between Croatian people and religion was further reinforced by the reported appearance of the Virgin Mary to a group of six Croatian children in 1981 in Medjugorje, Herzegovina. When the children's visions were made public, there was also an almost immediate political interpretation of the event. The symbolism and importance of phenomena like this are well expressed by Maria Warner (1985, p. 302) in her work entitled *Alone for all her Sex: the Myth and Cult of the Virgin Mary*:

> From the Church's point of view, the most important aspect of a vision was not a private ecstasy, but the public message of divine approval that the descent of Christ or the Virgin on earth communicated to all the faithful. Through the experience of an individual mystic a whole locality, where the vision had taken place, was thereby blessed.

One could easily replace "(f)rom the Church's point of view" in the above quotation with 'from the nationalist point of view' to provide an interpretation which would accurately reflect one of the impacts of the Virgin Mary's punctual apparitions in Medjugorje (Meštrović 1991, pp. 136-62). Many second generation Croatians feel 'special' because the Virgin Mary appears in what they see as their ethnic territory. Besides, Medjugorje has been a standard pilgrimage site for many Australian-Croatians since the Virgin Mary first appeared in 1981. The importance of Medjugorje's Virgin Mary was emphasised by all Croatian priests who took part in this research. One of them in fact tried hard to link our discussion with the phenomenon of the Virgin Mary, emphasising that a lot of Australian students from Catholic schools develop their interest in Croatia *via* learning about the Medjugorje phenomenon. While the interest of diaspora Croatians in the Virgin Mary is part and parcel of a global pan-Catholic interest in divine manifestations, it is also exploited for the purpose of maintaining the sense of identity of the Croatian ethno-national collectivities in the diaspora.

I have argued that diaspora settings are pervaded by nostalgic narratives which are amplified by the distant view. Diaspora media are highly instrumental in the process of creation and – more importantly – dissemination of such narratives. Some attention should thus be paid to the lyrics used in various songs which are to be heard on Croatian and Slovenian radio stations throughout Australia. They are interesting despite the lack of direct nationalist or political connotations. Slovenian writer, Drago Jančar (1993, p. 93), observed in relation to the 'sadness of exile', that in some "sugary alpine pop songs [...] the words 'Slovenia' and 'foreign country' are thoughtlessly used every third line." While Jančar's observation was not made in reference to the Australian-Slovenian or Australian-Croatian context, it nevertheless carries weight for them. Slovenian radio stations in Australia indeed often play songs which celebrate in verse the beauty of the Slovenian countryside, good-looking women, the forsaken homeland, and similar. Expressions of love for the homeland are usually couched in a form of eroticised nationalism (c.f. Anderson 1993 rev.ed., pp. 202-3). While Croatian songs celebrate similar things, the national and ethno-nationalist motifs are far more regularly included and their persuasive power is far stronger. Some of the songs directly alluded to the tragedy of war or referred to the territorial strength of Croatia. One song which was to be heard regularly on Adelaide's Croatian radio program between 1992 and 1994 went as follows: "Bosnian, Herzegovinian, the really Croatian woman... Mura, Drina and Cetina (rivers designating Croatian 'historical' territory, Z.S.), you are the Croatian homeland" (translation, Z.S.). This is not the only occasion on which women have been used as symbolic boundary-markers (c.f. Yuval-Davis and Anthias, 1989a, Yuval-Davis 1997). The extent to which the celebration of Croatian military strength appealed to Croatians in Australia can be well illustrated by the fact that between 1992 and 1994, the anthem of the Croatian Navy appeared to be one of the listeners' most frequent music requests on the Croatian radio program in Adelaide.

6.2   ... and historical

By far the most controversial issue relating to the symbolism of the Croatian past which enters contemporary discussion about Croatian national identity is the frequent appearance of the symbols of the old Independent State of Croatia (1941-1945). In the diaspora, one of the most controversial of such symbols is the picture of Ante Pavelić, its leader. In the literature, he is commonly referred to in relation to genocidal practices, mainly against the Serbs, during the existence of the Independent State of Croatia.[8] Many Croatian Clubs still exhibit a picture of Ante Pavelić on their walls, including the Croatian Club in Adelaide. A controversy surrounding this picture revealed itself in the first couple of interviews with second generation individuals, many of whom considered its presence as unnecessary and as representing something which is considerably outdated. According to the reports made by Croatian respondents, an increasing number of second generation Croatian individuals believe that the picture should be removed. And yet some of them do not problematise the picture's presence and simply refer to Pavelić as an historical figure who emerged out of the unfavourable circumstances of the Second World War:

Pavelić was a part of Croatian history. We can't change this. But we don't need to glorify him. He led Croatia during the period of time which provides us now with romantics. ... I have nothing against his picture [in the Club]. And I have nothing against Draža Mihajlović's (leader of Serbian pro-royalist Chetniks during the Second World War, Z.S.) statue in front of the [Serbian] church.

Q: What do you think about the picture in the hall of the Croatian Club?
A: Which picture? Are you talking about Pavelić?
Q: Do you think I am talking about his picture?
A: That's the one that is most debatable. The guy is still worshipped. I think he is not as much talked about in the community. It's more Franjo Tudjman now. Of course, there is still this sector in the Croatian community when they get drunk and they sing Pavelić's songs. Pavelić made a lot of mistakes. He sold Dalmatia,[9] didn't he? A lot of people realise he is not such a strong figure as he was before.
Q: Do you think Tudjman is more important than Pavelić?
A: Not really. Pavelić is still in people's hearts. He is just not spoken about as much.

The picture remains a highly disputed issue and some people do not want to disclose their opinions: "I don't want to talk about this. He was a Croatian giant. He made mistakes but he also wholeheartedly wanted to preserve Croatia". A second generation respondent who migrated to Australia with his parents as a little child in the 1960s remembers that when his father first went to the Croatian club he saw Pavelić's picture and "... that was a shock. That was it. He never went there again".

However, the tension surrounding the presence of Pavelić's picture reveals much more than just the political current within the diaspora. It provides insights into the role the 'political' migrants of the immediate post-Second World War period and their views play in the current situation. Their lobbying power is considerable enough to prevent even the barest discussion of the picture: "One issue that will never be discussed is whether Pavelić ['s picture] will stay up or not. That might take another fifty years. That will last longer than Yugoslavia". More precisely, the HOP is strongly opposed to any discussion on this topic. But, as one second generation respondent concisely stated: "To keep the peace you keep that picture".

The discussion in this chapter has revealed that the emphasis on ethno-national myths, simple exaggerations, self-praise, invented ethno-national identifications, the role of political parties and the power of symbolic expressions are necessary to establish a framework for understanding diaspora-based nationalist discourses. The 'distant view' allows these processes to follow a different development from similar ones in the homeland.

In the chapter which follows I intend to answer the question: how and to what extent are second generation individuals of Croatian and Slovenian backgrounds challenged by the ethno-nationalist ideas of the diaspora settings? More specifically still, how are these feelings and sentiments expressed in relation to groups which all come from the territory of the former Yugoslavia?

7 Notes

1. Their study is an analysis of Wallachians and Macedonians in Sweden and Denmark. Wallachians are the Romanian-speaking population of northeastern Serbia.
2. This example is particularly interesting as the respondent's argument implies that Croatian identity closely relates to Catholicism and that the two are almost inseparable. This argumentation is fairly common among those Croatians who have a strong sense of religious identity. However, these very same arguments commonly fail to mention that the alleged apparitions of the Virgin Mary are taking place in Bosnia and Herzegovina rather than in Croatia. The religious symbolism and appearance of the Virgin Mary are further discussed below in this chapter under the sub-heading 'The power of symbols'.
3. See chapter 3, section 3, 'Conforming to norms and standards in diaspora organisations'.
4. Ironically, in 1993 the Belgrade regime issued an inflatory 10 billion dinar bill which, as *Time Australia* (Anonymous 1993, p. 19) reported, was "graced with the face of inventor Nikola Tesla."
5. See Chapter 3, section 2, 'Politics, otherness and diaspora'.
6. Zemun is a Serbian city close to Belgrade, the Serbian capital.
7. See Chapter 5, section 5, 'Croatian respondents on Bosnian Muslims: search for 'true' ethnicity'.
8. See Hayden (1992a) for further discussion of Ustasha genocide and the role it played in building up the recent conflict.
9. The respondent refers to an agreement between Fascist Italy and the Independent State of Croatia. The consequence of this agreement was that Italy obtained possession of a substantial part of Croatia's coastal territory. The following communication of the American Minister in Belgrade, Bliss Lane, on May 17 1941 to the US Secretary of State

says: "Italian official source advises me that Italian aims in former Yugoslavia are as follows: Formation of Kingdom of Croatia with Duke of Spoleto as King, Pavelić to continue as Poglavnik; Italy to annex prefecture of Ljubljana, Susak [Sušak], Sibenik [Šibenik], Split and Dalmatian Coast from Bay of Kotor to Albania; Zara [Zadar] territory to be enlarged; Croatia to have 'all the rest' of Croatian and Dalmatian Coast including Dubrovnik but Italy to have all islands; King of Italy to be proclaimed King of Montenegro. ..." (quoted in Omrčanin 1989, p. 109).

5 Constructing the Other

> Obviously [I] distrust Serbians, but the other groups are not of particular interest.

When respondents in this study were invited to comment on other ethnic groups from the former Yugoslavia their answers implied that the fate of what was known as Yugoslavia is dependent on the fate of the most powerful, influential and/or the wealthiest ethno-national entities: Croatians, Serbs and Slovenians.

This triad is particularly interesting because it provides the impression that the destiny of Yugoslavia was determined by these three groups and that other groups were of no major significance. Respondents' emphasis on these three groups – which also reflects the content of this chapter – is not to be seen as an indication that the respondents were unaware of other groups constituting the federation of the former Yugoslav Socialist Republic. In fact, Croatian respondents made frequent references to Yugoslavs and Bosnian Muslims. However, these two groups were always mentioned only to be subsequently disqualified on the grounds that they do not represent what they considered to be the 'real' ethno-national categories. In other words, they were mostly seen as lacking legitimate historical reasons for their existence. In addition, the comments of Croatian second generation respondents in relation to these two groups were generally dismissive.

At this point it is useful to draw parallels with Adorno et al.'s (1950, p. 620) study, *The Authoritarian Personality* in which he and his colleagues explored the characteristics of people who encourage negative attitudes towards what they called specific 'outgroups', such as the Jews. One of the student participants in the study was quoted as saying: "Well, the Jews are a ticklish problem – not the whole race; they are both good and bad. But there are more bad than good." Adorno continues that "the 'problem' calls for a *solution*".

The student treated Jews not as subjects, but "as terms of a mathematical equation. To call for a 'solution of the Jewish problem' results in their being reduced to 'material' for manipulation" (ibid.).

The question on which I wanted to shed some light in my research was: to what extent do the answers of the respondents in this study resemble the answer of the student from Adorno's study quoted above? Do Croatians or Slovenians in Australia see any other groups from the former Yugoslavia (either living in Australia or in the ethnic homeland) as a source of irritation or as a 'problem' which requires a 'solution'? In other words, is the constructed Other perceived as 'polluting' the perceived purity of one's group? Is social contact with the Other desirable and tolerable? Most importantly, what is the basis for the construction of the Other? Is this construction process based on prejudice, the nationalist discourse of exclusivism, history or a combination of all these factors? In addition, how do members of these groups identify themselves? Do they identify themselves positively (in terms of their perceived self-identity: e.g. I am a Croat) or also negatively (by making references to what they are not: e.g. I am not a Serb). The *negative identification* of respondents may be a direct indication of negative attitudes towards other groups.

Parents definitely play an important part in constructing a stereotypical imagery of otherness. A Slovenian respondent said: "I have heard my parents saying something like: 'Croatians are crazy; they are all mad'. But they never spoke a lot about that". Although parents' negative and positive messages played a significant role in the construction and maintenance of otherness, the possibility of largely independent constructions of opinion in second generation individuals cannot be overlooked.

One of the questions in the questionnaire I distributed to respondents before the interviews took place was: "What do you think about other ethnic groups in Yugoslavia and in Australia?" This question was deliberately asked so as to enable a respondent to give as broad or as specific an answer as they wished. I was guided by a belief that *if* ethno-nationalist and related sentiments do exist among second generation individuals then I might find a considerable discrepancy between relatively 'neutral' statements in the questionnaire and far more negative sentiments which would be revealed during interviews. This proved to be a justifiable expectation. Indeed, very few respondents expressed negative sentiments about other groups in the questionnaires. Interviews, during which respondents had an opportunity to express themselves in a more elaborate way, by contrast, radically changed this picture. The answers in the questionnaires are classified in Table 5.1:

Table 5.1
Second generation responses to the question posed in the questionnaire: "What do you think about other ethnic groups in Yugoslavia and in Australia?"

	Croatians	Slovenians
Clearly negative response about others*	5	2
Ambiguity in response detected	7	3
Positive response about others	17	20
N/A	2	5
TOTAL	31	30

*   All Croatian respondents from this category targeted either Serbs or Yugoslavs. One Slovenian respondent identified both Serbs and Croats while the other one identified no specific groups but rather a generalised 'Southerner' (see below).

Most second generation respondents expressed tolerance of other groups. For example: "Their culture should be preserved" (Croatian), "Everyone has a right to live" (Croatian), "I think that every ethnic group, all people, have a right to practise their own way of life" (Croatian), "I feel quite neutral about other ethnic groups from Yugoslavia in Australia" (Slovenian), "I think that every ethnic group has a right to exist and practise their cultural beliefs and way of life as long as it doesn't interfere with the written law of the country or the state and extend out of the family unit" (Slovenian). In some cases there were examples of comments which were revealing of some underlying ambiguity towards other groups. Examples of this type of response were: "I have little contact with them and little to say about them; 'To each his own'" (Croatian). Later during the interview the same respondent expressed some clearly negative opinions about Serbs. Another respondent wrote in the questionnaire that "It is very important for all ethnic groups to keep their cultures and traditions going in foreign lands as well as in their homelands. I respect all people who respect me and what I am". This respondent later told me that Yugoslavs and Serbs 'naturally' deny respect to Croatians, and deserved no respect in return.

In the following section of this chapter I explore more systematically the way in which Slovenian and Croatian second generation respondents constructed the Other. Looking first at Slovenians, I will argue that they tend to identify the Other as an abstract entity. For practical purposes I shall call a member of this abstract entity a *Southerner* (*južnjak* in Slovenian). Indeed, 'Southerner' was the term most commonly used by respondents.

It is interesting that Slovenian respondents perceived no other group from the territory of the former Yugoslavia as 'the enemy'. And yet the symbolic boundary which designates the Other from Us was vividly present. This does not mean that they never mentioned the concrete names of other ethnonational groups, such as Croatians or Serbs. The point is that even when they did, little if any attention was paid to their distinctiveness.

1 Slovenian respondents on other ethnic groups from the former Yugoslavia: Southerners – the generalised Other

As Slovenia was the northernmost republic of the former Yugoslavia, Slovenians in Slovenia tended to portray individuals from other republics and members of other ethnic groups from the territory of Yugoslavia as abstract Southerners (sometimes also called 'Bosnians'). Little, if any, attempt was made to differentiate between different ethnic categories. The identity of the Other was constructed according to spatio-geographical logic. The Other is a symbolic fixation of a constructionist fantasy. In a more general discussion of the imaginary nationalist frontiers in the Balkans, Žižek (1992, p. 39) writes:

> For the right-wing nationalist Austrians, this imaginary frontier is Karavanke, the mountain chain between Austria and Slovenia: beyond it, the rule of Slavic hordes begins. For the nationalist Slovenes, this frontier is the river Kolpa, separating Slovenia from Croatia: we Slovenians are *Mitteleuropa*, while Croatians are already Balkan, involved in the irrational ethnic feuds that really do not concern us.

He later applies his argument to the Croatian and Serbian popular ideologies:

> For Croatians, of course, the crucial frontier is the one between them and the Serbians, that is, between the western catholic civilization and the eastern orthodox collective spirit, which cannot grasp the values of western individualism. Serbians, finally, conceive of themselves as

the last line of defense of Christian Europe against the fundamentalist danger embodied in Muslim Albanians and Bosnians. (ibid., p. 40)

Although Žižek's reasoning is accurate, there is a further notable difference between Slovenia and its defined South, on the one hand, and Croatia and Serbia and their respective 'South(s)' on the other hand.[1] The Slovenian 'South' was clearly an undifferentiated category (and if there were differences they were unimportant), while for Croatians, the South meant the Serbs, and for the Serbs it meant non-Christian fundamentalists, predominantly Muslim Albanians and Bosnians. This dialectic of otherness-building can be complicated even further, as Stjepan Meštrović (1994, p. 61) reveals:

> Thus, the Slovenes regard their border with Croatia as the border between the West and the Orient, respectively. Yet the Croatians regard themselves as Western and the Serbs as representative of Eastern culture. Moreover, even though the Slovenes claim in their media that the Balkans begin in Croatia, Croatians deny that they were ever a part of the Balkans, and they regard Slovenia as a satellite of Serbia! Thus, one hears the pejorative phrase, "Alpine Chetniks," among Croats when referring to their Slovene neighbours to the north.

In general, the term Balkan is associated with permanent ethnic antagonism, cleavages, corruption and instability. The Balkans is not only rich in symbolic frontiers but is also the place with which few – if any – really want to identify. The negative attributes of 'the Balkans' are commonly known in other parts of Europe as well. Bavarians humorously like to call Austria a part of the Balkans although no one takes this humour very seriously. In contrast, it would be hard to find anyone in Slovenia and Croatia who would be able to handle such a joke. When the European Union recently renamed the Committee on the Former Yugoslavia Republics and Yugoslavia, the Committee for the Western Balkans, the Croatian official press responded with a strong critique of the decision (e.g. Ströhm 1998, p. 1).

It needs to be emphasised that the notion of 'the Southerner' is not an invention of the Slovenian diaspora. It is commonly used in Slovenia even today to refer to people from other former Yugoslav republics. The Southerners and their cultural difference represent a symbolic threat to Slovenian culture. Not every cultural difference represents such a threat. And indeed, Slovenians never seem to be particularly concerned about being swamped by Austrian or Italian influences. The difference is constructed as threatening only if it is perceived as a source of symbolic pollution. This can be illustrated with a rather amusing example of an unimposing letter to the editor of a weekly magazine published in Slovenia. The author of the letter complained about the wide acceptability of various 'Balkan' dishes in Slovenia and explained how they are reminiscent of the post-Second World War 'intrusion' of the South in Slovenia. He wrote: "Let's finally get rid of Balkan 'grills' and let us make Slovenian cuisine the awakening of the conscience of those who like to eat and think in a Slovenian way" (Vičar 1993, p. 3, translation Z.S.). The writer assumes that the taste is not only fixed and perennial but also that Slovenian ethnicity and Slovenian taste-buds (indeed, the argument postulates the existence of these) coexist in some sort of happy fraternity. Defence of the national 'tradition' and 'traditional values' surfaces in various conservative contexts again and again.[2]

Operationalisation and manipulation of fixed national characteristics is not restricted to the sphere of popular culture or the yellow press. In July 1994 a well-published Slovenian poet, Tone Kuntner (1994), visited Australia to promote his book of poems entitled *O Homeland*. The main motif of the book was the propagation of loyalty to the homeland, the family and the nation – the three corner-stones of any ethno-nationalist discourse. Needless to say, the diaspora/migrant setting is a perfect place to market such homeland-flattering poetry. One of the poems which was immediately reprinted by the Australian-Slovenian newspaper *Glas Slovenije/Voice of Slovenia*: "To be a Slovenian, to love in a Slovenian way/is actually an unexplainable thing/as this is a matter of heart and being. To be a Slovenian is nothing else/but to think in a Slovenian way/to sing and speak Slovenian..." (translation, Z.S.)

The concept of a Southerner could be considered to be the very core of Slovenian post-Second World War nationalism. In post-Second World War Yugoslavia the question of the South and Southerners became an intrinsic part of Slovenian nationalist folklore. Slovenia, as the most economically developed region of Yugoslavia, attracted a substantial number of guest-workers (manual in particular) from the Yugoslav South. Flere (1991, p. 193) says that the "magnitude of this phenomenon cannot be accurately assessed but 200,000 would be a fair estimate." Salt and Clout (1976a, p. 221) estimated that about 25 per cent of the Slovenian workforce at the time was composed of internal migrants from the South. The tension these processes created is reported by Connor (1986, p. 28) who stresses that in 1982 the Zagreb magazine *Danas* wrote about polls in Slovenia showing that "some three-quarters of Slovenia's population oppose further immigration from Yugoslavia's other republics." The presence of these labourers from the Yugoslav South encouraged what Connor (1992, p. 209) elsewhere called the 'homeland psychology': "the hostility engendered by an intrusion of 'the native land' by nonnatives."

The Australian-Slovenian press responds vigorously to any information related to an increase of the non-Slovenian population in Slovenia. The refugees from Bosnia and Herzegovina from the recent war were seen as representing a latent danger because their presence could supposedly dilute the 'pure' and 'homogeneous' Slovenian national body. In accordance with these concerns, the suggestion followed in the Australian-Slovenian press that: "... Slovenians around the world should use their arguments against assimilation of refugees into the Slovenian environment" (Gregorič 1993b, p. 2). The reasons for this are, as suggested: 'Slovenia is too small', it faces 'economic difficulties', and also that the assimilation of refugees will 'decrease the proportion of Slovenian population'. A belief in the relative ethnic 'purity' of the Slovenian territory is widespread although the census data fall short of proving this. According to the 1991 census, the Slovenian component in the population of the Republic of Slovenia was 87.84 per cent and it has been in decline since 1945 (Zavod Republike Slovenije za statistiko 1992, p. 7).

It was noted above that in Slovenia the term Southerner is quite commonly used interchangeably with 'Bosnian' (*Bosanec* in Slovenian). This stereotypical label pays little attention to the fact that a 'Bosnian' or 'Southerner' could be anything from Croatian to Macedonian. The neglect of regard for differences between different ethno-national categories suggests that this construct depends more on the psychology of its users than the actual common traits of these different ethno-national categories. The South has been commonly perceived in a symbolic fashion as the personification of economic underdevelopment, hot-bloodedness and, most of all, otherness. Economic arguments were most commonly used in this context as it was believed that Slovenia contributed disproportionately to the Yugoslav federal budget. Belief in the (statistically confirmed) economic superiority of Slovenia was so strong that even the Slovenian tourist industry tried to attract tourists on the basis of Slovenia's advantageous economic position. The message was basically: Don't travel South, stop in Slovenia. As one Slovenian tourist guide-book stated, Slovenia "is economically the most developed republic in Yugoslavia. National production per capita in Slovenia is on average twice as high as the Yugoslav one. [...] Slovenia collaborates in one quarter of export business from Yugoslavia..." (Chamber of Economy of Slovenia 1988, p. 16).

How were these beliefs in the economic superiority of Slovenia within Yugoslavia transplanted to Australia? The logic of the 'economic superiority' argument was clearly detected among Slovenian second generation respondents and is revealed in the following examples.

> I don't really know a great deal about other ethnic groups in Yugoslavia. However, I know that the peoples down South are a real drain on the Yugoslav economy and that Slovenia has up till now subsidised these inefficient and, dare I say it, lazy people down South.

> Slovenia was supporting a lot of economy in Yugoslavia. I couldn't see this going on for too much longer in Slovenia without Slovenia getting a fair share of that wealth.
>
> On the Slovenian side [of the Slovenian-Croatian border] people are very, very industrious. ... Slovenians worked in the factories and in the afternoon they would take care of the animals in the barn or be involved with the handicraft etc. Croatians are much more relaxed.
> **Q:** Do you really believe the differences are so obvious?
> **A:** Yes. If it wasn't so obvious... then the Croats would not work only at work but also at home.
>
> My parents have always made comments about Croatians and Serbs being less than them, Slovenians. And also that Slovenians are workers, the brains, whereas the Serbs and Croatians are much more head-strong and temperamental.

Among Australian-Slovenians, the negative characteristics of the Southerners became, if anything, more pronounced. Slovenians in Australia have had less contact with other groups from the former Yugoslavia than Slovenians in Slovenia. Subsequently, it should not be surprising that the second generation had a relatively poor knowledge about these groups. More precisely, they were mostly incapable of differentiating between the specific groups.

> I didn't know much about other ethnic groups in Yugoslavia to be honest. I didn't know for example that there were Muslims as such or people who weren't Christians. That awareness has been more recent than something that I grew up with. I knew there were Macedonians, but I didn't know much about them and Montenegrins etc.

Slovenian second generation respondents tended to label Croatians, Serbs and others, without sustained arguments, as simply 'different'. Accurate knowledge about the groups concerned seems to be the least relevant consideration when rendering someone into the category of 'Other'. Interviews with second generation Slovenians confirmed this:

> If you go to Croatia or Serbia: that's Balkan. People there are different from the people in Slovenia.
>
> ... I always regarded [Croatians] as different and I really didn't know any other 'Yugoslavs'. Even though I didn't know them I didn't like them. Because of my father's attitude I thought they are to be disliked

even though I haven't experienced that. I got to know only one or two Serbs and they are both very nice people: they are generous, very happy, pleasant people to be with. But there was a lot of resentment on my father's part. They were considered to be people who were ruling Slovenia. I got the impression [from my father] that they are inferior in some respects.

One of the characteristics attached to the 'Southerners' is also their supposed aggressive nature. Salecl (1993, p. 102) once interestingly commented that it is not important what the Other does, for the Other's very existence is perceived as threatening. In Slovenia, belief in the 'evil' nature of Southerners is not uncommon, as one respondent explained: "None of my relatives likes Southerners whom they claim make their money worthless and who come to Slovenia to steal and commit crime". This reveals the very basic trait of any nationalist imagining of the Other, according to which the Other is the one who steals, commits crimes, works for the underground world, rapes 'our' women, etc. Slovenians are much more "cultured and pleasant" (in the words of one second generation Slovenian respondent). Another Slovenian said:

> Yugoslavs (in the sense of people from the former Yugoslavia, Z.S.) are known as having hot tempers. But we [Slovenians] are very cool, we have a very good temperament, I think. I think we are pretty good compared to other Yugoslavs. Compared to them we are fantastic. I think we are a lot more stable, it's easy to get along with us, we're friendly.

Because of the higher standard of living, the supposedly more 'westernised' way of life and their perceived difference from the groups from the South, it is often assumed that Central Europe, rather than the South, is the proper place for Slovenia to identify with. One respondent remarked that "Slovenia is like a province of Austria. Racially, [Slovenians] are different but really, they should be up there (a part of Austria, Z.S.) as opposed to down there (a part of Yugoslavia, Z.S.)." Although this statement reflects upon the situation in Slovenia, the basic characteristics of this belief are also to be perceived among Slovenians in Australia, regardless of generation.

As I have already mentioned, some second generation respondents have challenged their parents' position on this issue. Nevertheless, it also has to be noted that the stigma attached to this Southerner concept was strong enough to cause the complete distancing of a few second generation Slovenians from other ethnic groups from the former Yugoslavia:

> I have to admit that I was always embarrassed when I was asked if I am Serbian or Croatian. They haven't got a really good name for obvious reasons.
>
> I was never sorry that I was a Slovenian. I would have said that [I was sorry] if I was a Serbian or Croatian because they have given themselves such a headache. They are always fighting one another and it is common knowledge now in Australia that if you are Serbian or Croatian you don't get along. I think they are idiots because they are fighting in public.
>
> [Back in our school days] we had a few trouble-makers, Serbians... To my way of thinking, they are idiots. The same as Croatians. Both sides.

Did the brief military encounter in Slovenia in 1991 challenge this Southerner-concept among Slovenians in Australia? The answer is: not really. The only noticeable change was that at the beginning of the conflict, the Serbs emerged out of this Southerner-complex anonymity as the chief-Other. The identification of the Serbs in this way, however, had already begun to merge back into the generalised Southerner by around late 1993.

In summary, Croatian nationalist and right-wing fanaticism was perceived by second generation Australian-Slovenians to be nothing more and nothing less than what is characteristic of Southerners. This obvious phantasmagoric construction clearly served to reinforce the self-constructed boundary between the Westernised Slovenians on the one hand and the Balkanised Southerners on the other, between Us and Them, the clean and the polluted.

What is interesting is that among Australian-Slovenians, diaspora Croatians assumed the position of archetypical Southerners. This is very clearly specific to the Australian situation and cannot be extended to the situation in Slovenia. I cannot make any competent assessment of other Slovenian diasporas at this point. An important contributing factor for such an unfavourable portrayal of Australian-Croatians relates to the way in which they were treated by the Australian media, particularly in the 1960s and 1970s.[3] In Slovenia itself, Croatians are obviously frequently debated and mentioned in the media due to geographical proximity, a considerable degree of social and economic links between the two states, and unresolved political disputes, particularly those pertaining to unsolved maritime borders and ownership of the nuclear power station. But, Slovenians in Slovenia nevertheless do not perceive Croatians as representing the archetypal Southerners.

The basic feature of the image of Croatians constructed by the second generation Slovenian respondents was that they were 'powerful' and 'nationalistic'. Some Slovenians did not make any comments about them, but those who did invariably emphasised some negative attributes. How Croatians fit into the Southerner complex is revealed in the following comments of a second generation sister and brother whose relative is a Croatian:

> [My uncle] is a lazy man, untrustworthy. He is so nationalistic that it's painful. He did not allow his son to marry a non-Croatian. It might sound a very strong word 'brainwashed', but it is quite true. You must not have anything to do with anybody else if they are not Croatian. He is so dominant that my aunt can't do anything about it. I don't have anything to do with my own cousins because they consider themselves Croatians. I don't feel that way but they feel that way. They don't want to have anything to do with us. I actually feel very sorry for the kids because they are my only relatives in the whole of Australia. The kids work for him. But I think he [uncle] is more Bosnian from what my father tells me.

And the brother says about the same person:

> I always thought all Serbs and Croats are like my uncle who is a Croat. When you mention 'Yugoslav' to him, he says: "Oh, no way, I am Croatian, you know." And then he sits down and tells you never to mention... You know, he can go on forever. Anyway, he is Montenegrin. I just learned that. I've never been brought up like that. I am sure a lot of Croatian and Serbian kids were brought up like that. We never were and I believe there weren't many Slovenians brought up that way. I don't know. You would say Yugoslav and someone would say Slovenian. It wasn't such a big deal.

Interestingly, the relative mentioned in the above quotes becomes instantly compared and coupled with the Serbs (because of the presumed common characteristics). It is clear that to the respondent differences between Croatians, Bosnians and Montenegrins were/are negligible. Moreover, the symbolic border which delineated all non-Slovenian groups from one another in the interviews (Croatians, Serbs, Montenegrins and Yugoslavs) was shadowy and imprecisely defined. This is exactly how the undifferentiated Southerner is constructed; the 'border delineation' problem does not appear to be decisive.

The presumed 'fighting' nature of Croatians and the relatedness of this nature to 'old hatreds' carried on in Australia were often mentioned:

> I don't think old hatreds have a place here in Australia. [...] I have always known Croatians are very nationalistic but I don't have any first-hand experience. I know once my friends and I had one major argument about Tito. I would say that he also did something good for the country: he picked them up after the war. But to them, [Tito's regime] just betrayed Croatian people and everything else. ...

Those who had contact with Croatians through school or work would – with very few exceptions – mention the politicised nature of Croatian ethno-national identification in Australia and the difference in political rigour between both groups. Croatian ethnic identity and political beliefs were seen as inextricably linked. Furthermore, even the better preserved Croatian culture (compared to Slovenian) in Australia was seen as the result of a politicised Croatian 'nature'. A Slovenian first generation respondent said: "Croatians built their community on nationalism, so they have more chances [of survival] in Australia. We have not succeeded because we aren't nationalists".

Influential persons from Slovenian diaspora organisations were quite willing to speak about the functioning of Croatian communities in Australia. Although there has never been any open conflict between the two groups in Australia, the battle for prestige and symbolic capital was obvious. A first generation Slovenian respondent explained the supposed Slovenian prestige of Slovenians over Croatians in the following words:

> The Croatian Club [in Adelaide] is not run democratically. The committee is not elected democratically because you have to be a foundation member. The president of the Club could be selected from one out of maybe thirty families. They stick to nationalism much more than we do. We Slovenians have never been either Nazis or nationalists and we are not as sensitive about nationality as the Croatians and the Serbs. Slovenians were always merry fellows, no matter who the Master was. The most important thing was to have a full stomach and [enough money] for a jug of wine.

Of course, not all Australian-Slovenians hold this opinion about Croatians but it does represent a fairly commonly held view. During my research, I received many similar answers, particularly from people who assumed a place at the top-end of the diaspora hierarchy.

There is almost no official co-operation between Croatian and Slovenian organisations in Australia. One of the reasons put forward was, as one first generation respondent put it, "their breath of Ustasha". The numeric strength of Croatians, it is believed, adds up to Croatian unpreparedness for co-operation: "There is no official co-operation because we are a smaller group and I always have the feeling that whenever we get together, they look down upon us".

First generation Slovenian respondents were generally well equipped with untestable anecdotes about Croatians according to which they "are pretty chauvinistic. I don't know if it is true but apparently (sic!) in Canberra there was the message in the [Croatian] Club: 'Serbs and dogs forbidden'." Another respondent confidently affirmed: "I know that Croatians are extremists". This alleged Croatian extremism was generally characterised in a negative manner by Slovenian respondents.

The difference between Croatians and Slovenians was often described by Slovenian first generation respondents in terms of dichotomising argumentative endeavours: "Croatians are into politics and nationalism, whereas we..." When interviewing a first generation Slovenian respondent about the response of younger generation Slovenians to the war in their parents' homeland, and acknowledging the fact that many young Croatians actually become much more involved with their diaspora organisation for similar reasons, he said:

> No, [not Slovenians]. Slovenians are a gentle nation. But Croatians! They teach their children about Ustasha and Chetnics and this goes years back. [...] We are more good-hearted and our Slovenian songs are mostly about love, wine, good old times, sweethearts and the like. Croatians are more into the old political stuff. I know nothing about it, so how can I teach my children about this? This thing doesn't exist among Slovenians.

Another first generation Slovenian respondent very interestingly explained that an exaggeration of ethnic group strength, overestimating the preservation of their language and culture, istypical of Croatians in Australia. He continued:

> I have the following experience, [Croatians] want to show in public: 'we are big'. But I can assure you that [contrary to popular belief] the younger generation of Croatians doesn't speak Croatian but English. It's all that paper-tiger which looks malicious but it's just paper. [...] I worked with [Croatians] an awful lot and I tell you they are incredible... The noise that they produce is in their blood. When they

sing, they shout as much as their throats permit. The Croatian glory in which they themselves believe is worthless.

Both these examples show that Croatians were considered as 'something less', than Slovenians, that their noise and bravura were merely a façade they use to show off.

2   Croatian respondents on Slovenians

As a follow-on to the discussion of the Australian-Slovenian perception of Croatians, let us just briefly think about the way in which Slovenians featured in Croatian respondents' narratives. It is hard to estimate to what extent my own Slovenian background impacted upon rather favourable Croatian portrayals of Slovenians. It might have played a certain role.

The consistency of responses by Croatian respondents about Slovenians was considerable. Basically, Slovenians were not extensively covered in the interviews with Croatian respondents. This is a reflection of the marginal role Slovenians play in their concerns and interests. In general terms it could be said that the following statement by a second generation Croatian provides a common characterisation of Slovenians by Croatian respondents: "Slovenes: few in Australia – low profile – industrious." Another stereotypical characteristic which also regularly came up was – as one first generation respondent expressed himself – that Slovenians are "very quiet, modest, passive people". Another one said: "If you want me to stereotype a Slovenian, I'd say: hardworking, opportunistic, in a sense selfish in looking after Slovenian interests and not worried about the effects on Croatia." Yet another second generation individual said that Slovenians are "the only other group [from the former Yugoslavia] I could relate to".

Croatian respondents also commented on what they saw as the comparative advantages of Slovenians in the former Yugoslavia. They referred to the assumed 'ethnic purity' of the Slovenian nation. As already mentioned, a significant number of residents of Slovenia are non-Slovenians, yet Croatians usually talked in terms of Slovenia being "almost 100 per cent" populated by Slovenians. There were also suggestions that Slovenians, because of their 'better position' in Yugoslavia, also formed an alliance with the Serbs: "So, the Serbs let Slovenians do more or less what they wanted to – except that they had to give money. At the end, Slovenians got sick of that when they realised how much money that involved."

All the evidence presented so far suggests the existence of some distance between the two groups. There were no open conflicts between Croatians and Slovenians in Australia, but there were issues which helped to sustain the symbolic game of one-upmanship. In summary, Slovenians usually spoke negatively about Croatian nationalism, and Croatians about Slovenian selfishness.

3   Croatians on the 'practical identity' of Yugoslavs

As already mentioned, Croatian and Slovenian constructions of Otherness follow very different logics. For Slovenians, the Other is, broadly a generalised Other. To them, specificities separating and differentiating various Others from one another matter very little. In fact, they matter only to the extent to which they reinforce the stereotype and perception of Otherness. As we shall now see in the analysis of Croatian diasporic Others, it is precisely the *specificities* which matter and warrant individual consideration. Considering the well known tension and conflict between the Croatians and the Serbs, one might expect that the Serbs are the first and almost logical choice in an analysis of the Croatian diaspora construction of Otherness. However, it was the Yugoslavs who received much more critical commentary by the Croatian respondents than the Serbs.

In Chapter 3 some attention has already been dedicated to the question of Yugoslav identity. It has been suggested that the term Yugoslav constituted a volitional form of ethnic identity but that this meaning was not necessarily replicated in the use of this term by the respondents. In addition to this rather standard use, respondents negatively labelled as Yugoslav those individuals who were of Croatian ancestry but who were never part of the established Australian-Croatian diaspora network and only joined this network at the onset of ethnic conflict in the homeland. I suggested that the membership in Australian-Croatian organisations might have surged up to 30 per cent as a result of this process. In addition, people who in the past might not have paid much attention to the politics of ancestral identification might also have attracted the Yugoslav label.

Croatian respondents in this research unanimously believed that Yugoslav identity was brutally foisted upon Croatians in Yugoslavia. It is interesting to note, however, that 'Yugoslav' as a census category was not included in official censuses in Yugoslavia until 1961 (Sekulić et al. 1994). The analysis by Burg and Berbaum (1989, p. 538) also points to the "reluctance to formally encourage the emergence of Yugoslav identity" by Yugoslav authorities. Evidence of this can be found in the official instructions to census-takers which, in 1981, stated that "if a citizen wishes to record Yugoslav as an answer to this question, the census taker is obliged to record even that answer, although by this the citizen does not declare membership in a nation or nationality" (ibid.).

The reality is thus in complete contrast with the general belief of the respondents. To be sure, in 1981 more people (5.4 per cent) than ever before in Yugoslav censuses declared Yugoslav as their ethnic identity (Sekulić et al. 1994, p. 85, c.f. Burg and Berbaum 1989, p. 536). Burg and Berbaum (ibid.) interpret this fact as evidence of "shared political identity" and an "indicator of political integration and diffuse regime support". It is interesting to reflect upon this statement in the light of subsequent events.

The Yugoslav identity was considered to be a pure fabrication of the Titoist regime which was striving towards a uniform socialist culture and the elimination of diversity. Croatian respondents interpreted the Yugoslav identity as an indicator of *specific* support for a hegemonic ethnic power (Serbs) and a dominant ideological power (communist ideology).

The question of Yugoslavs in this research proved to be a Croatian rather than a Slovenian concern. None of the second generation Slovenian respondents was concerned with *any* of the aspects of Yugoslav identity. Slovenians usually did not consider Yugoslav identity as having a particular political meaning. When asking a second generation Slovenian respondent about different ethnic groups from the former Yugoslavia, I asked: "What about Yugoslavs?" And the answer was: "Who are the Yugoslavs?" Many Slovenian respondents confessed that when asked about their ancestry, they used to say 'Yugoslav'. This "unfortunate fact", or even a "slip of a tongue" – so considered by various first generation Slovenian respondents – must not be confused with the question of Yugoslav identity as understood by Croatian respondents. There is, of course, a big difference between not questioning the concept of Yugoslav identity and denying its existence.

The political loading of the term, however, was a key issue for the Croatian interpretation of Yugoslav identity. Only a few second generation Croatians failed to display negative feelings towards self-declared Yugoslavs. According to them, these feelings are shared by their parents' generation: "I think that my father thinks that something like [Yugoslav identity] doesn't exist". A second generation Croatian respondent (who was not *a priori* critical of Yugoslav identity) explained her father's experience upon arrival to Australia: "My father used to say: 'I came from Yugoslavia', but [other Croatians] would say: 'There is no Yugoslavia. Yugoslavia doesn't exist.' He used to say: 'You people are mad. What's going on here?'" Although respondents would frantically debate the supposed evils of the state of Yugoslavia they could simultaneously philosophically deny its existence. If there is such a determination to deny the existence of a state, one can imagine the intensity of feelings when such a person encountered an individual who dared to, no matter how vaguely, identify with that state. Respondents, in this sense, denied that identity can be chosen rather than primordially given. Individual volition in defining one's ethnic identity was not an acceptable possibility. There is a distinct tendency towards the deification of Croatian identity by a majority of respondents. Being of Croatian descent means that one partakes in "generations of shared historical experience" and any attempt at distancing oneself from this is considered a betrayal.

The ongoing issue Australian-Croatians have with people who identify as Yugoslav can only be understood historically. Interestingly, in the period between the two World Wars, Croatian immigrants to Australia were the champions of the idea of Yugoslavism and Yugoslav unity. Many Croatian inter-war organisations in Australia were left-wing oriented (c.f. Tkalčević 1992, pp. 41-70). This is not surprising because the ideology of Yugoslav unitarianism was very common among the Croatian intelligentsia (c.f. Banac 1992) and the Croatian working class in the early twentieth century. However, and as the reader would know, immigrants from the post-Second World War period operated with a radically different set of political ideas which were in sharp contrast with the pro-Yugoslav left-wing orientation of established Croatian organisations. There was no possibility and willingness for ideological or political compromise between the two. There is also no evidence that individuals moved from the Yugoslav-unitarist position in the pre-Second World War era to the Croatian-nationalist position in the post-Second World War period. In other words, the Australian-Croatians in the pre-Second World War period were almost the exact opposite of Croatians who arrived after the Second World War.

What actually happened with those ethnic Croatians in Australia who chose to identify as Yugoslav? The Croatian respondents in this research generally believed that such people have betrayed the richness of Croatian cultural experience and the continuation of a certain historical process and that they substituted this cultural tradition with something that is recent and morally corrupt. In the words of a second generation Croatian: "Yugoslavia has existed for a couple of decades only; it hasn't got a history as a country and you call yourself Yugoslav! These sort of people I don't respect. I haven't met any of them but I don't respect them. For me, they don't exist".

What is the reason for the Croatian hostility towards the concept of Yugoslav identity? Why is this type of identity so disputed to have led some Croatian respondents to deny that something like Yugoslav identity actually exists?

> Because of the type of person that I am, I tend to get on well with most people, this includes other ethnic groups. However, I don't get on well with people who call themselves 'Yugoslav' as I believe there is no such thing. This usually starts an argument. However, if Yugoslavs or Serbs don't bother me, I won't bother them. If they do, then so do I.

When I challenged the respondents by pointing out that many Yugoslavs are actually people with Croatian ancestry, they usually skipped over this difficulty with their argument, while acknowledging their awareness of the fact. They could not accept the idea of multiple identification in this particular case.

Some Croatian respondents maintained that being a Yugoslav is basically a position of naïveté. It is the position of someone "who is sitting on the fence". With the break-up of the former Yugoslavia, many people of Croatian background who used to call themselves Yugoslav or who attended social functions in pro-Yugoslav oriented Clubs in Australia, became involved with Croatian organisations. Their 'sudden' presence caused a high degree of suspicion among the 'older' members of Croatian clubs. They were given various names with pejorative meanings: Yugos, ex-Yugos, parachutes, born-again Croatians, part-time Yugos, turn-arounds, 'this year Croatians' and so on. The debate among second generation Croatians in *Klokan* magazine is particularly illustrative of different dimensions of this 'sudden appearance'. One Letter to the editor expressed disappointment over some Croatians in Australia who:

> ... have a negative attitude to the people they call 'born-again Croatians'. Just because an individual had the wrong political allegiance in the past, or has only recently discovered his or her Croatian identity, does not mean they are less Croatian than the rest of us. (Hrketic 1992, p. 3)

This critique centres on the process whereby a group's out-member becomes (due to the boundary shift) a group's in-member, leading to a resistance to 'intruders' by the established members. Two responses to Hrketic's letter deserve mention as they are indicative of the points of contention within Croatian-Yugoslav relations. The first response by Simat (1992, p. 3) goes: "In my terms, to be a Yugo was to be a *traitor*, nothing more and nothing less. To be a Yugo, for me, also constituted being a Serb." He argued that few young Croatians can comprehend ("particularly [not] the young '*reborn*'") the extent of "Yugoslav-Serb propaganda, infiltration and assassination campaign" against Croatians. He continues,

> Croatians were *naturally* ostracised. [...] The aim of the communist dictatorship in 'Yugoslavia' was to *wipe out the total existence of Croatia and its people and the fact that it ever did exist.* ...Yugos now ironically call themselves Croatians and, funnily enough, as if they all received bad bouts of *amnesia* or something which caused them a loss of memory, they all *conveniently* forget the fact that they

were Yugos and portray themselves as being proud Croatians all their lives. [...] If you are an ex-Yugo, please, don't be *hypocritical* about it. Just *admit to it, talk about it (not too loudly* though) and this way you will gain a lot more respect... (emphasis added, Z.S.)

Simat's example evokes the old Christian belief: as human beings have to live with responsibility for the Fall of Man in the Garden of Eden, so the 'ex-Yugo' has to live with (and admit/confess to) his 'mistaken' identity in the past, too. The second response (Knezevic 1993, p. 3) is more straightforward, and it directly links the question of 'born-again Croatians' with the Serbs in the context of the defence of honour: "I hate Serbs. I hate the very name and the very existence of a Serb. They started World War I and now are aiming for World War III... How can you forgive a 'born-again Croat'? It would be an *insult to forgive* the so-called Yugos..." (emphasis added, Z.S.).

The emphasised text in the above quotations shows a potential (and actual) ideological component in the Croatian portrayal of the Yugoslav. There seems to be no possibility left for compromise. A deep-seated sense of historical experience which cannot be transcended or skipped over is drawn on to justify a separation between the two groups.

The main weakness of the former Yugoslavs who are approaching the Croatian community – as perceived by Croatian respondents – is their changing identity which makes them unpredictable and unreliable. Their new loyalties and identity are the consequence of *practical considerations* rather than *genuine identity transformations*. A typical explanation would be: "Their national awakening does not originate in deeper and frank initiatives. These are the 'turnarounds' according to the current need. The very same people will change their loyalties the moment the political situation changes again" (first generation respondent). This can be illustrated as follows:

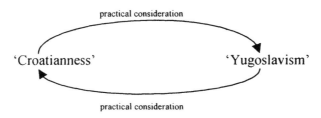

Figure 5.1   Essentialising a 'Yugoslav'

The Yugoslav is seen not only as a deception of prescribed 'real' origins. In addition, Croatians who for any reason call themselves Yugoslav challenge the most crucial rules of the ethnic game in its most serious form: it is a step beyond primordiality as prescribed by the popular ideology of a given Croatian diaspora collectivity.

The joining of established Croatian diaspora organisations by the 'former Yugoslavs' caused mixed feelings and responses in Croatian diaspora organisations. Although they have been accepted as new members, they have largely not been entrusted with decision-making positions within these. One of the well-known first generation Croatians said:

> The reactions of those people who have always been within the community are not good and they don't like to see these new people taking leadership roles at the expense of Croatians who have always been in the Croatian community and never pro-Yugoslav. They are accepted on the level of being a member of the Croatian community. But I don't think the community will be willing to accept them at the upper levels.
>
> It is true that [Yugoslavs] are not as accepted in the community as other Croatians. I always say: they should be welcomed but we also should have reservations towards them. You never know who they are. I was saying yesterday... that now the 'Red ones' (another name for the 'former Yugoslavs', Z.S.) have started to confess and want to become Christened.

Being a Yugoslav is more than just being a person with mistaken past political affiliations. It is the label commonly attached to anyone who breaks the rules of conformity. Accordingly, many of the respondents in this study who became active in Croatian diaspora organisations due to the war, were often referred to by people from the leadership structure as 'Yugoslavs'. In particular, young, second generation Croatians whose parents were not active members of the community were often dismissed as 'former Yugoslavs'. It did not matter that they possibly never identified as Yugoslavs; this detail is beyond the concern of those who label. At this point I can again refer to my already reported fieldwork experience. As mentioned in Chapter 3, on the occasion of my visit to the Croatian club in Adelaide I was asked to sign the visitors' book. When I asked why this was necessary, a person whom I didn't know said: "I know you are a decent guy. But recently Yugoslavs came in and caused a fight." I was obviously immediately suspected of being a potential Yugoslav. When I later recounted this incident to my informant, I asked him to clarify who had been engaged in that fight, the answer was: "Ha-ha-ha... They were our own people." Transgressing the boundaries of behavioural acceptability was translated into the language of political marginalisation.

The Croatian respondents frequently volunteered to compare the Serbs and the Yugoslavs. There was relatively little divergence in opinions as far as the principles and criteria for this comparative evaluation were concerned:

> My father used to say: 'At least, if they are Serbian, that's fine, they say they are Serbian.' But he couldn't stand anyone who used to say they were Yugoslav.
> **Q:** What about you?
> **A:** I was the same. [...] I never accept just Yugoslav. And then they would say: my mother is from there and father is from there. And I'd say: "So, you are Croatian!", and they: "Same thing – Yugoslav." And I: "Of course, not." And I'd get into an argument. I was always like that. It was like my father said: you respect the Serbians because they at least admit who they are but he always thought Yugoslavs were communists. And I have retained that attitude my whole life.
>
> I can tolerate Yugoslavs less than I can tolerate Serbs. A Serb is a Serb, he could call himself a Serb and I respect him for that. I always said I would respect a Serb, whereas a Yugoslav I can't accept because to me they are ignorant.
>
> Our parents never gave us lessons about how to behave towards Serbians and Yugoslavs. But when their friends came over and they spoke about these things, I think we started to understand that it was not good to mix with them. However, we were never told or forbidden anything in that respect. Nevertheless, we understood and accepted their attitude. Declaring yourself to be Yugoslav is the worst possible thing. If a Serbian says that he is Serbian, he is proud of that and he has the right to be proud. But being a Yugoslav to me is the same as being a scheming fox and no better than a scheming fox.
>
> **Q:** What do you think about the so-called Yugoslav group?
> **A:** Well, that was different. That's what we were told not to respect. You respect Serbian, Macedonian, Slovenian, Bosnian, but the one that called himself 'Yugoslav' – you have to watch. And anyone that called himself a Yugoslav was an enemy. When I was growing up the chief enemies were Yugoslavs, not Serbians. Serbians weren't mentioned that much. They are Serbians, we are Croatians – big deal.

It is easy to draw a conclusion on the basis of this information: the enemy is respected if it has a readable identity but this does not change its status to a friend. It does, however, make the antagonism predictable and resembling chivalry. But the Yugoslavs are not perceived in such a manner by Croatians even if they honestly believe in their association with Yugoslav identity. The choice of Yugoslav identity is not perceived as justifiable even if the person is of mixed parentage between, for example, a Serb and a Croat. In this case a child from such an interethnic liaison could choose Yugoslav identity as a form of compromise. Croatian respondents would perceive such a compromise as serving the purpose of instigating antagonism rather than neutralising identity.

Labelling oneself as a Yugoslav could be treated by Croatians as a direct provocation: "If I came out in conversation with someone and said I am Croatian and then he came out with 'I am a Yugoslav...' I'd treat that as a direct provocation because they are actually denying Croatian nationality by saying that."

It seems that the very existence of Yugoslavs almost warranted a negative response among the respondents. I now propose to test the Croatian-Australian respondents' assumption that the Serb is better than the Yugoslav. Just how 'good' is 'better'?

4   Croatian respondents on the Other: the Serbs

Slovenian respondents made comparatively fewer comments about the Serbs than Croatian respondents. Both generations of Slovenian respondents referred to them mostly in the comments which allowed me to easily classify them under the rubric Southerners. The first generation Slovenians portrayed the Serbs more positively than they did the Croatians. It is interesting to note that Slovenian 'political' migrants generally have very favourable views towards Serbs. I mentioned to one such 'political migrant' that he constantly privileges Serbs over Croatians. He replied:

> Yes, I always liked them more. The Serbs were far away [during the Second World War]. The Serbian Orthodox community in Slovenia at the time was something small. ... a couple of Serbian officers. Their children were born in Slovenia and they spoke Slovenian. Some of them fought on our [Slovenian Home Guard] side and they were very good. You see, there were many things we could not see then.

It is also known that during the Second World War the Slovenian Bishop Rožman acted against the interests of the Croatian Independent State. The Serbs in Serbia hosted hundreds of Slovenian families which were exiled by the Germans during the war. Bishop Rožman, who was reportedly wary of the emergence of possible anti-Slovenian sentiments in Serbia and the effects this would have on the exiled Slovenian families, wanted to prove his commitment to Serbian interests. For this reason he formed a Commission which collected documents about Serbian suffering in the Independent State of Croatia and sent them to Pope Pius XII who subsequently sent a cheque for one million Deutsch Marks to Serbia *via* Bishop Rožman. The money was intended for "those Orthodox who suffer oppression" (Kolarič 1977, p. 169, c.f. pp. 164-70).

Only ten out of 31 second generation Croatian respondents showed no explicitly aggressive anti-Serbian bias. This is the question of a nationalist identity politics *par excellence*. The key to our understanding of Croatian attitudes towards the Serbs (and *vice versa*) could be described as the search for and imposition of differentials. Hirschman (1987, p. 557) emphasises that *physical* and *cultural* markers, employed in mechanisms of differentiation of one group from another, can be not only ambiguous but also subject to change across generations. He says that "(f)or ethnic groups to persist, such markers must be reinforced by social arrangements and practices that solidify group identity and heighten divisions between groups" (ibid.)

How do these markers fare if applied comparatively to Croatians and Serbs? Physical markers between Croatians and Serbs – as is commonly the case between neighbouring groups – are not easy to establish. Only one respondent mentioned that Serbs possibly look different, although his comment reveals nothing about the nature of this 'difference'. It shows, however, the respondent's ability to combine stereotypical and ideological constructions of the Serbs:

> ... Wait. Some of them really look different. Two Serbs that I've met... One is dead and he really looked different; it would be derogatory to describe him (laugh), so I won't get stuck into that. But the other one that I met in Croatia – he looked really odd, too... I don't know if that is bias or what. But then again, I read the Serbian paper and I see all these Serbian beauty-queens and stuff like that. They are pretty sexy looking. So it can't all be... (laugh)

Hirschman (1987, p. 557) also suggests that language and religion serve as "especially strong factors in maintaining divisions that reinforce cultural definitions of ethnicity." While I have already indicated the ambiguity and manipulability of *religion* as a marker in the previous chapter in relation to Nikola Tesla, there is similar ambiguity concerning *language* as a marker and I shall devote some attention to this issue.

The second generation Croatian respondents had difficulties explaining the difference between the Croatian and Serbian languages. The description of these differences was usually limited to the difference in scripts (Croatian uses Latin and Serbian Cyrillic), and differences in words or dialects. The Australian-Croatian diaspora organisations exercised a considerable amount of pressure to make sure that its members acknowledged Croatian rather than Serbo-Croatian as their mother tongue. One Croatian female respondent, a rather 'visible' and successful individual in the Australian-Croatian diaspora who took Serbo-Croatian as a matriculation exam, said: "In the Club I don't say I finished Serbo-Croatian, but I say Croatian and don't go into that any further. Some people there simply wouldn't understand why I let myself be humiliated to that extent. Matriculation was more important to me."

Only a few respondents admitted that they cannot recognise the difference between the Serbian and Croatian languages:

> I can understand both very well. It's the same as the difference between water and ice. They look quite different but they are fundamentally the same. This is the only way I can describe it.

> No, I can't see the difference between the Croatian and Serbian languages. Only the other day someone said: you shouldn't say *hiljadu* [thousand] but *tisuča*. And I said: "But I've been saying *hiljada* for a long time." I didn't know that was Serbian.

While some respondents found it hard to articulate anything except the most obvious differences between the languages, they still maintained that the languages are separate and different. My main interest at this point lies not in the exploration of the linguistic dimension of this separateness, but with the manner in which Croatian respondents constructed and operated with this difference. This difference clearly functioned as a marker and mechanism of ideological reinforcement of the boundary. Armstrong (1982, p. 8) provides us with an historical parallel:

> Most often symbolic boundary mechanisms are words. Such words are particularly effective as traffic lights warning a group member when he is approaching a barrier separating his group from another. This intense power of a few symbolic "border guards" is illustrated by early Yiddish. It was basically an Old High German dialect, but rigorously excluded certain words in the German environment that had specifically Christian connotations. For example, *seganon*, "to bless," was rejected because it derived from Latin *signare*, "to make the sign [of the cross]", in favour of retaining the neutral form "*bentshn*" from Latin *benedicere*, "to speak well," which earlier

Jewish communities had incorporated in Southern Laaz, their Romance dialect.

If the differences between languages are hard to detect and maintain, then words, as 'symbolic border guards', start to play a decisive role as the following second generation respondents indicate:

> One has to be careful not to make a mistake [when speaking Croatian]. For me that was never a problem because my parents were very strict with that. My father was always 'on watch' to detect any Serbian word... I've got books at home which list words and explain which are Croatian and which Serbian, how they are to be used, etc.

> From what my parents told me – we'd say *bijelo* (white, Z.S.) and *kruh* (bread, Z.S.) and [Serbs] would say *belo* and *hleb*. Just odd words. That was from what my parents told me... Even now, if I hear both [languages] on the radio ... to me a lot of it is the same.

> The difference is in the meaning of many words. For instance *vlak* (train, Z.S) for *voz*, *kašika* (spoon, Z.S.) for *žlica*...

Historically, political ambitions and the desire of Southern Slavic peoples for unity exerted considerable pressures on language policies. The tendency towards amalgamation of Slovenian and Croatian languages in the 19th century was very short-lived. The relationship between Croatian and Serbian languages is more complex. It has been the subject of intense philological controversies since the middle of the 19th century. In the Kingdom of Serbs, Croats and Slovenes, the Croatian language was under considerable pressure to conform to the syntax and lexical attributions of the Serbian language (Samardžija 1993, pp. 5-12). These problems were obviously amplified by the influence of the Serbian language within the same kingdom. The previous Austro-Hungarian set-up was far less threatening to the Croatian language as the two most influential languages – German and Hungarian – were very different from it. When Ustasha came to power in 1941 they made Croatian language purism one of their ideological cornerstones. Ante Pavelić argued that the purity of the Croatian language had suffered less over the past centuries together than in the period between 1918-1941 because allegedly in this period: "the simplest, the ugliest, the worst Balkan words became (...) a constitutive part of Croatian language" (ibid., p. 14). The Ustasha regime orchestrated a major revamping and purification of the Croatian language. A linguist Franolić (1984, p. 102) writes:

In the Independent State of Croatia (April 1941-May 1945), Croatian linguistic purism manifested itself again: new words were coined to replace international terms. Thus neologisms *brzoglas, krugoval, promička, slikokaz* replaced telefon, radio, propaganda, kino. On the other hand, words coined in the 19th century, which fell out of use, were brought back into use and assumed meanings to handle new ideas or objects; e.g. *samovoz* 'automobil', *slikopis* 'film', *svjetlopis* 'photography' etc.

After the Second World War, the Croatian and Serbian languages were again amalgamated into Serbo-Croatian although allowances were made for variations in vocabulary and script. Most importantly, Serbian and Croatian versions of Serbo-Croatian were easily intelligible to speakers of both groups.

Croatian independence in 1991 actualised the need to widen the gap separating the two languages. The appearance of Brodnjak's (1992) *Rječnik razlika imedu sprskog i hrvatskog jezika* (Differential Dictionary of Serbian and Croatian) fits into the context of emphasising the markers of differentiation (c.f. Klaric 1992, p. 7). Some words are invented, others reactivated from pre-Second World War Croatian. The effect of Brodnjak's new vocabulary is basically that of "accepting Serbo-Croatian as Serbian language and searching for and creating the Croatian words" (ibid.) This is almost identical to what was happening to the Croatian language during the existence of the Independent State of Croatia (1941-1945).

How important the differentiation of the two languages is can be seen from an interview with the coordinator of the SBS Croatian Radio Program in Sydney (Milic and Velcic 1994, p. 4). The Croatian language radio coordinator was criticised for using vocabulary which "sometimes departs from the standard literary Croatian." The interviewee interestingly responded that she was "lining up *the most up to date vocabulary* from Zagreb" (emphasis added, Z.S.), pointing to the vibrant dynamics of the codification of recent changes to the Croatian vocabulary.

The following story told by one second generation Croatian respondent clearly shows how important language is as an identity component:

> My arrival in Croatia. I got there and I asked two people the way to Korčula (the Croatian island, Z.S.). And they said: "Where are you from?" – they noticed my accent, broken, not very good, and I told them that I am from Australia. And one said: "*Oh, dobro ti srpsko govoriš*" (Oh, you speak very good Serbian, Z.S.). I couldn't handle that. I said: "*Pička materina, to nije srpsko, ja govorim hrvatsko*

koliko možem." (Fuck you. This is not Serbian. I speak as much Croatian as I can, Z.S.)

Most Croatian émigré literature directly or indirectly mentions Serbs as somehow inferior. Korsky (1983, p. 40), for example, when describing the geostrategical position of Serbia says: "Serbian national territory is closeted, monotonous and poor" and therefore presents the Other in a subordinate way, even in a sphere which is fundamentally beyond the reach of human influence. Omrčanin's (1989, pp. 614-25) description of the "tragic point[s] for the Serbians" reads: "... the experiment of trying to subjugate Croatians ended in disaster. We do not invoke any lesson learned by Serbians from the experiment, because Serbians cannot learn it." And last but not least, in 1991, *The New Yorker* (Viorst 1991, p. 74) published an article in which the Croatian president, Dr. Franjo Tudjman, was quoted as saying:

> Long before Shakespeare and Moliere, our writers were translated into European languages. The Serbs belong to the East. Their church belongs to the East. They use the Cyrillic alphabet, which is Eastern. They are an Eastern people, like the Turks and the Albanians. They belong to the Byzantine culture.

This comment resembles the logic of the Slovenian construction of the Southerner and adapts it to the local political repertoire. But there is a difference in their approach in the sense that Tudjman's 'Easterner' label is more clearly individuated and very seldom used in a public discourse. In fact, the Easterner featured only in one single statement by a first generation Croatian participant who explained that:

> Serbian religion is different from Croatian. Also their culture is completely different from Croatian. They are the East, full of Balkanisms, where everything is done through the back door. They are the sort of nation where a husband, the Serb, kills his Croatian wife. They are an ungrateful nation.

The existence of a Serb is therefore threatening even in the most intimate relationship and the above respondent has chosen to use a moralistic stand to describe it. Only as a uniform totality can they be unanimously characterised as: "perfidious, megalomaniacs, ... [they] hate Croats with a vengeance" (second generation Croatian). This reveals the respondent's inability to experience a Serb as an individual. Each Serb – to paraphrase Levinson

(1950, p. 94) – "is seen and reacted to as a sort of simple specimen of the stereotyped, reified image of the group".

Just before the military conflict in the Balkans arose in 1991, a second generation respondent had visited Croatia and spoke about the Serbs he met as follows:

> ... some were very good on the surface. Some of them were intelligent although they didn't want to discuss problems because the war was starting and it was a good idea not to – especially on the small boat [that I was travelling on]. They were into rock-'n-roll, having a good time, drugs...; I met other Serbs, too, who were extremists. Croats are perhaps violent and aggressive because Serbians are aggressive. You don't know whether it's the chicken or the egg.

The interpersonal distance between Serbian and Croatian individuals is not set by any predetermined factors. Although the antagonism between Croatians and Serbians may seem to be ever-present and all-pervasive, it would be a mistake not to allow for the possibility of mutual interpersonal understanding between members of the two groups: "[X] was the name of the person that was of Serbian descent and we had a very good relationship [in school]. He would never say that he was a Yugoslav; he'd always say he was a Serb. And I always said I was Croatian." Another second generation Croatian respondent commented as follows:

> When I was in a Croatian dance group we'd perform at the Festival Theatre or somewhere. There was the Croatian dance group and the Serbian dance group and we'd always say: "Oh, they are the Serbs," and they'd say: "Oh, they are the Croats."

These examples are reportedly more of an exception, however. Even if a relationship between a Croatian and Serbian developed, it was never reported as a pristine, wholeheartedly intimate experience of friendship. The only exception is one second generation Croatian respondent whose girlfriend was Serbian but who was nevertheless found stating, as already quoted above, that Serbs are "perfidious, megalomaniacs" who "hate Croats with a vengeance".

There were not many occasions for second generation Croatians to make contact with Serbian individuals. School or 'coincidence' were most often mentioned:

> I've met Serbs by accident, yes. One guy that I was working with was Serbian and he was quite friendly towards me... and he was derogatory towards Croatian nationalism but I wouldn't rise to the bite, you

know. I actually helped him out on a couple of occasions when needed it because he was a drinker and a womaniser.

Other venues, such as the soccer ground, usually provided less positive experiences:

> As soon as I heard [our soccer team was getting a new player whose mother was a Serb] I thought: here we go, something is going to happen here. I said to him straight away: "Listen! You played for Beograd [soccer team] – he said he was a Yugoslav – just stay out of my way; just don't talk to me because there could be a fight. Let's just keep it to soccer." And he ended up being all right. We ended up being friends as close as a Serb and a Croatian can get. I respected the fact that he was a soccer player. But as for now, I have nothing to do with him. I can't stand it, really. I can't see any Serb for a long time.
>
> I remember being at a soccer game. A Croatian female... happened to be sitting next to me. So, we were sitting there behind the goal-keeper and watching the game. She had (that was 10-15 years ago) the Croatian team's flag. By coincidence, I was next to her and her girlfriend. The others from our group just disappeared. And the Belgrade supporters happened to be sitting next to us! Great! She provoked them and then I was expected to help her out. In revenge, [Serbs] tried to burn her flag and then I had to step in. That was probably the only time that I met Serbs.

One of the respondents replied to my question: "Do you have any Serbian friends?" with laughter, adding: "All I knew was that the Serbs existed but actually I didn't know anyone that was Serbian."

Respondents described a few very interesting encounters with Serbs. The following is taken from an interview with a respondent who met a Serb in Malaysia in 1991. This Serb presented him with a postcard of the famous Croatian coastal town of Dubrovnik, saying: "This is where I am from. This is Serbia."

> He didn't know I was Croatian. ... He just blurted it out like an idiot. Unbelievable! I told him that I was Croatian when he was leaving; and I told him my parents were from Dubrovnik.
>
> He didn't like the war. The war hadn't started yet but it was definitely building up towards it. This was an example of a lunatic perhaps. You can't say Serbians are like that. He is the only Serb that

> I met and see what I was meeting? And this is not what I wanted to believe Serbians are like. I wanted to find out but not like that.
>
> I realised he wasn't an aggressive person, not a Chetnik. But although he didn't seem to be a Chetnik, he still talked like this. And he was an intelligent person, in his 30s. He wasn't some kind of stupid person from God knows where. He was what I call an intellectual!

In some instances second generation respondents openly expressed their negative attitudes towards Serbs: "Serbs – hate them. They leave me alone, I'll leave them alone". Yet, a group of young Croatians interviewed in a group session was unanimous when one of them said: "Serbs provoke us everywhere: in the car-parks, on the soccer ground, they are threatening over the phone. We fight each other. Some Croatians say we are very nationalistic, but we fight the Serbs while they just put their heads down". This statement was the only clear first-hand account suggesting that there is an amount of pro-active planning and readiness for street violence between the two groups. However, Croatian respondents justified their use of violent methods by alleging the other side's responsibility for provocations. The above statement, made by one individual in a group with others wholeheartedly supporting what he was saying, was actually talking about violent encounters with the Serbs as a means of defending Croatian honour and pride. The radicalism of particular Croatian groupings and individuals was more commonly acknowledged and referred to indirectly: "I don't hate Serbians. I hate what they are doing but I don't hate them. But some of my Croatian friends... they really hate them. That must be from a very early age."

A respondent who mentioned that he finds it easy to deal with the Serbs on an inter-personal level was asked to estimate to what extent he believes his attitudes are valid for the rest of the second generation Croatian population. He replied:

> I know a lot of Croatians who if you just mention the word 'Serbs', they reach for a gun, I guess. They are very negative. It is very difficult for me to speak about other Croats. Now (1992, Z.S.), they are extremely defensive and aggressive about it. But stereotypically speaking, the Croatian mentality sees no ending [to the Croatian-Serbian conflict]. [Croatians] have no resolution. All they see is conflict, a lasting conflict, a vicious circle of violence and submission. They don't seem to have the ability to say: "How do we resolve this issue?"... They don't have the answer. They only deal with conflict and simple mechanisms of conflict. I also think they

don't appreciate the sensitivity of Serbian people. They don't understand about Kosovo, they really don't.

In all analyses presented in this chapter, the attitudes of Croatians towards Serbs are substantially influenced by the opinions prevalent in Australian-Croatian diaspora organisations. The 'Serbian question' is the one which was most successfully promoted in these settings by those who declared themselves to be 'political migrants'. Several respondents said without hesitation that their parents taught them not to trust Serbs and to dislike them. The following examples allow us a glimpse into the cross-generational transmission of ethno-nationalist ideas.

> Q: Have you ever been told by your parents to avoid the Serbs?
> A: Not really. Not by my parents. As far as they are concerned, they brought me up in the right way: I should know what is right or wrong myself. They never said: "Watch out for the Serbs." I knew that for myself. I didn't have to wait for someone to tell me to stay away.

> [My father and I] don't talk about Serbians every day. When he says something about Serbians I don't contradict, I just say: "Yes, you are right dad." Whether I agree with him or not, I always say: "You are right dad." It's for the sake of peace in our house.

> I was indoctrinated [by my father] to be very anti-Serbian. I didn't know why. So, it was a very political upbringing. I have been raised to feel animosity towards the Serbian ethnic group in Yugoslavia, but have never really felt any dislike...

My research provided plenty of evidence of the attempted transmission of anti-Serbian sentiments from the first generation migrant parents to the second generation. However, this transmission process is complex. While prejudice is transmitted across generations, there is also evidence of reflexive attitudes among the second generation. This is seen in their questioning of Croatian 'knee-jerk' reactions against Serbs. One first generation respondent commented: "We always had a bit of a catastrophe whenever we played Beograd soccer team. You get kids that just go crazy. Some of the parents instilled in them 'hate Serbs, hate the Serbs'. Some of these children don't even know why or what the history is. Nothing. They are just stupid; 'They are the Serbs! We hate them!'" The following respondent also indicates a degree of reflexivity and thoughtfulness:

> I was definitely told by my parents not to make friends with Serbs and to be careful, to distrust them.
> **Q:** Did you accept that?
> **A:** Yes, I did accept that. My father was very good. He always justified even to us children 'why'. I believed, I trusted my parents that Serbs are not interested in establishing equality with Croatia not even in this country. I believed that but I always tried to find out why. So, I was quite open minded to Serbians or whoever.

What exactly is the role of Australian-Croatian diaspora organisations in maintaining negative attitudes towards Serbs? One respondent commented on the impossibility of developing a really close personal relationship with a person of Serbian background: "I would be an outcast. And I see that. Maybe that's wrong but that's reality. I treasure my community... but I don't develop any close relationships [with Serbs]. They realise I am a Croat and I realise they are Serbs. We respect each other and leave it at that. There is no hatred or anything like that."

The war not only challenged but also radicalised Croatians' views about Serbs. A person who described himself as being positive "towards blacks, towards anyone" was surprised when his girlfriend reportedly said: "'When I first met you, you were always positive towards Serbs. You only disliked the supporters of the government.' And she said to me recently: 'Your attitudes have changed, you seem to be generally anti-Serbian.' I hadn't really noticed that and I was surprised when she said that". This is a very important statement since no other respondent disclosed this change in his/her attitudes more clearly. One needs to be aware that there is much we cannot know on the basis of asking questions of respondents at a moment of historical turmoil.

A first generation Croatian referred to a Serb whom he knew and with whom he was on speaking terms and reported that after the conflict erupted it all became different: "We still say 'hello' to each other but we both know: he is a Chetnik and I am Croatian". One could hardly imagine a more radical metamorphosis of the constructed Other.

Such views are not typical, however. If the last two examples represent a type of strengthening of negative emotions towards the Serbs, the two which follow represent its moderate antipode:

> I don't find Serbs offensive. Not even now. I know a lot of Serbians who don't bother me at all. Just because you are a Serb doesn't mean you hate Croatians necessarily. But it is very hard to be a friend with someone when you know they are one thing and you are the other.

I disapprove of people who say: "O.K., I want Croatia to be free but I don't want any Serb living there." I totally dispute this point and I would be against anyone saying: *istjerati sve Srbe iz Hrvatske!* (expel all the Serbs from Croatia!, Z.S.) I find it really stupid and anti-Croatian.

The overall pattern of the Croatian sample suggests a strengthening of negative sentiments due to the war. Yet the very existence of some 'tolerant' statements destroys the stereotypical image of an all-embracing hatred of the Serbs by the Croatians. While I paid particular attention to the Croatian construction of the Serbs, it is likely that research into Australian Serbs would reveal a similar intensity of prejudices towards Croatians. Some indication of such negative attitudes are to be found in Procter's (1997) study of Australian-Serbs.

5 Croatian respondents on Bosnian Muslims: search for 'true' ethnicity

Bosnian Muslims appeared to be of completely marginal concern to the Slovenian respondents. To Croatian respondents, however, the 'Muslim question' appeared in a twofold form: as a problem of defining Muslim *identity* and as a problem of defining their *loyalties*. Only one second generation Croatian respondent did not know who the Muslims were: "The Muslims are Albanians, the Muslims are also Montenegrins..." Many Croatian respondents' answers contained controversial claims of which respondents appeared to be fully aware.

The oscillation of attitudes of Croatian respondents about the Muslims affected the Muslims themselves. One of the Muslim informants mentioned that many Muslims who used to attend functions in the Croatian club later passed over to the Bosnian club which is a place where most Bosnian Muslims go. The period during which I conducted the bulk of the interviews with Croatian respondents was one in which the old Croatian conviction that Muslims are in fact Croatians of Islamic faith was becoming eroded. The belief that Bosnian Muslims are really only Croatians of Islamic faith was gradually being replaced by an awareness that Muslims not only demand the right to have their own separate identity recognised but also that they try to assert their own particular interests. Respondents sounded rather ambiguous about the Muslims:

> ... I even like Bosnians. We Croatians think that all Bosnians are Croatians because Bosnia and Herzegovina always used to be a part

of Croatia... Being a Muslim to me is just another faith – not another nationality. Religion is not so important to me.

Q: Who are the Muslims?
A: This is a good point. My attitude was always: Yes, they were Croatians many, many centuries ago, being isolated they developed their own culture, they are not Serbs they are not Croatians. I always treated them as individuals who are unique but are a part of ourselves. They are not Croats in a sense but they still should be a part of the Croatian nation. I have noticed that many Croats marginalise them, which is unfortunate.

Not surprisingly, the identity of Bosnian Muslims and their origins are subject to scholarly (e.g. Vucinich 1974, Friedman 1996) and political scrutiny. There are two types of approaches to the 'Muslim question'. The first type sees identity as a product of historical process and accepts the changes in identification of individuals and the fact that ethnic identity is situationally conditioned and self-constructed. The second type ceaselessly searches for the 'real' (i.e. Croatian) origin of the present-day Muslims. It is hard to resist the assessment that the latter are in fact trying to reinvent and/or rediscover a historically justifiable sameness between Croatians and Bosnian Muslims. As Đodan (1994, p. 144) argues: "Bosnia-Herzegovinian Muslims can not be Serbs because they factually are not. They are completely different from the Serbs by their religious beliefs and ideas, by their cultural life... The individual can betray their blood and the nation due to self-interest and selfishness. We call such people with a derogatory term traitors and renegades" (translation Z.S.). In other words, the underlying idea of Đodan's interpretation is that if Muslims would only open their minds to the 'proper' interpretation of history and disregard their current self-indulgent Muslim-identity fantasies, they would be able to rediscover their Croatianism.

The thesis that Muslims are Croatians of Muslim faith again confirms the usefulness of the notion of the 'distant view', discussed in the previous chapter. The search for the 'real' ethnic origin of Bosnian Muslims was neither encouraged nor generally considered of foremost importance in the former Yugoslavia. In fact, the category "Muslim in the national sense" was introduced in the Yugoslav census only in 1971, which is almost three decades ago (Burg and Berbaum 1989, p. 538). One of the leading representatives of the Bosnian Muslim community in Australia told me that he was very surprised when he got to Australia and heard that Bosnian Muslims are supposedly Croatians. While his alleged surprise might be something of an exaggeration, the official treatment of the Muslim question in Yugoslavia was vastly different from the kind of attention this question attracted in diaspora circles. In the eyes of the Australian-Croatian diaspora establishment Bosnian Muslims were *expected* to see themselves as part of a Croatian nation. It would be quite possible to argue that Croatians in Croatia perceived Bosnian Muslims – contrary to the view held among Croatians in Australia – as a separate ethno-national category.

Korsky's (1983, p. 107) suggestion that Muslims were given a separate identity simply because they could not be Serbianised easily enough is an obvious oversimplification. Yet, it is not possible to deny that "both Serbs and Croats have laid claim to Bosnia [during the Second World War] on ethno-linguistic and historical grounds" (Schöpflin 1973, p. 125, c.f. Connor 1990, p. 95).

In the Croatian diaspora, the opinions of 'political' migrants of the immediate post-Second World War period determined and conditioned the treatment of Muslims. One of the leading figures of the Australian-Croatian diaspora stated in relation to this: "There were only a handful of Muslims in the Croatian community. We always had to handle them with kid gloves because they were under the patronage of the HOP."

There were some pragmatic implications behind this Ustasha altruism. Namely, if Muslims are Croatian, then the land they occupy is also Croatian. The Muslims, these "purest of all Croats" (quoted in Friedman 1996, p. 122) were brothers and allies for all practical purposes. This was confirmed in the contemporary context during an interview with one of the Australian HOP representatives:

> The main aim of [the HOP] is to get the border on the river Drina. Then we'll be able to negotiate and to preserve Croatian culture. We also want to have a good relationship with Muslims because we believe we are one people and we don't accept Muslim nationality.

What is being articulated in the above statement is the strategy typical of the times of the existence of the Independent State of Croatia. There is plenty of evidence that the Independent State of Croatia drew considerable support from the followers of Islam. Not surprisingly, Ante Pavelić made it clear that to him Bosnian Muslims are the 'blossom of Croatianness'. As one respondent put it: "My father always said that a Croatian from Bosnia is worth two Croatians from Dalmatia".

But Bosnia and Herzegovina (more specifically Herzegovina) is not only of concern to Croatian right-wing political parties in Australia. My interview with high ranking members of the HDZ is illustrative. During the interview they mentioned that one of the major concerns of the party is the Croatian population of Bosnia and Herzegovina. Both respondents obviously tried hard to avoid this subject but when I inquired further they looked at each other, wondering who was going to answer. A part of the answer that followed was: "... We work along the lines that the interests of the Croatian people in Bosnia and Herzegovina are looked after. We work against any other force which might be willing to break down our community there."

Only a few second generation Croatian respondents perceived Muslim nationality as unconditionally acceptable. Some were radically against it, but a majority mentioned that Muslim nationality is "ridiculous", that "one's religion can not be one's nationality". The following examples show that behind the rhetoric of accepting Muslim nationality, there is often another less positive aspect:

> **Q:** Who are the Muslims from Bosnia?
> **A:** Muslims from Bosnia are Muslims from Bosnia! After the Second World War they got their own national status... no matter that before they were Croatians. They have their own flag and I recognise this. I recognise them just as I recognise Serbs and Slovenes.

And then immediately after that a different explanation by the same respondent:

> They got their own [national] identity through religion. To me that's crazy! As if I got my [national] identity because I am a Catholic. That's crazy; that's religion! The only country in the world which recognises Muslim nationality! If they want to be Muslims – that's their problem. I can't understand that and yet I accept it.

From my observation, a substantial number of Croatians in Australia feel reluctant to accept Muslim nationality and many of them would not disagree with Mehmedagic's (1992, p. 9) claim that the "religiously Islamic masses of Bosnia and Herzegovina" should return "to their true ethnicity – which is of course – Croatian." A unique counter-argument to this popular dogma was given in Klokan's 'Letter to the Editor' saying:

> We criticise [Muslims] for being the last kid on the block, yet this would be like Iran claiming Croats to be Iranians, the principle is the same even though the time frame is quite different. The point I'm making is that the more we say Muslim=Croat the less likely it is that this will come true. (Glavan 1993, p. 1)

Since the Second World War, the majority of those Yugoslav Muslims who migrated to the United States of America "during the refugee phase call themselves Muslim Croats" (Thernstrom et al. 1980, p. 186). The same could be claimed for Australia. It is documented that Croatian communities financially supported the establishment of the Croatian Islamic Association (Tkalčević 1992, pp. 94-5) and the official links have been nurtured. As Tkalčević says: "The basic approach of the Croatian Islamic Association to the immigrants of Islamic faith was to explain the historical fact that in Bosnia, Herzegovina and Sandžak, Croatians always lived and they were forced to accept Islam under the Turks" (ibid., p. 95, translation, Z.S.). These debates about the 'true essence' of Bosnian Muslims are important for understanding of the possible points of contention and reasons for the breakdown of the alliance between the Muslims and Croatians in the recent military conflict. Slaven Letica (1993, p. 34), the former adviser to the president of Croatia, maintains that president Tudjman relied in his decision-making:

> ... on some sort of confidential research by Edvard Kardelj[4] from the 1960s which found that if Muslims were forced to choose between Serbians and Croatians, 70 per cent of them would choose Croatianness. According to this logic he expected that there will automatically be brotherhood and unity between the Croatians and Muslims.

President Tudjman's public statements reveal his intolerance of the Muslim separateness: "Croatia and Bosnia constitute a geographical and political unity, and *have always formed* a joined state in history" (quoted in Cohen 1993, p. 97, emphasis added, Z.S.). Such mistaken expectations and assumptions which were also common in Australian-Croatian diaspora merely exacerbated political divisions.

In the mainstream Croatian diaspora organisations, the contradiction of the Croatian identification of Muslims is also clear when one is reminded of the exclusive Catholic symbolism of the invocation: "God and the Croatians" from the previous chapter. Also, the customary way of referring to Bosnia and Herzegovina in the Croatian-Australian media was to talk about Herzeg-Bosnia rather than Bosnia and Herzegovina. This clearly suggests the privileging of the Herzegovinian area of Bosnia and Herzegovina where there is a substantial non-Muslim Croatian population.

6   From 'public' to 'private'

This chapter has explored how members of both groups construct and nurture the existence of the Other. The main difference between the two groups has concerned two issues. First, Slovenians clearly homogenised the Other. For them, the differences between individual groups from the territory of the former Yugoslavia were negligible and they paid very little attention to these. For Croatians, however, the Other was always carefully defined as a Yugoslav, Serb or Bosnian Muslim. Second, the Other which Australian-Slovenians constructed was not very vividly present in either the collective or individual imagination. The Other was almost distant and marginally relevant to individuals' views on identity politics. The Other(s) which Croatians constructed, however, were very strongly present in the collective imagination of individuals and diaspora groups. Their Other(s) featured as being alive and well and thus a factor to be accounted for in the game of identity politics.

There is one big puzzle emerging from this documentary evidence gathered during the fieldwork. What happened to the Jews? Why are they absent from the list of Croatian Others? It is well documented that the old type of Croatian nationalism fed on its antagonism not only towards Serbs but also towards Jews. These two goups were the main targets of Ustasha pogroms during the Second World War. Why is it that the Jews simply did not figure in Croatian diaspora narratives? In fact, on only two occasions did my respondents and informants mention Jews. To a certain extent, this might reflect the absence of the Jewish question from the list of relatively immediate concerns. But it is hard to dismiss president Tudjman's embroilment with the Jewish community in Croatia and, initially at least, a rather thorny relationship between the newly independent Croatia and the Israeli state soon after the proclamation of Croatian independence in 1991 (Hudelist 1997). The representatives of the radical right in Croatia whom I interviewed in early 1998 were quick to explain that anti-Semitism was never on the agenda of Croatian nationalists. According to the same sources, anti-Semitism was 'forced upon' Croatian Ustashe by the German Nazis. The fact that Pavelić's wife was Jewish, as well as some of his close collaborators, should also attest to this. It is difficult to accept such an argument in the light of historical facts. The absence of the Jews from the diaspora construction of the Other is clearly something which requires further analysis.

The present chapter has dealt with issues which pertain to the public manifestation of ethno-nationalism. The chapter which follows, however, will explore the functioning of ethno-nationalism related behaviour at the level of privacy and intimacy.

7   Notes

1   In his interview for the *New Yorker* (Viorst 1991), Franjo Tudjman, the president of Croatia, used an ideological complement for the Southerner: the Easterner.

2 Similarly, albeit in a different context, the Slovenian Home Guard soldiers are inclined to believe that during the Second World War they essentially "defended traditional culture, as formed by the national community through centuries" (Stanovnik 1991, p. 6).
3 See Chapter 2, section 6.4, 'The myth of return'.
4 Edvard Kardelj used to be considered the 'second man' during Tito's ascendancy. He was an undisputed official ideologist of the policy of socialist self-management.

6 Marriage choices

> Love might be blind but it can't be stupid.
> (Second generation Croatian on marrying a Serb)

This chapter takes a step further in the present exploration of nationalism in the diaspora context. Whereas the previous two chapters dealt with rather public manifestations of ethno-nationalism, the present one explores the extent to which such ethno-nationalist politics influences more intimate, inter-personal relations. I shall specifically focus on the question of partnership and marriage choices among second generation migrants. To what extent do ethno-national ideas and feelings really influence and determine the choice of a (marriage) partner? Insofar as they do, how profound is this pattern in the second generation context? Which mechanisms of influence and control are employed by parents and respective diaspora organisations to encourage the choice of (marital) partner of a particular background? Is there rebellion among the second generation against norms of inmarriage, and if so does it evoke any corrective measures by parents or diaspora members?

Issues of intimacy, sexuality, and partnerships can be analysed from a variety of perspectives. This chapter specifically concerns those relationships between men and women which could potentially lead to the formation of a heterosexual marriage/partnership. Part of the reason for this is that none of the respondents was openly homosexual. But even more importantly, nationalism in general tends to be preoccupied with the encouragement and propagation of virility and natalism and thus supports reproductively-oriented sexualities (c.f. Parker et al. 1992, p. 6). In short, homosexuality tends to be perceived as counter-productive to the interests of the nation. In extreme cases, nationalist fantasies tend to equate homosexuality with the enemy.[1] This is clearly illustrated in the concluding remarks to a book by Croatian diaspora intellectual, Omrčanin (1989, p. 624), who wrote that the

Independent State of Croatia (1941-45) was considered in "the friendly orbit of nations as a sovereign state and could not be run by the Yugo Bolsheviks and the homosexuals, Communists, and moles of Great Britain."

In this book I have chosen to talk about intermarriage and inmarriage.[2] The former refers to marriages and partnerships between individuals from different ethnic groups, while the latter refers to marriages and partnerships between individuals of the same ethnic background. In Australia, there is a popular belief that some ethnic groups discourage intermarriage because of a vaguely defined 'nationalism' but this is also the point where our knowledge of this phenomenon stops. Most of the existing relevant research in this area concentrates on patterns of intermarriage, and the variables affecting differential intermarriage rates for different ethnic groups (e.g. Price 1989, pp. 18-25).

Let us now turn to some characteristics of the second generation research sample and other issues relevant to this discussion.

1 The key factors which impact on in(ter)marriage in diaspora settings

The marital status of second generation respondents at the time of interview is as presented in Table 6.1:

Table 6.1
Marital status of respondents at the time of interviews

	Croatians		Slovenians	
		%		%
Single	14	45.2	23	76.67
Married	17	54.8	7	23.33
Inmarried	12	70.6	0	0
Intermarried	5	29.4	7	23.33
Total respondents	31	100.00	30	100.00

The most striking difference between the two samples is that Croatian respondents are more likely to be married. One of the reasons for this is the lower medium age of Slovenians in the sample (28.3 years of age) compared to Croatians (30 years of age). From my observations, second generation Croatians do tend to marry younger than Slovenians. It is interesting to observe that none of Slovenian respondents was inmarried at the time of research and that there was a relatively high proportion of inmarriage in the Croatian sample.[3] Further information gathered through records of Croatian and Slovenian religious institutions in Adelaide, Melbourne and Sydney confirmed that second generation Croatians are comparatively far more likely to inmarry than are second generation Slovenians. The table above thus resembles the overall patterns in Croatian and Slovenian diasporas in Australia.

Even though inmarriage is quite common among second generation Croatians it is also important to note that respondents do not embrace the idea of inmarriage without hesitation. Some respondents had negative views on inmarriage and these views in turn influenced their respective marriage strategies. Support for inmarriage is not necessarily an indication of a complete absence of negative views about inmarriage. The negative views about inmarriage fit three broad categories. The first view can be identified as *assimilationist* and *hegemonist* for it portrays inmarriage as a form of retrograde social behaviour. Interestingly, this view was most likely to be advocated by respondents of mixed ethnic backgrounds. A respondent whose mother was Slovenian and father a fifth generation Australian commented that encouraging marriage within an ethnic group is simply an "unofficial form of Apartheid". He expressed a concern for the future of Australia if inmarriage trends persist in non-English speaking background populations. According to him, inmarriage is the way to form small ethnic enclaves which seem 'very divisive' for Australian society as a whole.

The second approach can be named *liberal* for it emphasises the possible constraints upon freedom of choice if inmarriage is promoted. This argument regards differences in ethnic affiliation, class and social status as irrelevant or at least of secondary importance: "I don't think you should really be encouraged to marry within your racial group. It seems to me that this takes away a freedom of choice. Intermarriages are fine. Love counts".

The third view relates to the personal philosophies of some respondents. This view concerns *social status* and was most commonly found among individuals who perceived themselves, and were in turn perceived by other members of a diaspora group, as 'high achievers'. Their acquired and/or desired social status encouraged their distancing themselves from the rest of the co-ethnic population. For such a person, a conscious choice of a spouse from the mainstream society symbolically reinforces the person's standing above the rest of diaspora membership. The importance and sensitivity of this distancing is particularly felt in small diaspora groups. An example of this view is a male respondent who was raised by his parents to become 'somebody', and what he said about Slovenian girls in the community was quite revealing:

> Most Slovenian girls didn't really attract me. They were somehow different. I was very lucky I had a very good education and a lot of Slovenian girls were very simple girls. They didn't have any ambitions. They have been basically brought up to get married and have children.

Ironically, this respondent's own sister explained to me that she was raised by her parents to become a "very simple girl". Her university studies were not encouraged and as her mother reportedly put it: "No, you are a girl and you don't need any more education." It was even suggested she should marry a doctor because: "That would make me something then, that would give me the position"..

In both groups there was much more expectation placed on a son's than a daughter's educational and professional achievements. The division of labour within the household is usually in line with gender stereotypes and freedom of movement is greater for male than female children. As the following example of a Slovenian female reveals, parents have placed different sets of expectations on their male and female children:

> I was expected to be a teacher, but it wouldn't have mattered if I wasn't because I could always get married and my husband would look after me. Whereas my brother... There was a lot of expectation upon him to become a professional and I think that's why he dropped out of College and he didn't do anything for years.

The assimilationist/hegemonist, liberal and social status arguments outlined above can – at least in theory – lead to three different marriage strategies which discourage marrying within an ethnic group. Table 6.2 shows the way in which I attempted to construct respondents' responses. Not all respondents were unambiguously classifiable and thus not all responses are included in this presentation as their positions often assumed an in-between position.

Table 6.2
Arguments against inmarriage: categorisation of respondents in relation to their use of assimilationist/hegemonist, libertarian and social status arguments

	Croatians	Slovenians
Assimilationist/Hegemonist	0	3
Libertarian	14	17
Social Status	0	2
TOTAL OF RESPONSES	14	22

I would like to make several comments in relation to the categories in the above table. First, while the assimilationist/hegemonist approach could relatively easily be identified on the basis of questionnaire and interview material, the social status category is based on my own assessment. Second, both respondents who fit the 'social status' category are successful professionals who do not expect to draw their clientele from their own ethnic group. Obviously, there is an easily identifiable counter-position to this: an individual's high social position (e.g. medical practitioner) could be an incentive to inmarriage. Inmarriage in this latter case could be seen as a public gesture of recognition of a person's own ethnic loyalties as well as a sign of their commitment to the ethnic group which can provide clientele. Third, while 14 second generation Croatian respondents clearly argued along the lines of a libertarian position, five of them married partners of sole Croatian descent and an additional two had partners with at least one Croatian parent. This reveals to the discrepancy between the rhetorical position and practical action.

Although it is difficult to clearly define reasons for the high intermarriage rate among second generation Slovenians, I would like to emphasise the following points. First, a sufficient number of potential second generation Slovenian marriage partners, due to the small size of the eligible group, is simply unavailable. No other factor conditions the frequency of occurrence of inmarriage more than this one: "It would be very hard to find a Slovenian woman, to be honest. Our parents always criticised us, you know: "Find yourself a Slovenian girl." But where are they? That's it." Second, there is a very pronounced tendency among the second generation to move away from Slovenian diaspora organisations. And third, the relative absence of strong political and ethno-nationalist beliefs provides no additional incentive for marriage.

Interviews with second generation Slovenian individuals who were born to parents from the first wave of post-Second World War migration in the 1950s were more likely to desire a Slovenian partner than those born later. The period of the 1960s and 1970s (the time of most intensive socialisation of those born in the 1950s) was a peak-period for immigration of Slovenians to Australia. This, nevertheless, failed to produce a noticeable increase in inmarriage rates. In the 1980s in particular, a decline in Slovenian-Australian settings became blatantly obvious, mostly due to the aging of first-generation migrants and minimal migrant intake of Slovenian migrants willing to socialise in diaspora organisations.

However, many Slovenian respondents complained that besides the limited choice which the migrant setting provides there are other reasons which might also account for the low rate of inmarriage: "It seems to me that Slovenian girls wouldn't mind marrying Slovenian guys. It just seems to me that Slovenian guys don't want to marry Slovenian girls." Such mutual complaints by both Slovenian females and males against each other were always accompanied by other critiques directed against the opposite sex. These critiques were sometimes expressed rather emphatically, particularly among those who were still single despite being well into what is conventionally regarded as a marriageable age. While conducting fieldwork among Slovenians in South Australia I was told on several occasions that Slovenian males do not dance and socialise with Slovenian women. Part of the reason was the 'Australian tradition', according to which "guys are very male, they don't need women – they drink. The male has to drink and not to hang around women". The encouragement of inmarriage could thus be seen as being partly related to negative stereotypes which many respondents' parents had about Australians in general, and Australian women in particular. The father of a Croatian respondent was reportedly trying to be as convincing as possible: "Australian woman won't cook you food and a Croatian woman would look after a man much better." A Slovenian respondent's mother expressed her sentiments about Australians in a more subtle way for she "suggested that it would be nice if I found a Yugoslav (sic!) or an Italian girl. She always thought it would be better to marry someone non-Australian. It is just because of the family ethic". It may be that her discrete suggestions about her preferences for her son's marriage partner were based on her own misfortune with her former husband who was an Anglo-Australian.

Although the Croatian population in Australia far outnumbers the Slovenian population, Croatian respondents put forward similar concerns related to the scarce availability of partners within the diaspora. Respondents from both groups indicated another factor which limits the chance of inmarriage. This was expressed by a Croatian respondent in the following terms: "I would like to have a Croatian boyfriend, but because I have grown up with most of the males at the Croatian Club I find it hard to be more than friends". A Slovenian respondent commented similarly: "A lot of the children that grew up together see each other as brothers and sisters". The same respondent remarked that she found the petty gossip (which makes individuals more the objects than the subjects of information) very discouraging of her attempts to get closer to other Slovenian males. The diaspora institutional framework may therefore be obstructive of the very processes which it is supposed to encourage:

> If you speak to someone of the opposite sex from your community for a half an hour, all the people would say that you'd get married. Of course, all they want to do is just to say hello, to be friends. But because some of the older people talk like this, kids just steer away from the community. They'd rather go out with Australians, because they are not so watched, I suppose.

The barriers to inmarriage imposed by a sense of limited local opportunities are often crossed by attempts to find a suitable co-ethnic partner interstate or overseas. The latter was found to be quite a popular option among Croatians: "The only chance is to get to know someone from another city. I just got to know someone from Sydney. You need to search and hope to find someone". Travelling back to the parents' homeland to find a partner is also common although the anecdotal evidence suggests that Croatians tend to be more interested as well as more successful in these adventures than Slovenians.

Children of marriageable age are often sponsored by their parents to visit the homeland on the pretext that they should get to know their relatives better and to learn about their roots, culture and heritage. Second generation respondents believed that what their parents often hope for is that their child might become involved with someone of the same ethnic background: "I think my father was expecting me to find a husband in Croatia when I went over there for a trip." Unfortunately, nothing came of it.

One respondent said that generally nothing is too expensive for parents to achieve a positive outcome:

> **Q:** Do you think your parents would be happy if you married a fellow Slovenian?
> **A:** They'd be ecstatic! They would pay for everything I wanted. But they want me to marry someone with a good job behind him. A Slovenian doctor would be wonderful.

Parental concern that their children may later settle in their homeland did not feature very prominently in our discussions. Nor did they pay much attention to whether their children's partner was Australian-born or from overseas.

'Ethnic' stereotypes undoubtedly affect marriage choices. When a Croatian male respondent said: "I can see myself fitting in quite easily with an Australian-Croatian female but not a Croatian female". In other cases, stereotypes arise from the actual experience of marriage or partnership. One of the Croatian female respondents' former partners was a Muslim from the former Yugoslavia (as a Muslim he was considered by her parents as 'one of their own') which was very acceptable in her family. However, "he was very, very traditional: he was the man, he was the boss. Plus, he was quite violent – he wasn't scared of knocking me around".

The process of migration or displacement does often cause the reinforcement of conservative and traditional values (c.f. Watson 1977, p. 4, Pettman 1992, pp. 51-2). Pallotta-Chiarolli (1989, p. 50) states in relation to first generation Italian migrants that "if they had remained in Italy, they would have shown a greater flexibility in modifying their value system, 'moved with the times' in their known environment." Parents' preferences for the children's partners to be of the same ethnic and cultural background is usually in relation to their static interpretation of their own culture. A Croatian respondent explained this concisely: "The [ethnic] community has this ability to retain old values. [Many migrants] came here with a 1950-1960 mentality and now they impose these values upon their children". The 'old ways' brought from homelands often go through the very same process of 'displacement' from the native settings as the migrants themselves.

The very question of sexuality was portrayed as a controversial subject where tradition and taboos play an important role. As respondents from both groups explained, it was often simply a topic which was to be avoided. A Croatian male said:

> At no stage in my life did my parents say anything about sex. Ever. Except when I was about sixteen. I think my dad wanted to check how much his son knew about the facts of life. He was repairing a bike chain and said: "I think this male bit goes into this female bit. Do you understand what I mean by this, son?" And I said: "Yes, dad, of course I do." "That's good", he said. And that was it.

A Slovenian female respondent had something similar to report:

> When I was seventeen, my father said: "You are old enough to get married." Just like this, overnight. Before that I was forbidden to go out, to get to know boys, but when I was seventeen I was supposed to get married. Ufff! Terrible!

A few Croatian respondents explicitly talked about Croatian sexual morals as 'very conservative', which reinforces the notion of virginity, although everyone knows that "sex happens before [marriage] as well". The most significant ideal believed to be promoted was that "all good Croatians should marry other good Croatians". Interestingly, several respondents asked me (as a person familiar with the situation back 'home') if sex roles in the homeland are still as clearly defined as their experiences in the confines of their respective Australian diaspora settings suggest.[4]

A Croatian second generation respondent who met his Croatian wife overseas said: "... only then I got the idea of finding a Croatian woman – where am I going to find the best Croatian woman if not here!? Here are the best Croatian women!". The notion of a good Croatian woman requires clarification as it implies that a 'good' Croatian woman fits certain criteria. There is definitely a politics of reputation at work which encourages the moulding of young individuals to conform to traditional roles and expectations (Bottomley 1979, p. 74, Pallotta-Chiarolli and Skrbiš 1994, Baldassar 1999). Moreover, I was able to detect a tendency among some parents to uphold the upbringing which promotes keeping women at home for purposes of household "status and/or decoration" (Bottomley 1984, p. 103).

2   'Pragmatism' in the functioning of intimacy

The majority of Slovenian respondents said there was no pressure upon them to marry another Slovenian, although nearly all of them agreed that their parents would be more than happy to see this happen.

The frequent occurrence of inmarriage among second generation Australian-Croatians, however, clearly indicates the efficacy of family, friends and informal networks which stimulate and assist these processes. Several Croatian respondents said their parents never put any pressure upon them to marry a Croatian but nevertheless ended up marrying one. A Croatian female who married a Croatian said it happened "by luck. ... I asked him out and we started going out from then". The importance of informal community networks will be discussed below, but the relevance of friends and family is shown in the following examples:

> My parents never told me to marry a Croatian woman. I wasn't looking for a Croatian woman. It just happened. We met in Adelaide through a Croatian friend.

> Personally, I think I will end up marrying a Croatian. And most of my friends are Croatian and everywhere I go are Croatian people. Even if I went out to a movie, it would be with Croatians.

One Croatian second generation respondent explained to me how in the 1980s he was approached by his friends and asked to 'sign the papers' (i.e. marriage certificate) for their female relative from Croatia. She was visiting Australia at the time and her marriage to the respondent would entitle her to stay in Australia permanently. He agreed after hesitating for a considerable time. His comments on his decision during our interview require elaboration. He explained that at first he reportedly saw her purely as 'one among many' female sexual objects: "She was beautiful. All in black, from hair to underwear." However, what really determined his decision in the end was the fact that she was from the same part of Croatia as he was and that "her parents were respected people". Learning about her 'pedigree' turned out to be a rudimentary operation. He later continued: "It is funny how many girls I had – and before the beginning I saw an end. So, I decided to marry her..." Clearly, love had a secondary relevance (although he said he loved her) and he would refuse to marry her if she was not Croatian or if her reputation might have been questioned. Her Croatianness provided a safety net which made risk-taking justifiable. The attitude of this respondent resembles Baldassar's (1999) description of the attitudes of some Australian-Italian males who think that Australian girls are 'for sex' whereas Italian girls are 'for marrying'.

This point is worth stressing as Croatian male respondents often claimed they have different standards and requirements for Croatian and non-Croatian girls. Furthermore, they felt they should have different responsibilities towards them. Again, a considerable amount of predetermination is at work:

> I had different girlfriends: Croatians, Australians,... It depended who I came across. I wished to have a Croatian in the end. (Croatian respondent, married to Croatian)

> The only girls I went out with were Australian. My parents had [a small business], so she (his present Croatian wife, Z.S.) always came [there]. Even when I was going out with other girls I still said I am going to marry this one. I always said that – all the way along.

One should not underestimate the fact that inmarriage in second generation contexts usually occurs voluntarily, due to an individual's belief that ethnicity-related factors (e.g. life-style, similarities in culture, religion) play such a crucial role that marriage to a person of a different background could be perceived as functionally impossible. A Slovenian female was very straightforward: "Mixed marriages? Alright for those who want them. I don't think I could cope, though." Another Slovenian thought "it would be nicer to marry a Slovenian. It would be good, it would be less complicated", although she later married a non-Slovenian. A Croatian male respondent said that "the way I was brought up, the way I am now and the culture that has been put into me... Another person from another society can't even start to understand this sort of upbringing". Or, as two Croatian respondents categorically stated: "Croatian wife – that's the only one I wanted" and "I dare say I would probably never marry anybody but a Croatian." Not all respondents who were looking for a fellow ethnic partner were able to answer with similar degrees of assertiveness.

Only one Slovenian respondent, according to my inquiries, found herself in a situation where she felt she ultimately had to obey parental coercive directions. Comparatively, there were many more Croatian respondents who reported being in this type of situation. The Slovenian respondent who tried hard to please her father in his demands to find a suitable Slovenian partner finally succeeded, although the relationship did not last:

> I liked him. My father got to know him but when he found out which family he came from, he started to dislike him. Although he was Slovenian and Catholic... But he had long hair, a motorbike, we had parties non-stop. Now I know the reasons why my father didn't like him. He was concerned. My mother had already passed away at the time; he didn't know whether I was a good daughter or not... and he started to hate him. I thought: "What am I supposed to do to find the right one?" I gave up! I was desperate, you know.

A similar degree of parental coercion echoes in the following statement by a Croatian female respondent:

> **Q:** Did you want to find a Croatian man?
> **A:** Yes. Yes. I did. Because that's what I was supposed to do, you know? I thought there would be too many problems with my family if I didn't find a Croatian.

Another Croatian female, well aware she should find a Croatian partner, faced a basic dilemma: "How am I going to meet a Croatian? It was really very, very hard." Luckily, a young Croatian came to visit his uncle in one of the big Australian cities:

> ... it was at the Croatian Club. It was his second day in Australia and he came to the club with his uncle. He was a very handsome man, dark. I saw him – oh! – from one side of the room and I said: "I am gonna get this man! He is new, he is young – only 21. I went out of my way, virtually forced myself to get to know him. Luckily, he was the right man. We have been married now for [x] years and he often says that I hooked him.

One Slovenian respondent explained that she desired an affair with a member of a group of young Slovenian musicians who came to perform in Australia in the early 1990s. Some unmarried Slovenian girls engaged in a bitter dispute over who was going to offer and provide accommodation for them. They were hugely disappointed when these young musicians (most of them married), arriving from Melbourne, brought Australian-Slovenian females with them. The respondent with whom I spoke did not deny the existence of 'the battle over scarce resources':

> **Q:** Do you think that these people who came from Slovenia wanted to make use of... [she interrupts, Z.S.]
> **A:** Yes. They can get what they want and then go back. I would like to go to Slovenia to meet a Slovenian. I've had enough of all this here.

Not all respondents can assimilate similar experiences so easily. I witnessed an outburst of emotions when I asked a second generation female respondent the following: "If you had to choose between two men of the same qualities and beauty, one Slovenian and one Australian... Would you prefer the Slovenian one?"

> [quietly] Yes. [silence, crying]
> It is hard for me to talk about this. [silence]
> Two years ago, I had a Slovenian boyfriend and I experienced how good it is to have fun, to love, to go dancing, to talk about Slovenia in Slovenian... Yes, I saw how different it is with a Slovenian. I can relate to certain things in Slovenian much easier, although I have problems with more complicated words. It is so familiar to me. I laughed as I never have before. You can have fun in English as well... However, I believe that if your partner is of the same origin, nation, language... It is just wonderful. (translation, Z.S.)

Some respondents incorporate a substantial degree of pragmatic thinking when making decisions about marriage. A Slovenian male respondent of marriageable age mentioned his intention to undertake a trip overseas to find a Slovenian woman. "I have never been told by my parents to marry a Slovenian woman. Not directly". Although his parents did not expect this, as he said, I found a more subtle reason for his persistence in finding one. He explained that his sister married an Australian and that this had a negative effect on his parents. In other words, he understood that his parents would prefer him to marry a Slovenian. Simultaneously, it became apparent that he was also worried about jeopardising his ability to inherit his parents' considerable wealth. Two years after the interview, he indeed made a trip overseas and married a Slovenian woman.

'Getting married' *per se* is considered an important issue and children are often expected to be married at a certain age. This issue is particularly sensitive to more traditional parents. A Croatian respondent in his late twenties said his parents did not care any more if he married a Croatian or not as he has already passed what is considered to be an ideal marriageable age. Thus, all his parents desire now is: "They would like to see me married. Full stop". A Croatian respondent claims her father "always thought a girl should be married at the age of eighteen, nineteen or twenty. By the time I was 23-24 my father thought: you better take what you can get." Her father's high expectations for his daughter to marry to a Croatian became irrelevant. Thus, when she informed him she was going to marry an Australian he said: "Well, it's time... As long as you get married". This is an example of issues of patriarchy and family honour clearly over-riding the primacy of ethnicity.

'Living together' with a partner is not considered to be appropriate to 'traditional' parents. Ideally, a partnership should be confined within the institution of marriage. A Slovenian respondent revealed: "They wouldn't like me to live with a woman without being married. It is a very big issue for [my parents]". His sister, who lived with her de facto and their child, was considered an outcast by her parents because of her 'inappropriate' conduct. The parents' ideal as described by many respondents is well captured in the sarcastic words of the following Croatian respondent who described his parents' happiness when his sister married a Croatian from Croatia in the 1980s:

> Oh fantastic! He is from a good family from Dalmatia, just down the road [from where my parents are from]... [My sister and him] married early, they met in High School, family lived around the corner, and there was money behind them. They got married after a comfortable number of years, had no children for a number of years, they saved money for a house, they are financially secure. Now they have three children and they are all cute, all intelligent, all speak Croatian.

The story of this young couple reveals their perfect conformity with both the standards of the diaspora community and their parents' hopes and wishes. They not only preserved their ethnic strength by inmarriage and producing children who are brought up conscious of their Croatian background, but they also comfortably function as part of mainstream society. It is important to acknowledge, however, that subtle coercive mechanisms are not always perceived in a negative way by the second generation. Some respondents conceded that they find them quite useful as they maximise their chances of finding a fellow ethnic partner.

3   The construction of marriage markets

The discussion in this section concerns both male and female individuals because both are involved in making partnership and marriage choices and both are potential transmitters of ethno-nationalist beliefs. Despite this, there are some further issues about women's relationship to ethnicity and nationalism which need to be noted. Kandiyoti (1991, p. 429) suggests there are "relatively few systematic attempts to analyse women's integration into nationalist projects." This is in a way surprising since women are indeed central figures of nationalistically driven discourse and are called in as "mothers, educators, workers and even fighters" (ibid., pp. 432-3, c.f. Salecl 1992). The role women may play in nationalist projects is, however, always contextually specific. Yuval-Davis and Anthias (1989b) emphasise women's specific roles as biological reproducers of members of ethnic collectivities, their role in reproducing the boundaries of ethnic/national groups, their centrality in the ideological reproduction of the collectivities, their role as signifiers of ethnic/national differences, and as active or symbolic participants in national, economic, political and military struggles.[5] In short, women are not solely simple 'victims' of all sorts of oppressions but also play an important role in exercising control over other women and thus enabling the transmission of (often radical) political ideologies (Yuval-Davis 1993, p. 630).

There are additional issues which should not be lost sight of in the analysis of diaspora settings. One is them is the relevance of the experience of isolation by first generation migrants. A Slovenian respondent explained why his mother never visited Slovenia. According to him, her feelings of isolation in Australia were so strong that he said: "I wonder if my mum would've come back to be honest". Another is the reinforcement of traditional and patriarchal values (inmarriage inclusive) as a result of the migration experience and/or efforts to preserve the diaspora distinctiveness and strength. Both these factors *may* also have strong nationalist undertones. Obviously, the support for inmarriage *per se* in diaspora settings is not necessarily an indication of the ethno-nationalist bias of ethnic group members and it may stem from other social and situational factors. In short, the frequency of inmarriage in migrant settings is not to be seen as a *direct* index of ethno-nationalism.

It could be expected that migrant groups which discourage the 'contamination' of their imagined ethnic purity for cultural or political reasons will more or less aggressively promote inmarriage. Such an aim could be achieved by encouraging a supply of marriage partners from what I define as a *privileged market* or *privileged sub-markets* (Figure 6.1).[6]

Figure 6.1   Reconstruction of marriage markets

I wish to make two comments at this point. The first relates to the very notion of the 'marriage market' while the second relates to the question of the permanency of marriage market positions.

It is true that the marriage market in the Croatian and Slovenian diaspora contexts is not governed by the price mechanism. Yet exchange does take place. Symbolic exchange replaces the role which money plays in commodity markets and it takes place at two different levels. The first level is the exchange between the 'newcomer' and the partner's family. Evidence of the success of this exchange in the case of intermarriage is when the 'newcomer' accepts the symbolism of an ethnic culture (e.g. learning of the language or some of the phrases of that language, observing religious festivities, expressing an appreciation of the culture). The reward for such efforts is given in terms of positive recognition which also necessitates the second level of exchange which takes place between the family and the diaspora community. This is the secondary exchange. Just as the 'newcomer' needs to be groomed into the family, the family is seeking symbolic recognition for their child's intermarriage by visually grooming the 'newcomer' into the established web of diaspora relations. The absence or minimisation of critical gossip may well be taken as an indication of symbolic recognition and acceptance.

The four identified 'marriage markets' are not permanent and universal formations. It may be possible that what is perceived as a deprivileged market by first generation migrants is simultaneously perceived as a privileged market or privileged sub-market by second generation individuals. Likewise, what is perceived as an anathema market in the diaspora setting could well function as (at least) a privileged sub-market in the homeland. This latter point (which I return to in the last part of this chapter) can be illustrated by comparing the numbers of mixed marriages between Serbians and Croatians in Australia and in the former Yugoslavia. Hayden (1992b, p. 1379) reports, for example, that Croatia (before the break-up of Yugoslavia) had an "intermarriage rate of 17 per cent overall [and that] the rate in some heavily mixed regions approached 40 per cent." Naturally, because of the specific ethnic mixture, "(m)ost of these marriages were between Serbs and Croats, the very groups most heavily antagonistic to each other during the civil war of 1941-45." Unfortunately, there is no corresponding data available on intermarriage between Croatians and Serbs in Australia. Although it is clear that such interethnic marriages did take place, it is fair to speculate that due to the specific profile of diaspora groups, their proportion was drastically lower than in Yugoslavia.

3.1 Privileged marriage market

The privileged heterosexual marriage market consists of members of the opposite sex within the same ethnic group. Class and status are obviously considerations, but ethnic identity is the determining factor in this classification.

The traditional and most radical means of supply of partners from the privileged market in many cultures is the arranged marriage. The act of arrangement itself takes different forms but it normally accounts for the compatibility of potential spouses in terms of religion, social class and ethnic background. While some of these elements could be considered with more and some with less dedication, the very form of arranged marriage enables the maintenance and transmission of traditional norms, roles and regulations.

Anderson (1993 rev.ed., p. 76) mentions how the ruling classes from the pre-bourgeois period generated their cohesion by various means. In this context he poses a puzzling question. Namely, "if the King of England married a Spanish princess – did they ever talk seriously together?" Providing they managed to produce lawful descendants and consequently enabled a symbolic passing of legitimate traditions, the question of their communication problems is amusingly interesting but only marginally relevant.[7] Arranged marriages do differ from Anderson's example of cross-dynastic royal marriages to a large degree as they are usually not cross-cultural and there is compatibility in terms of religion, ethnicity and language involved. However, the logic behind Anderson's example and arranged marriages in general is concurrent: purpose counts more than romantic love.

Rex and Josephides (1987, p. 37) explain in relation to the Greek tradition of *proxenia* which is a form of arranged marriage: "Prior to any introduction a discreet investigation takes place to ensure that the person in question is suitable, that is that they come from a respectable family..." Some respondents did mention that their parents' marriages were the result of various arrangement efforts of their friends and neighbours either from overseas or Australia. As most of these examples depart from the traditional arranged marriages, they would probably be more accurately described as assisted marriages. For example, a respondent's father was introduced to his future wife through correspondence with his friend in the homeland.

> [My parents] corresponded for about a year. Actually I read all their love letters the other day. All letters started off like: "My dear lady" or "My dear gentleman." And later it was: "My dear [mother's name]" and "My dear [father's name]." After a year she came here.

The story of a Slovenian respondent reads similarly:

> My father wrote a letter to his father that he'd like to marry a Slovenian woman. His father wrote him back saying he'd found someone but he needed to pay for her ticket to Australia. They exchanged photographs... That's how she came down.

It must be emphasised again that the occurrence of assisted marriages should be understood not only as being a consequence of diaspora-enforced traditionalism but also as a result of the gender imbalance of many diaspora groups. The practice of marriage arranging was rather common in the early post-Second World War period. Price (1963, p. 258) called such spouses 'wharf-side brides' and explained they were the 'girls' who came to Australia to be "met by their fiancees and married, if not in the church nearest the wharf, at least within a few weeks of arrival."

3.2 *Privileged marriage sub-market*

The privileged marriage sub-markets usually contain some but not all of the privileged market's characteristics (e.g. same religion, language, similarities in cultures). A privileged sub-market always functions as a second preference to the privileged market. The following comment made by a Slovenian respondent explains the construction and functioning of such a sub-market:

> For me, it would be good [if my partner was Slovenian] but by the same sort of measure Italian girls are just as good, I think. As long as there is a similar sort of upbringing, it doesn't really matter too much to me. I'd probably say I'd prefer any kind of decent ethnic girl rather

than Australian. But that doesn't mean Australian women are all bad. And if there was a good Australian girl, I'd go out with her for sure.

This respondent expects a commonality between himself and his potential partner to be grounded in similarities in upbringing which are in turn, closely (but not exclusively) related to 'Europeanness'.

Religion is one of the most important elements determining the choices of partners among both second generation Croatians and Slovenians. In some cases, the importance of religion often overrides the importance of a partner's ethnic background, although these two factors are sometimes intertwined. A Croatian respondent said: "If I married any other nationality it wouldn't worry [my parents] very much, providing that she was a Catholic". Or as a Slovenian female respondent stated in relation to her parents' coercion about her marriage: "They always said 'Make sure he is a Catholic and make sure, if you can, that he is Slovenian. It would be nice.' They knew there weren't that many around". Religion was not only the parents' concern. Second generation individuals who emphasised the significance of faith in their lives share this concern with the parents:

> I guess, deep down, I would prefer to marry a Croatian woman. There is also a notion of calling in life, having a Catholic-Christian faith. I believe that one is called into a particular way of life and I'd like to think that I would be called into such a life with a Croatian woman. (Croatian male, single at the time of interview, now married to a Croatian)

3.3 Deprivileged marriage market

Between the privileged sub-market and the anathema market there exists the de*privileged market*. Access to this market is not forbidden and yet it is looked upon with considerable skepticism and distrust. This category is particularly interesting as it is often perceived as very broad. In this research the 'Anglo-Australian' mainstream society often functioned as such a category. The opinions of respondents and their parents about 'Anglo-Australians' were particularly stereotypical and negative.

A Croatian respondent commented on his sister's decision to go out with "an Australian guy. [My parents] don't really like it. I also think she could do better than that..." This particular respondent later revealed that his sister's boyfriend supposedly "had some strange ideas", but the main reason for his dislike was the boyfriend's emphatic Australianness. A reported vast majority of respondents' parents had negative views on 'typical Australians' – who are usually typified as young males with tattoos and earrings (c.f. Cahill and

Ewen 1987, p. 27). Part of the source of this stereotype may come from first generation experience with blue-collar employment. There were also strong indications in my research that second generation individuals who entered the labour force soon after completing their primary schooling were more likely to perpetuate this image of a 'typical Aussie'. Stereotyping is not the exclusive domain of those less educated as the following example of a person with completed secondary education reveals. He described his former Australian girlfriend as 'typically Australian' and therefore:

> ... totally different [from myself]. She was always broke, never had any money. Never worried about the future. Whereas, I think I am different to that. I don't throw my money around, I plan more for the future. She was untidy... She never used to go to church. A lot of little things.

The evidence suggests that stereotypes which influence marriage choices work across the important divide between 'Anglo-Australian' and non-English speaking groups as well as within groups themselves.

3.4 Anathema market and factors which influence its performance

> [My parents] never drummed into me that I have to marry a Croatian, although they said that it would be the best for me. I know when it comes to the crunch: it can't be a Serb.

There is one segment of the marriage market which is particularly important in analyses of nationalist discourses and which I call an *anathema market*. This represents a stigmatised, discouraged and even forbidden option. In the context of our discussion about ethno-nationalism it has to be noted that membership of the anathema market is usually and strictly (although not permanently) defined according to ethno-national (e.g. the Serbs) characteristics. The more articulate the notion of an anathema market among ethnic group members the more likely it is that it will impose demands on individuals.

One of the pre-conditions for the existence of an anathema market is the coercive power of parents and diapora organisations to exercise a degree of coercive power. A comparison of Croatian and Slovenian diaspora settings in Australia reveals a clear difference in the ways that pressure is exerted. The fieldwork evidence suggests that there is far less coercion in this sense among Slovenians than among Croatians. A Croatian respondent was able to state assertively her chances of marrying a Croatian: "I am very certain this will happen because of my involvement with the Club. Croatian people have many resources and lots of relatives who would make sure this happened." The Australian-Slovenian setting lacks these often politicised organisational mechanisms, and young people are far less actively involved with diaspora organisations. To put it plainly, Slovenian youth did not hang around the Slovenian Club in Adelaide during my fieldwork. There was no entertainment provided for them either. By contrast, Croatian youth had their own entertainment in the Club and even without this, there was always a considerable number of young Croatians around. The Club was in fact described to me as a place where young Croatians occasionally fall in love with each other. The poor lighting in the parking area was reportedly welcomed by those who form more or less intimate relationships. As one Croatian respondent put it: "the father of a friend of mine would go around the car park of the Croatian Club with his flash light."

Parents and/or the family are a relevant consideration in marriage choices. A belief that 'by marrying a person you also marry the partner's family' is still occasionally mentioned by second generation Croatians and Slovenians. Parents can, under certain circumstances, step into the relationship between their child and a potential partner and play the role of an unwelcome arbiter:

> When I started to go out with [my present husband] my parents were over the moon and his parents had been to our house. But the second time we went out, I didn't like him. And my mother said: "You can't discredit me now." You know... like, you got to stick to him. I was really upset. I just couldn't believe it.

The above quotation probably represents one of the most radical interventions one can envisage. It basically means that the respondent had to remain in the relationship against her will simply because of the honour of the family which might be in jeopardy if the relationship broke up. As Bernardi (1982, p. 5) writes, young people could be expected to "protect the good name of the family and maintain good relationships with all the people their parents have accepted within their friendship."

Relatively few parents exercise their power to that point. There are, needless to say, other ways of asserting pressure upon a child's decisions. A Slovenian respondent who told her parents she wanted to marry an Australian and non-Catholic despite their opposition was given a symbolic statement by her mother: "We don't want to pay a lot of money for your wedding." More commonly, parents who want to prevent the type of situation which would potentially lead to intermarriage often encourage contacts with other children of the same ethnic background. Some parents use more discreet ways of dealing with this issue. For instance, a Slovenian respondent was never directly told to find a Slovenian wife. And yet he was often told: "They have a nice daughter. What do you think of her? You must get to know her a bit better". One male second generation Croatian respondent's mother actually went as far as to try to line him up with some "Croatian girls, women or whatever." This is not an isolated example. An established young Croatian professional said that many Croatian mothers tried to line him up with their daughters: "Girls liked me but mothers even more. I went out for strange dinners arranged by mothers on many occasions."

Last but not least, parents try to utilise various other avenues to maximise the possibility of falling in love with someone who would fulfil the requirements of a similar ethnic background, shared religion and, if possible, an equivalent socio-economic status:

> My father was talking to me even today... I am looking for a house to rent and my father works with this Croat who's got [a couple] of daughters. One of them has separated from her husband, absolutely beautiful woman, absolute dynamite. The idea was that by simple relationship to [her father] who would be my potential landlord... potentially he might become my father-in-law by renting out this house.

What happens if the potential marriage partner is unacceptable to parents and members of a diaspora? Besides, who are the potentially unacceptable partners in the context of the present inquiry? Is a discussion about the anathema market relevant to Croatians as well as to Slovenians in Australia?

The second question can be answered without dispute. The Australian-Croatian anathema market basically consists of Serbs and Yugoslavs. The general prejudice against Serbs as described in the previous chapter becomes magnified and evokes far more powerful imagery when related to marriage, partnership and sexuality. The existence of the constructed Other therefore influences both the behaviour and performance of individuals on the marriage market.

This is not the case with Slovenians. Although they tended to render other ethnic groups from the former Yugoslavia into the negatively stereotyped category of 'Southerners', the negative imagery was not at all magnified if applied to marriage situations. On the contrary, individuals from the 'Southerner' category were commonly and easily perceived by most of the respondents as a more or less acceptable marriage partner. Two of the Slovenian second generation respondents are in fact married to persons born in the former Yugoslavia but who are not Slovenians. One of the Slovenian respondents acknowledged that she used to have a boyfriend who was a Serb. Their relationship broke up because he reportedly tried to mould her into his image of a Serbian woman. He would not allow her to go to the Slovenian church. "Serbia was everything to him. The reason we split up was because 'Serbia was it'."

Undeniably, there is an interesting and remarkable difference between second generation Croatians and Slovenians in relation to marrying partners of other ethnic backgrounds from the former Yugoslavia. Slovenians do not refer to an anathema market at all although articulated preferences in relation to other marriage markets could be recognised.

Among the Croatian respondents, the very idea of intermarriage with a partner from an anathema market was seen as commensurate with treason to the family name as well as the nation. A case in point is a father of two Croatian respondents who called his children *Janičari* [the Janissarys][8] because they have married non-Croatian partners. The father would always tell the "story of how the Turks came in and took the children to another land and they then came back and killed their own families." Undeniably, this is a very powerful allusion and clearly is a description of the situation where one has been 'stabbed in the back' – a dishonourable and unacceptable mode of conduct. However, one should bear in mind that the respondent concerned did not marry a Serb or a Yugoslav, the representatives of the anathema market – she simply married an Anglo-Croatian.

Politics and nationalist emotions can intersect deeply with marriage and personal life. For example, when a Croatian second generation female respondent introduced her Muslim boyfriend to her father, not only did she not mention that her boyfriend used to call himself a Yugoslav, but also took care to instruct her boyfriend about the politically correct answers the father expected to hear: "And the first thing my father said to my boyfriend when I brought him home was: "What do you think about Tito?" That was the first question... Luckily, I had told him before not to say anything about Yugoslavia. So, that was O.K."

Croatian respondents often said that parents simply would not allow them to marry a Serb or Yugoslav if such a situation arose. One parent commonly used the following words when discussing a daughter's marriage choices: "When you get married, make sure you bring me home a Croatian. Don't bring me home a Serbian, first of all, *Australac* [Australian], Englishman or a Jew". This statement warrants specific mention as this was one of the two occasions in my research when the Jews were mentioned. Again, I would like to emphasise how puzzling it is that anti-Semitism, an integral part of the Ustasha nationalist discourse and genocidal practices, is largely absent from the modern Croatian diaspora nationalist discourse.

One of the highest-ranking Croatians in the Australian-Croatian diaspora commented on his daughter's choice of an 'Australian' husband by establishing a hierarchy of racial preference:

> Of course, my wife and I would prefer a Croatian. Nevertheless, the other day I spoke to a friend of mine who said: "And what if he was yellow, black or a Serbian?" And I said: "Well, if you wish to know I would prefer it if he was black or yellow than a Serb." (translation, Z.S.)

Likewise, a Croatian respondent whose father was described as non-racist ("I need to qualify this as well: on the topic of Yugoslavia he is a completely different person.") said:

> I know my father would be perfectly happy if I married a black, but not a Serbian female. He wouldn't care if my wife was Asian, black, whatever – but not a Serbian. From my point of view, she would need to be a fairly exceptional person to be interested to risk my life and her life falling apart; and the circumstances now... I wouldn't allow this situation to develop.

It is little wonder that the reaction of second generation individuals to the existence of an anathema market is usually self-protective and consists of the simple avoidance of situations which could lead to potentially intimate relationships. Marriages between Croatians and Serbs in Australia are not common and are seen as unacceptable by the respective diaspora settings. In marriages of this kind, couples often live their own lives, isolated from the diaspora organisations. Only one second generation respondent explained that he had a relationship with a Serbian woman but this was not something he shared with his friends from the Croatian Club. He explained his involvement in this relationship as an act of naïveté and recognised that he would be totally rejected by the Croatian community if found out. The pressures of the diaspora setting and parental expectations (as stated earlier in the interview) were two crucial elements which subsequently led to the break-up of the relationship. It could be said that the respondent saw no possibility of compromising his standing in the Croatian Club, her Orthodox religion ("There is no way that I would go to the Serbian Orthodox Church.") and his and her parental expectations.

Most commonly, respondents claimed there is really no possibility for them to get involved with a Serbian person on an intimate level. An individual might be attractive, but he/she is "first a Serb" and this is what takes away all attraction:

> No, no, no! I wouldn't do that. That wouldn't happen. Not with a Serbian. If it was anyone else...

I am not against mixed marriages, neither are my parents. However, they will not allow me to marry a Serbian or Yugoslav. This doesn't bother me because I wouldn't even think about marrying them.

You are joking! If [I had a Serbian girlfriend] I would definitely need to find new parents! That's true. My parents couldn't even think of me not marrying a Croatian. They couldn't even think of an Australian wife.

I am sure my father wished me not to have anything to do with the Serbs. Sometimes he would openly say that. If I wanted to marry a Serb? No, I wouldn't be allowed to. Only if I escaped from my family. If that happened my father would have refused to recognise me as his daughter.

Q: So, you can't imagine having Yugoslav or Serbian friends?
A: No. Never. Never. I couldn't imagine myself going anywhere where they are. Unless I went to a Night Club and I met somebody there. I always wondered what it would be like if I did meet a Serb and he really seemed to be nice. But no. As soon as I find out he is a Serb – no. That's just the way I was brought up.
Q: You said "Not a Serb."
A: Not a Serb.
Q: Would you like to underline this?
A: Yes, I would. Everything you've been brought up to believe in... I talk to them, we get along fine but you just both know where you stand. It's as simple as that. It's not just a fear of your dad or your family. When you meet someone that you go out with, you have to be compatible. He's been brought up to dislike what I am all about. Unless you both escape to an island I just can't see it working.

To the majority of Croatians an anathema marriage market is an *existent* and *functioning* reality which is not to be experimented with. It is likely that these feelings are mutual in the Serbian diaspora in Australia although this needs to be tested in empirical research.

The *a priori* negative portrayal of individuals from the anathema market is perpetuated by parents and the diaspora organisations. Priests are an important mediating mechanism in this respect. The data obtained from some Croatian Catholic priests clearly reveal a complete lack of any evidence of intermarriage via a religious ceremony between Croatians and Serbians. Croatian priests would not marry such a couple, as one of them confessed.

The refusal to perform such service had little to do with Catholic religious requirements but rather with the nationalist prejudices of the priests. Often, Slovenian priests did this job. As one Slovenian priest commented: "I married many mixed couples. Croatian and Serbian in particular. Croatian priests are rather conservative as far as this goes."

4   The future of marriage choice

There are two questions which automatically call for an explanation. First, are these parental and community beliefs, norms and expectations simply and uncritically accepted by second generation individuals? Second, to what extent do second generation Croatian individuals intend to impose stereotypically negative beliefs about Serbs and Yugoslavs upon their own children (an emerging third generation)?

It was observed that many respondents from both groups reject traditional religious and moral codes associated with their parents and diaspora organisations. During interviews it became apparent that a majority of respondents share modern views on pre-marital sex, parental control and similar issues. Rebellion and resistance were manifested in different forms. A Croatian respondent who grew up in the 1960s identified strongly with the 'flower-power' movement and said he "rejected any sort of pressure". Most commonly, children rebelled by making the simple decision that they would not marry a fellow ethnic partner: "My intention was actually not to go out with the Croatian guys. After my major romance I didn't want to go out with another Croatian because he was a real male chauvinist pig and that's what I expected from all of them." Or, as another respondent said about her Croatian husband: "The first time I met my husband I said: 'No! He's really nice but because [he is Croatian] ... no!' I think it was my own way of rebelling." Both respondents rebelled for one specific reason: the fact that they both identified their own ethnic culture as intrinsically patriarchal. Despite this, they both married Croatian men.

Parents often create circumstances which call for rebellion. One Slovenian female respondent explained how her father "basically hit [my Australian boyfriend] and chased him off the premises saying: 'I don't want to see you again.' But [my parents] over-react with everything." This type of authoritarianism is in relation to the touchy subject of 'bringing the partner home'.

A comparison of parental and second generation views on individuals from the anathema market reveals an interesting feature. What can be observed is a remarkable degree of similarity in opinions between the two. The degree of acceptance of parental and community messages by the children in relation to this is far higher than in relation to many other issues which concern marriage and sexuality. Why are these ideas so successfully transmitted to the second generation and why are some other issues more easily discarded as unimportant or less vital? To put it simply, marrying a Serb is perceived as an act against honour, pride and common sense. It is a symbolic gesture of defeat.

What marriage between a Croatian and a Serb or a Croatian and a Yugoslav signifies to Croatians in Australia can best be explained by using the Palestinian saying about Israelis: they "beat us at the borders but we beat them in the bedrooms" (quoted in Yuval-Davis and Anthias 1989b, p. 8). While this saying relates specifically to the comparatively much higher birth rates of Palestinians than Israelis, it is mentioned here because its meaning extends beyond the fact of the simple capacity to multiply: as the Palestinians contaminate the Israeli ideal of territorial purity by their very presence and existence, so the intrusion of the Other into the Croatian national 'body' through marriage, contaminates their symbolic community.

The intimate spheres of everyday life provide and evoke the most colourful imagery. At this point it should be stressed that several male respondents acknowledged they could imagine a Serb as a potential sexual partner but not as a marriage partner. The distinction between the two is crucial. 'Making love to' evokes images of possession and occupation, while rendering the Other of the opposite sex a fertile field for exercise of power. It evokes the image of an emotionless and non-binding encounter whose strength and significance lie in the fact that such an encounter safely takes place on the other side of 'enemy' lines.

Preoccupation with the sexual relationships between members of different collectivities is, for a nationalist, the most natural activity (c.f. Yuval-Davis 1993, p. 628). In the nationalist imagination, there is an undisputed and strong correlation between two beliefs: the first is that an ethno-national unit needs to preserve its purity and strength; the second is the belief that intermarriage contributes to the weakening of such strength. Individuals from the anathema market in particular are to be treated as a segregated entity for all practical purposes.

None of the Slovenian respondents claimed that they would explicitly try to influence their child's decision regarding a future partner, and the already loosely defined marriage market categories thus became diluted even further. As for the Croatians, the second generation respondents quite often said they would like to see their child married to a Croatian although there was a distinct lack of 'sharpness' compared to first generation parental authoritarianism. As one respondent stated: "It was crazy what my parents did to me." Many Croatian respondents would easily agree with the following statement made by a fellow Croatian: "Everything is mixed here [in

Australia] so it is stupid to marry only from the Croatian group. I wouldn't force them." Such a lenient statement should not mislead, as the anathema market remains intact *despite* the generational change. In the second generation Croatian context, some of the distinctness of a privileged sub-market remains strongly present, particularly in relation to religion. However, in general, the privileged-market and deprivileged market become extremely fluid or even vanishing categories. The main reasons for this loosening of marriage market categories are to be attributed to the second generation's exposure to the mainstream Australian environment. A second-generation Croatian respondent said explicitly to her daughters (third generation) that they are not expected to marry Croatians, although – somewhat contradictorily – this expectation remains in the background:

> My daughter's first boyfriend was an Australian and there were functions, discos at the club. They used to fight because he wouldn't come. He thought it was stupid that we carried on the way we did. Even in a Croatian Disco they throw in Croatian music. He thought it was stupid. But because of that they broke up. So, what I thought of twenty years ago happened to my daughter. She got the lesson. After that, she had two boyfriends and they've both been Croatians. So, she had this lesson from the start. I was never allowed that lesson: it had to be a Croatian, there was no choice.

A Croatian respondent revealed that he retained all the ideas of his father. He would like to see his children married to Croatians: "Basically, I'd like to see this but everything is in their hands. I would like this. It would be easier for me as well. And also, I think it would be easier for them." Although his wife strongly disagreed with this, he still said he will insist on sending them to a Croatian ethnic school and making them join the folklore group: "If you mix your children with Croatians they have got a better chance of marrying one of them."

The anathema market is the only segment of a marriage market which clearly retains its power and characteristics across the generations. While a clear majority of Croatian respondents would accept a non-Croatian partner, they clearly stated there is no compromise regarding the supply of marriage partners from the anathema market:

> I would recommend my daughter not to mix; that cannot be good. The Croat and the Serb cannot live together: different religion and language. And the religion is very important.

> I can't really say to my kids: look, you have to marry a Croatian. There may not be many of them around. As long as it's not a Serb it doesn't worry me. Their religion has to be the same – it has to be Catholic. But it depends. I'd like them to marry a Croatian but we'll have to wait and see.

The recent conflict in the Balkans reinforced the characteristics of an anathema market. It has not, however, put any new ethnic groups in the anathema market. The Serbs and the Yugoslavs have been well established determinants of the Croatian anathema market for decades. Simmel (1964, p. 93) wrote that the war situation makes groups of people intolerant: "They cannot afford individual deviations from the unity of the coordinating principle beyond a definitely limited degree." It could be expected that it will take at least another 'diaspora' generation to witness change in the Australian-Croatian construction of their anathema marriage market.

It is important to note the differences between both samples of respondents. They show not only a difference in the intensity of ethno-national sentiments among different groups but also the differential location of these sentiments.

Analysis of ethno-nationalism in the second generation setting would be incomplete without an analysis of the sphere of 'intimacy'. This chapter set out to link 'private' issues around choice of marital partner with the more 'public' issues of ethnicity and politics. It is therefore not possible to separate 'public' and 'private' spheres in exploring ethno-nationalism in a diaspora setting. Rather, ethno-nationalism, under certain conditions, envelops and inter-penetrates both.

5   Notes

1   Mosse's (1985) study on *Nationalism and Sexuality* represents one of the most interesting analyses in the field as it infuses sexuality with an ethno-national dimension.

2   There is much disagreement between different authors about the most appropriate terminology relating to marriage and ethnicity. Spickard (1989, p. 20) is critical of the term 'mixed marriage'. Barron (1972, p. 5) is reluctant to use the term intermarriage and prefers the neologisms 'heterogamy' and 'homogamy' preceded by appropriate descriptive terms, such as 'racial', 'religious' or 'national'. Gordon (1967) differentiates between interfaith, interracial and interethnic intermarriage. Jones (1993, p. 3) defines interethnic marriage "as one in which spouses were reared in culturally distinctive environments"

but his definition seems to be too narrow as it equates with and predetermines the relationship between ethnicity and culture.

3. One Slovenian second generation respondent did marry a Slovenian from Slovenia two and a half years after being interviewed. This goes against the established record of incidence of inmarriage in the specific research setting where the respondent lived at the time.

4. The question of sex roles was often accompanied with another one related to music. Most respondents found it hard to believe that younger generations in Croatia and Slovenia are exposed to the same kind of 'music terror' as exercised by ethnic radio stations in Australia. Many expressed amazement when told about the subversive role which musical sub-cultures played in the former Yugoslavia and were shocked when told of my adolescent admiration of the Sex Pistols.

5. Theweleit's (1987) comprehensive study of German *Freikorpsmen* which deconstructs the transformation of women into the key element of fantasmic imagining is probably the most radical case in point.

6. The term 'privileged sub-market' derives from Bourdieu's (1977, p. 54) *Outline of a Theory of Practice* and his discussion on arranged marriages.

7. Anderson's rhetorical question brings to mind Shakespeare's (1965, p. 158) conversation between Henry V and Katherine, Princess of France in *Henry the Fifth.*

"*Katherine*: Is it possible dat I sould love de ennemie of France?

King Henry: No, it is not possible you should love the enemy of France, Kate; but in loving me you should love the Friend of France: for I love France so well, that I will not part with a village of it – I will have it all mine. And, Kate, when France is mine and I am yours, then yours is France, and you are mine.

Katherine: I cannot tell wat is dat.

King Henry: No, Kate? I will tell thee in French,...."

8. Janissary (or Janizary) – a former body of the Turkish infantry. It constituted one of the main parts of the Turkish army during the time of Turkish dominance in the southern Balkans. The majority of these soldiers (called Janissarys) were forcibly recruited children of Christians (so called 'boy tax') and converted to Islam at an early age. Some of them were trained for higher administrative posts (c.f. Arnakis 1974). There are numerous folk-tales which talk about the tragic fate of Janissarys who came back to their own country as soldiers, unknowingly killing their own parents and burning their own villages.

7 Conclusion

This study provides no more than a snapshot of some of the processes of long-distance nationalism which, in my opinion, is set to gain even greater prominence in the future. Our increased ability to transgress time and space enables a more efficient transmission of nationalism across the globe. We live in an era in which cultures and cultural identities, no less than nations and national identites are globally present. In other words, globalisation tendencies have the capacity to elevate local interests, loyalties and identities to a global level. The distinction between local and global is definitely becoming blurred.

It is difficult – if not impossible – to elucidate a universal pattern of long-distance nationalist interaction. Diaspora groups vary by size, historical experiences and memories, the state of current events and many other factors. In fact, they do not necessarily share the reality of the long-distance transmission of ethno-nationalism. The comparison of Croatians and Slovenians proves to be useful in this respect. They are neighbouring ethnic groups with considerable shared historical experiences in the pre- and post-Second World War period. I have tried to outline historical differences in as much detail as I thought necessary to inform the overall argument. What might have surprised the reader somewhat are the considerable and relatively consistent differences between the two groups. Generally speaking, Australian-Croatians are far more influenced by ethno-national discourses than are Australian-Slovenians. The significance of nationalism in the Australian-Croatian context is reflected in the success of the transmission of nationalist attitudes from the migrant generation to second generation individuals. Australian-Slovenian diaspora identities are comparatively free of intense and collectively defined nationalist biases. The most important thing which can be learned from these differences is an awareness of the variability and specific conditioning of ethno-nationalist feelings.

The main goal of this book was to reveal the logic of ethno-nationalist processes and the way in which they are capable of survival and nurture in diaspora environments. Clearly, it is difficult to isolate any particular sphere of diaspora life which would be solely responsible for the transmission of ethno-nationalism. Instead, one needs to look at the intersecting powers of individual identities and histories, family environment, the organisational structure of diasporas, the interactive processes between homelands and diasporas, as well as the social climate and pressures existent in the host society. I have tried to keep all these different factors in mind throughout this book.

There is no doubt that diaspora politics is often a controversial kind of politics. Nationalism in these settings often lives a life of its own, semi-independent from developments in the homeland, but constantly making reference to it. The manipulatory powers of homeland political establishments can be considerable and – as I have tried to explain in relation to Croatians – designed to produce the desired effects. Just a few months before the submission of this manuscript I was given an opportunity to undertake research in Slovenia which enabled me to gain some useful insights into the government's position on this topic. Developments in Slovenia are going in quite the opposite direction from those in Croatia. In Slovenia, the government wants to keep the internal politics of Slovenian diaspora at bay and at a safe distance from mainstream political influence.

It is the interest of Croatian political parties to exercise some form of influence over Croatian diaspora. After all, this is relevant to electoral contests. Twelve out of ninety-two seats in the Croatian parliament are reserved for the so-called 'diaspora vote'. It is true that this diaspora vote includes Croatians from Herzegovina but this makes Croatians abroad no less included in political calculations of homeland establishments. It is not insignificant that so far the dominant HDZ has managed to attract more than half of the diaspora vote. The Slovenian diaspora, on the other hand, has no seats reserved in the Slovenian parliament and Slovenians outside the borders of the Republic of Slovenia are difficult to mobilise. During the 1997 elections only 2033 Slovenians living in other countries decided to cast their vote – more than half of these were in Argentina. By any measure, this is a relatively insignificant turn-out.

But diaspora politics is not just controversial – it is also an interesting kind of politics. Disporas are the breeding places for the creation of idealistic beliefs pertaining to the past, the present and a possible future. Some examples, like those pertaining to the idealisation of Slovenia's and Croatia's supposedly heroic pasts, were mentioned in this book. They are more than simply amusing because they reveal deep-seated emotions which are the driving force of diaspora identity politics.

This book gives no conclusive answers relevant to groups beyond those explored. This is an ethnographic study with some intrinsic limitations. It would be interesting to conduct similar analyses on other diaspora groupings as well as research into other related processes. It would be useful to explore additional questions. For example, does anything like long-distance regionalism exist? Strong regional divisions in Italian diasporas might suggest that it does. How is this regionalism transmitted through generations and what are the similarities with long-distance nationalism? Similarly, it could be productive to think about religious fundamentalism in this manner as well. Of course, fundamentalism differs enormously from nationalism, but in the contemporary context one might discover numerous similarities: from its ability to transgress the limitations of space (religious fundamentalism can thrive in Rome and New York no less than in Teheran), to its utilisation of modern technologies.

Two questions and/or dilemmas are persistently present when one deals with the question of long-distance nationalism. Let me examine them in turn.

The first question relates to the implications which processes described in this book have for the host environments. More particularly, how and to what extent does long-distance nationalist politics affect Australian society or, in fact, any immigrant society? Does long-distance nationalism have a potentially destabilising effect on these societies? Or is this something which is greeted by silent disinterestedness on the part of the host society? Is this disinterestedness allowed as a part of the quasi postmodern politics of freedom and choice?

Some of the above questions would require a book-length answer. As for Australia, the long-distance nationalist politics of diasporas is silently accepted. Over the past ten years, Australia has been the site of fund-raising, political agitation, street protests, public flag-burnings, 'unexplained' arson attacks, and political lobbying. East Timorese, Greeks, Slav Macedonians, Croatians, Serbs, Albanians, Kurds and Jews, to name but the most obvious few, were involved in some of these activities. Regardless of the content, these activities were fairly clearly connected with long-distance nationalist politics. Pragmatically speaking, they caused relatively little damage and disturbance of public law and order. As the reader of this book will hopefully agree, a vast proportion of the politics of this sort is hidden from the inquisitive public eye. It happens in diaspora organisations, over the phone, fax and the internet and in circles of friends. But that does not mean that this kind of politics is totally inconsequential. It resulted in votes for foreign governments, funds to support overseas political parties, funds for the purchase of military equipment and – to a much lesser extent, I dare to say – financial assistance for refugee populations.

This brings us to the second question which relates to the ethics of long-distance politics and I feel tempted to repeat the aforementioned dilemma contained in Anderson's work (1992a, 1992b, 1994). There seems to be little to add to Anderson's account. In fact, my research proves precisely what Anderson claims about the nature of long-distance nationalist participation.

Such participation indeed creates a serious and unaccountable politics. There is nothing innocent about it, although this is easily overlooked. Most long-distance nationalists (including a number of my respondents) believe that *their* politics is the right kind and that what they do is precisely what they should be doing. They invariably believe in the righteousness of their cause. The illusion and rigidity of this stand becomes clear when one studies their opponents. They, too, believe in the righteousness of their cause.

It is more than obvious that long-distance nationalist politics has significant implications for the politics of host country governments. The increasing significance of long-distance nationalism in the contemporary world will force governments to carefully rethink their role in regulating these processes. Indeed, should such processes be curbed, and if so, how? The liberalisation of dual citizenship laws (e.g. in Germany) has been long awaited. But is it possible that such liberalisation brings with it the potential seeds of political instability? These questions are important ones and the answers would go beyond the intention of this book. What is certain is that these questions will not go away. It is hard to predict a shortage of work for social scientists in this area.

The now famous arrest of the Kurdish PKK separatist leader, Ocalan, in February 1999 brought the various aspects of the theme covered in this book into sharp focus. Ocalan was a high-flyer in diaspora politics. He was able to control and coordinate the financial, political and military activities of the Kurdish rebels. But it was the simple use of a mobile telephone which allowed his captors to discover his hiding place (Stevens 1999, p. 17). The reaction of diaspora Kurds to his arrest was globally organised. The protests were not only co-ordinated with the help of modern communications technologies but were also promptly transmitted to global audiences. There is plenty of evidence in press releases at the time of how nationalist identity politics assumed central stage in this whole process. Nejla Kanteper, a 14-year old Kurdish girl from London, set herself on fire to protest against the oppression of her people without a homeland. She was reportedly "... [r]aised on a steady diet of Kurdish separatist literature and satellite television beamed into her living room" (Farrell 1999, p. 6). This story comes as no surprise to anyone who deals with manifestations of modern nationalism. It is hoped that the reader of this book will find it easier to understand how anything like this is possible.

Post scriptum

People, it is said, are creatures haunted by death. This metaphor seems appropriate for people affected by violent forms of nationalism as well as for the people considered in this book. The writing of this book was haunted by the threat of wars, war itself and the miseries and death it brings. The submission of the manuscript of this work was constantly delayed to allow me to 'catch up' with developments unfolding in the homeland. Even at the final submission date I was again confronted with a reminder that my efforts to keep track of changing political realities in the Balkans were all in vain.

At the end of March 1999 the NATO allies started to wage a selective military campaign against Yugoslav strategic targets. This not only unleashed a humanitarian crisis of a scale incomparable with any other post-Second World War crisis in Europe but also provided another set of circumstances which could demonstrate the effects of long-distance nationalism at work.

Throughout my intellectual engagement with Slovenian and Croatian diaspora politics, I was aware of how important it was to gain some insight into the diaspora politics of the other groups from the former Yugoslavia. Clearly, the Serbs were perfectly suited to this task considering Croatian and Serbian political antagonisms as well as the rather powerful stigmatisation of Serbs by Croatians evident in my research. But it is only now that Serbian diaspora politics have begun to play a more decisive role. In Australia at least, this current conflict has mobilised the Serbian population and engaged it in numerous forms of protest. These protests, as well as stories of Serbian migrants who decided to take up arms to defend their homeland, fill the local press. The same applies to Albanians. They have mobilised their own resources and have managed to enthuse potential Kosovo Liberation Army fighters to a much greater extent than Serbs have managed to mobilise theirs. These mobilisations are not confined to first generation migrants. We again witness the phenomenon of – in this case Melbourne-raised youngsters – who are willing to defend the homeland they have never seen. There are some diaspora individuals who are prepared to engage directly in the conflict. They are, however, a minority. The vast majority of long-distance nationalists vent their emotions at the safe distance provided by diaspora environments.

Obviously, the main Serbian antagonists in the present conflict are not Croatians but Albanians. Furthermore, Croatians are not directly affected by the most recent conflict except that most would deem NATO engagement in Yugoslavia as anything but objectionable. But what the current situation provides is almost a replica of the Croatian diaspora mobilisation described in this book.

The recent developments are almost programatic for the intellectual engagement with diaspora politics in general and the potency of long-distance nationalism in particular. Only time will tell to what extent long-distance nationalist politics may become inseparable from nationalist projects in general. We can only hope that future projects like this will be less haunted by death.

8 Bibliography

Adorno, T.W. et al. (eds) (1950), *The Authoritarian Personality*, Harper and Row: New York.
Ahlin, N. (1993), 'Turjaške zgodbe', *Zaveza*, No. 10, pp. 36-44.
Alborghetti, I. (1998a), 'Tuđmanov govor vrlo nas je vrlo zabrinuo: Washington će tražiti dodatna objašnjenja!', *Globus*, 27 February, Zagreb, pp. 4-7.
Alborghetti, I. (1998b), 'Dinku Šakiću treba suditi u Zagrebu, a ne u Beogradu ili Jeruzalemu!', *Globus*, 24 April, Zagreb, pp. 6-7.
Ališič, M. (1992a), 'Družijo jih le prazniki', *Slovenske novice*, 24 November, Ljubljana.
Ališič, M. (1992b), 'Razdeljeni Slovenci', *Slovenske novice*, 25 November, Ljubljana.
Ališič, M. (1992c), 'V Adelaidi kot psi in mačke', *Slovenske novice*, 26 November, Ljubljana.
Anderson, B. (1992a), 'The New World Disorder', *New Left Review*, No. 193, pp. 3-13.
Anderson, B. (1992b), 'Long-Distance Nationalism: World Capitalism and the Rise of Identity Politics', *Wertheim Lecture*, CASA, University of Amsterdam.
Anderson, B. (1993 rev.ed.), *Imagined Communities: Reflections on the Origin and Spread of Nationalism*, Verso: London and New York.
Anderson, B. (1994), 'Exodus', *Critical Inquiry*, No. 20, pp. 314-27.
Ang, I. (1994), 'On Not Speaking Chinese: Postmodern Ethnicity and the Politics of Diaspora', *New Formations*, No. 24, pp. 1-18.
Anonymous (1991), 'Osnutek programa Svetovnega slovenskega kongresa', *Slovensko pismo* Vol. 1, No. 5-6, pp. 26-7.
Anonymous (1992), 'Kdaj dva milijona Slovencev?', *Rodna gruda*, No. 4, p. 7.

Anonymous (1993), *Time Australia*, 4 October, p. 19.
Anonymous (1998a), 'Čovjek od rječi', *Bilten Ministarstva povratka i useljeništva*, No. 17, June, pp. 3-5.
Anonymous (1998b), 'High Number of Croat Immigrants', *Croatia Weekly*, No. 7, 26 February, p. 10.
Anonymous (1998c), 'Remembrance of Bleiburg and the Way of the Cross', *Croatia Weekly*, No. 19, p. 2.
Anwar, M. (1979), *The Myth of Return: Pakistanis in Britain*, Heinemann: London.
Applegate, C. (1990), *A Nation of Provincials: The German Idea of Heimat*, University of California Press: Berkeley.
Armstrong, J.A. (1982), *Nations Before Nationalism*, The University of North Carolina Press: Chapel Hill.
Arnakis, G.G. (1974), 'The Role of Religion in the Development of Balkan Nationalism', in Jelavich, C. and Jelavich, B. (eds), *The Balkans in Transition*, Archon Books: Hamden, pp. 115-44.
Australia Bureau of Statistics (1993a), *Basic Community Profile: South Australia*, Catalogue No. 2722.4, 1991 Census of Population and Housing: Canberra.
Australia Bureau of Statistics (1993b), *Basic Community Profile: Australia*, Catalogue No. 2722.0, 1991 Census of Population and Housing: Canberra.
Australian Bureau of Statistics (1994a), *Language Profile: Slovenian Language, South Australia*, Catalogue No. 2803.4, 1991 Census of Population and Housing, Ethnic Communities Package: Canberra.
Australian Bureau of Statistics (1994b), *Language Profile – Croatian and Slovenian Languages: Birthplace by Sex, Australia*, Catalogue No. 2803.0, 1991 Census of Population and Housing, Ethnic Communities Package: Canberra.
Baldassar, L. (1997), 'Home and Away: Migration, the Return Visit and Transnational Identity', *Communal/Plural*, No. 5, pp. 69-94.
Baldassar, L. (1999), 'Marias and Marriage: Ethnicity, Gender and Sexuality among Italo-Australian Youth in Perth', *Journal of Sociology*, Vol. 35, No. 1, pp. 1-22.
Banac, I. (1992), 'Emperor Karl has Become a Comitadji: The Croatian Disturbances of Autumn 1918', *The Slavonic and East European Review*, Vol. 70, No. 2, pp. 284-305.
Barron, M.L. (ed.) (1972), *The Blending American: Patterns of Intermarriage*, Quadrangle Books: Chicago.
Basch, L. et al. (eds) (1994), *Nations Unbound: Transnational Projects, Postcolonial Predicaments, and Deterritorialized Nation-States*, Gordon and Breach Publishers: Amsterdam.

Bavčar, I. et al. (1993), 'Milanu Kučanu, predsedniku Republike Slovenije!', *Delo*, 23 June, p. 3.
Bernardi, S. (1982), *Second Generation Italians in Australia: An Ambivalent Generation*, Catholic Intercultural Resource Centre Paper: Melbourne.
Bertelli, L. (1985), 'Italian Families', in Storer, D. (ed.), *Ethnic Family Values in Australia*, Prentice Hall: Sydney, pp. 33-73.
Bertsch, G.K. (1973), 'The Revival of Nationalisms', *Problems of Communism*, No. 22, pp. 1-15.
Birsa, I. (1994), *Slovenians in Australia*, Simkin, K. (ed.), Birsa Melbourne and La Trobe University: Melbourne.
Blainey, G. (1984), *All for Australia*, Methuen Hayes: Melbourne.
Bottomley, G. (1979), *After the Odyssey: A Study of Greek Australians*, University of Queensland Press: St. Lucia.
Bottomley, G. (1984), 'Women on the Move: Migration and Feminism', in Bottomley, G. and De Lepervanche, M.M. (eds), *Ethnicity, Class and Gender in Australia*, Allen & Unwin: Sydney, pp. 98-108.
Bottomley, G. (1992), *From Another Place: Migration and the Politics of Culture*, Cambridge University Press: Melbourne.
Bourdieu, P. (1977), *Outline of a Theory of Practice*, Cambridge University Press: New York.
Breuilly, J. (1982), *Nationalism and the State*, Manchester University Press: Manchester.
Brodnjak, V. (1992), *Rječnik razlika izmedu srpskoga i hrvatskog jezika*, Školske novine, Zagreb.
Budak, L. (1988), 'Post-War Croatian Settlement', in Jupp, J. (ed.), *The Australian People: An Encyclopedia of the Nation, Its People and Their Origins*, Angus and Robertson: Canberra, p. 342.
Bureau of Immigration Research (1990), *Birthplace, Language, Religion 1971-86*, Census Applications: Canberra.
Burg, S.L. and Berbaum, M.L. (1989), 'Community, Stability and Integration in Multinational Yugoslavia', *American Political Science Review*, Vol. 83, No. 2, pp. 536-54.
Cahill, D. and Ewen, J. (1987), *Ethnic Youth: Their Assets and Aspirations*, Australian Government Publishing Service: Canberra.
Calwell, A. (1972), *Be Just and Fear Not*, Lloyd O'Neill: Hawthorn.
Campbell, J.K. and Sherrard, P. (1968), *Modern Greece*, Ernest Benn Ltd.: London.
Castles, I. (1990), *Census 86: Data Quality Ancestry*, Australian Bureau of Statistics: Canberra.
Ceferin, S. (1998), 'Dr. Edi Gobec, Slovenec v svetu', *Misli/Thoughts*, June, pp. 137-8.

Chamber of Economy of Slovenia (1988), *Slovenia – i – Information*, Centre for Tourist and Economic Promotion: Ljubljana.
Clout, H. and Salt, J. (1976), 'The Demographic Background', in Salt, J. and Clout, H. (eds), *Migration in Post-War Europe: Geographical Essays*, Oxford University Press: London, pp. 7-29.
Cohen, E. (1982), 'Persistence and Change in the Israeli Kibbutz', in Kamenka, E. (ed.), *Community as a Social Ideal*, Edward Arnold: London, pp. 123-46.
Cohen, L.J. (1993), *Broken Bonds: The Disintegration of Yugoslavia*, Westview Press: Boulder.
Colvin, M. (1996), 'Stumbling Away From Peace', *The Australian*, 30 September, p. 9.
Connor, W. (1986), 'The Impact of Homelands Upon Diasporas', in Sheffer, G. (ed.), *Modern Diasporas in International Politics*, Croom Helm: London and Sydney, pp. 16-46.
Connor, W. (1990), 'When Is a Nation?', *Ethnic and Racial Studies* Vol. 13, No. 1, pp. 93-103.
Connor, W. (1991), 'From Tribe to Nation?', *History of European Ideas*, Vol. 13, No. 1-2, pp. 5-18.
Connor, W. (1992), 'The Nation and Its Myth', *International Journal of Comparative Sociology*, Vol. 33, No. 1-2, pp. 48-57.
Constantinides, P. (1977), 'The Greek Cypriots: Factors in the Maintenance of Ethnic Identity', in Watson, J.L. (ed.), *Between Two Cultures*, Basil Blackwell: Oxford, pp. 269-300.
Corsellis, J. (1997), 'The Slovene Political Emigration 1945-50', *Dve domovini/Two Homelands*, No. 8, pp. 131-59.
Danforth, L.M. (1995), *The Macedonian Conflict: Ethnic Nationalism in a Transnational World*, Princeton University Press: Princeton.
Davis, F. (1979), *Yearning for Yesterday: A Sociology of Nostalgia*, Free Press: New York.
Dench, G. (1975), *Maltese in London: A Case Study in the Erosion of Ethnic Consciousness*, Routledge and Kegan Paul: London and Boston.
Djilas, A. (1991), *The Contested Country*, Harvard University Press: Cambridge and London.
Dular, J. (1993), 'Argentina, tako daleč in tako blizu', *Delo: Sobotna priloga*, 7 May, Ljubljana, p. 26.
Dusevic, S. (1993), 'Can Our Community and Klokan Survive?', *Klokan* Vol. 4, No. 2, p. 15.
Đodan, Š. (1994), *Bosna i Hercegovina – Hrvatska djedovina*, Meditor: Zagreb.
Etzioni, A. (1995), *The Spirit of Community: Rights, Responsibilities, and the Communitarian Agenda*, Fontana Press: London.

Farell, S. (1999), 'Children with Passion for Their People', *The Australian*, 19 February, p. 6.
Fink, B. (1984), 'Slovensko domobranstvo in njegova prisega', *Vestnik/Noticero*, Vol. 35, No. 1, Buenos Aires, pp. 3-19.
Flere, S. (1991), 'Explaining Ethnic Antagonism in Yugoslavia', *European Sociological Review*, Vol. 7, No. 3, pp. 183-93.
Forsythe, D. (1989), 'German Problem and the Problem of History', in Tonkin, E. et al. (eds), *History and Ethnicity*, Routledge: London and New York, pp. 137-56.
Franolić, B. (1984), *An Historical Survey of Literary Croatian*, Nouvelles Editions Latines: Paris.
Friedman, F. (1996), *Bosnian Muslims: Denial of a Nation*, Westview Press: Boulder.
Gans, H.J. (1979), 'Symbolic Ethnicity: The Future of Ethnic Groups and Cultures in America', *Ethnic and Racial Studies*, Vol. 2, No. 1, pp. 1-20.
Gellner, E. (1983), *Nations and Nationalism*, Basil Blackwell: Oxford.
Genorio, R. (1993/94), 'Geographical Dimensions of Slovene Emigration Around the World', *Slovenija*, Vol. 7, No. 4, pp. 59-62.
Gitmez, A. and Wilpert, C. (1987), 'A Micro-Society or an Ethnic Community? Social Organization and Ethnicity Amongst Turkish Migrants in Berlin', in Rex, J. et al. (eds), *Immigrant Associations in Europe*, Gower: Aldershot, pp. 86-125.
Glavan, L. (1993), 'Muslim=Muslim', *Klokan*, Vol. 4, No. 3, p. 1.
Glazer, N. and Moynihan, D.P. (1965), *Beyond the Melting Pot: The Negroes, Puerto Ricans, Jews, Italians, and Irish of New York City*, The M.I.T. Press: Cambridge, Massachusetts.
Glenny, M. (1992), *The Fall of Yugoslavia*, Penguin Books: London.
Gluckman, M. (1963), 'Gossip and Scandal', *Current Anthropology*, Vol. 4, No. 3, pp. 307-16.
Gordon, A.I. (1967), *Intermarriage: Interfaith, Interracial, Interethnic*, Beacon Press: Boston.
Graham, P. (1997/98), 'Canadian Warlord', *Saturday Night*, No. 112, pp. 56-96.
Gregorič, S. (1993a), 'Editorial/Uvodnik', *Glas Slovenije*, Vol. 1, No. 5, 7 July, p. 2.
Gregorič, S. (1993b), 'Slovenija moja (rojstna) dežela', *Glas Slovenije/Voice of Slovenia*, Vol. 1, No. 11, 29 September, p. 2.
Gregorič, S. (1994), 'S ponosom reči smem: Slovenec sem', *Glas Slovenije/Voice of Slovenia*, Vol. 1, No. 21, p. 7.
Harris, N. (1991), *National Liberation*, I.B. Tauris: New York.

Hayden, R.M. (1992a), 'Balancing Discussion of Jesenovac and the Manipulation of History', *East European Politics and Societies*, Vol. 6, No. 2, pp. 207-13.
Hayden, R.M. (1992b), 'Yugoslavia's Collapse: National Suicide with Foreign Assistance', *Economic and Political Weekly*, Vol. 27, No. 27, 4 July, pp. 1377-82.
Hirschman, C. (1987), 'The Meaning and Measurement of Ethnicity in Malaysia: An Analysis of Census Classifications', *The Journal of Asian Studies*, Vol. 46, No. 3, pp. 555-82.
Hobsbawm, E. (1984), 'Introduction: Inventing Traditions', in Hobsbawm, E. and Ranger, T. (eds), *The Invention of Tradition*, Cambridge University Press: Cambridge.
Hobsbawm, E.J. (1990), *Nations and Nationalism Since 1780: Programme, Myth, Reality*, Cambridge University Press: Cambridge.
Hobsbawm, E. (1991), 'Introduction', *Social Research*, Vol. 58, No. 1, Spring, pp. 65-8.
Hobsbawm, E. (1993), 'The New Threat to History', *The New York Review of Books*, Vol. 40, No. 21, pp. 62-4.
Hoffman, G.W. (1973), 'Migration and Social Change', *Problems of Communism*, No. 22, pp. 16-31.
Holborn, L.W. (1956), *The International Refugee Organization: A Specialized Agency of the United Nations*, Oxford University Press: London.
Holton, R.J. (1998), *Globalization and the Nation-State*, Macmillan Press: London.
Horvatic, D. (1994a), 'The Contribution of Croatians to Western Culture I', *Klokan*, Vol. 5, No. 1, pp. 3-6.
Horvatic, D. (1994b), 'The Contribution of Croatians to Western Culture II', *Klokan*, Vol. 5, No. 3, pp. 11-14.
Hrketic, S. (1992), 'Born-Agains Again', *Klokan*, Vol. 3, No. 10, p. 3.
Hudelist, D. (1997), 'Goldstein', *Globus*, 12 December, pp. 32-6.
Hugo, G. (1989), *Atlas of the Australian People: South Australia*, Australian Government Publishing Service: Canberra.
Ivanković, N. (1998), 'Šušak's last message', *Croatia Weekly*, Vol. 1, No. 18, p. 1.
Jančar, D. (1993), 'Slovene exile', *Nationalities Papers*, Vol. 21, No. 1, Spring, pp. 91-105.
Jenšterle, M. (1995), 'Mit o nespremenjeni domovini', in Gantar Godina, I. (ed.), *The Confrontation Between Myth and Reality on the Arrival of the Emigrants to a New Land*, ZRC SAZU: Ljubljana, pp. 17-26.
Jevnikar, M. (1996), 'Slovenski domovi v Južni Ameriki', *Dve domovini/Two Homelands*, No. 7, pp. 97-112.

Jones, F.L. (1993), *Are Marriages that Cross Ethnic Boundaries more Likely to End in Divorce? An Aspect of Ethnic Stratification in Australia*, Paper presented at the Trondheim Meeting of Research Committee 28 of International Sociological Association, 20-22 May.

Jupp, J. (1988a), *The Australian People: An Encyclopedia of the Nation, Its People and Their Origins*, Angus and Robertson: North Ryde.

Kandiyoti, D. (1991), 'Identity and its Discontents: Women and the Nation', *Journal of International Studies*, Vol. 20, No. 3, pp. 429-43.

Kay, D. (1995), 'The Resettlement of Displaced Persons in Europe, 1946-1951', in Cohen, R. (ed.), *The Cambridge Survey of World Migration*, Cambridge University Press: Cambridge, pp. 154-8.

Kazich, T. (ed.) (1989), *Serbs in Australia: History and Development of Free Serbian Orthodox Church Diocese for Australia and New Zealand*, Monastery Press: Canberra.

Kesic, E. (1996), 'Genius in the Shadows', *Klokan*, Vol. 7, No. 3, p. 15.

Klaric, S. (1992), 'The Croatian Language – Free at Last', *Klokan*, Vol. 3, No. 5, p. 7.

Klausner, S.Z. (1991), 'Diaspora in Comparative Research', in Manachen, M. (ed.), *Eretz Israel, Israel and the Jewish Diaspora Mutual Relations*, Center for the Study of Religion and Society: Lanham, pp. 194-221.

Klemenčič, M. (1993), 'Reactions of Slovene and Croatian Immigrants: The American Press and Scientists about the Events in Slovenia and in Croatia Prior to Their Recognition', in Devetak. S. et al. (eds), *Small Nations and Ethnic Minorities in an Emerging Europe*, Slavica Verlag: Munchen, pp. 333-7.

Klinar, P. (1993), 'Tolerantni etnični pluralizem', *Večer*, 21 October, p. 14.

Knezevic, P. (1993), 'Always Croatian', *Klokan*, Vol. 4, No. 1, p. 3.

Kolar-Panov, D. (1996), 'Video and the Diasporic Imagination of Selfhood: A Case Study of the Croatians in Australia', *Cultural Studies*, Vol. 10, No. 2, pp. 288-314.

Kolarič, J. (1977), *Škof Rozman*, Vol. 1-3, Družba Sv. Mohorja: Celovec.

Korsky, I. (1983), *Hrvatski nacionalizam*, Ateneo Republicano Croata: Buenos Aires.

Kovacevic, M. & Gladovic, M. (eds) (1990), *Croatians in Australia: As Printed by the Sydney Morning Herald*, Croatian Resource Centre: Sydney.

Kuntner, T. (1994), *O domovina*, ČZP Kmečki glas: Ljubljana.

Kuropas, M.B. (1991), *The Ukrainian Americans*, University of Toronto Press: Toronto.

Lendvai, P. (1972), 'Yugoslavia in Crisis', *Encounter*, August, pp. 68-75.

Letica, S. (1993), 'Prazna bencinska kanta', *Mladina*, 14 September, pp. 32-5.

Letica, S. (1998), 'Tko je veći državnik: Tito ili Tuđman?', Globus, 1 May, pp. 42-7.
Levinson, D.J. (1950), 'The Study of Anti-Semitic Ideology', in Adorno, T.W. et al. (eds), *The Authoritarian Personality*, Harper and Row: New York, pp. 57-101.
Lieberson, S. and Santi, L. (1985), 'The Use of Nativity Data to Estimate Ethnic Characteristic and Patterns', *Social Science Research* 14, pp. 31-56.
Lovrić, J. (1998), 'Hrvaška: po vojni vojna', *Razgledi*, 13 May, p. 13.
Malešević, S. and Uzelac, G. (1997), 'Research Note. Ethnic Distance, Power and War: The Case of Croatian Students', *Nations and Nationalism*, Vol. 3, No. 2, pp. 291-8.
Margolis, M.L. (1995), 'Transnationalism and Popular Culture: The Case of Brazilian Immigrants in the United States', *Journal of Popular Culture*, Vol. 29, No. 1, pp. 29-41.
Marrus, M.R. (1985), *The Unwanted: European Refugees in the Twentieth Century*, Oxford University Press: New York.
Martin, J. (1965), *Refugee Settlers: A Study of Displaced Persons in Australia*, The Australian National University: Canberra.
McDowell, C. (1996), *A Tamil Asylum Diaspora: Sri Lankan Migration, Settlement and Politics in Switzerland*, Berghahn Books: Providence, Oxford.
Mehmedagic, E. (1992), 'To Return the Moslems to Their Original National Ethnicity', *Klokan*, Vol. 3, No. 11, pp. 9-10.
Meštrović, S.G. (1991), *The Coming Fin de Siècle: An Application of Durkheim's Sociology to Modernity and Postmodernism*, Routledge: London and New York.
Meštrović, S.G. (1994), *The Balkanization of the West: The Confluence of Postmodernism and Postcommunism*, Routledge: London and New York.
Milic, M. and Velcic, D. (1994), 'SBS Radio: Interview with Natasha Talmacs', *Klokan*, Vol. 5, No. 3, pp. 3-6.
Miličević, J. (1998), 'Iz Canberre došla sam u 'Tigrove'', *Bilten*, 15 April, p. 17.
Miller, D.E. and Miller, L.T. (1991), 'Memory and Identity Across the Generations: A Case Study of Armenian Survivors and Their Progeny', *Qualitative Sociology*, Vol. 14, No. 1, pp. 13-38.
Ministarstvo povratka i useljeništva (1997), *Vodić za povratnike u Hrvatsku*, Zagreb.
Morley, D. and Robins, K. (1993), 'No Place Like *Heimat*: Images of Home(land) in European Culture', in Carter, E. et al. (eds), *Space and*

Place: Theories of Identity and Location, Laurance and Wishart: London, pp. 5-31.
Mosse, G.L. (1985), *Nationalism and Sexuality: Middle-Class Morality and Sexual Norms in Modern Europe*, The University of Wisconsin Press: Madison.
Naficy, H. (1991), 'The Poetics and Practice of Iranian Nostalgia in Exile', *Diaspora*, Vol. 1, No. 3, pp. 285-302.
Nowotny, H. (1994), *Time: The Modern and Postmodern Experience*, Polity: Cambridge.
O'Neill, J.J. (1980), *Prodigal Genius: A Life of Nikola Tesla*, Granada Publishing: London.
Omrčanin, I. (1989), *Anglo-American Croatian Rapprochement*, Samizdat: Washington.
Pallotta-Chiarolli, M. (1989), 'From Coercion to Choice: Second-Generation Women Seeking a Personal Identity in the Italo-Australian Setting', *Journal of Intercultural Studies*, Vol. 10, No. 1, pp. 49-63.
Pallotta-Chiarolli, M. and Skrbiš, Z. (1994), 'Authority, Compliance and Rebellion in Second Generation Cultural Minorities', *Australian and New Zealand Journal of Sociology*, Vol. 30, No. 3, pp. 259-72.
Paric, L. et al. (1997), *Croats in the Australian Community*, Bureau of Immigration, Population and Multicultural Research: Melbourne.
Parker, A. et al. (eds) (1992), *Nationalisms and Sexualities*, Routledge and Chapman & Hall: New York and London.
Pascoe, R. (1992), 'Place and Community: The Construction of an Italo-Australian Space', in Castles, S. et al. (eds), *Australia's Italians: Culture and Community in a Changing Society*, Allen & Unwin: Sydney, pp. 85-97.
Peric, M. (1993), 'Editorial', *Klokan*, 2 February, p. 1.
Peristiany, J.G. (1974), 'Introduction', in Peristiany, J.G. (ed.), *Honour and Shame: The Values of Mediteranian Society*, The University of Chicago Press: Chicago, pp. 9-18.
Petersen, W. (1987), 'Politics and the Measurement of Ethnicity', in Alonso, W. and Starr, P. (eds), *The Politics of Numbers*, Russel Sage Foundation: New York, pp. 187-233.
Pettman, J. (1988), 'Whose Country Is It Anyway? Cultural Politics, Racism and the Construction of Being Australian', *Journal of Intercultural Studies*, Vol. 9, No. 1, pp. 1-24.
Pettman, J. (1992), *Living in the Margins*, Allen & Unwin: Sydney.
Price, C.A. (1963), *Southern Europeans in Australia*, Oxford University Press: Melbourne.
Price, C.A. (1989), *Ethnic Groups in Australia*, Australian Immigration Research Centre: Canberra.

Procter, N. (1997), *A Stone in My Heart: Hermeneutic Ethnography of Serbian Australian Culture and Health During the Balkan War 1991-96*, unpublished PhD thesis, Flinders University: Adelaide.
Proudfoot, M.J. (1957), *European Refugees 1939-52: A Study of Forced Population Movement*, Faber & Faber Ltd.: London.
Prpic, G.J. (1971), *The Croatian Immigrants in America*, Philosophical Library Inc.: New York.
Rein, R. (1993), *The Franco-Peron Alliance: Relations Between Spain and Argentina, 1946-1955*, University of Pittsburg Press: Pittsburg and London.
Republički zavod za statistiku (1992), 'Stanovništvo prema narodnosti po naseljima', *Dokumentacija, No.* 881, Zagreb, p. 9.
Republički zavod za statistiku Republike Hrvatske (1991), 'Stanovništvo prema vjeroispovedi: prethodni rezultati, po općinama', *Saopćenje Republičkog zavoda za statistiku Republike Hrvatske*, Vol. 28, No. 21.4, Zagreb, pp. 6-7.
Rex, J. and Josephides, S. (1987), 'Asian and Greek Cypriot Associations and Identity', in Rex, J. et al. (eds), *Immigrant Associations in Europe*, Gower: Aldershot, pp. 11-41.
Rimmer, S.J. (1991), *The Cost of Multiculturalism*, Flinders Press: Bedford Park.
Royal Institute of International Affairs (1963), *Nationalism: A Report by a Study Group of Members of the Royal Institute of International Affairs*, Frank Cass and Co.: London.
Safran, W. (1991), 'Diasporas in Modern Societies: Myths of Homeland and Return', *Diaspora*, Vol. 1, No. 1, pp. 83-99.
Said, E. (1991), *Orientalism*, Penguin Books: London.
Salecl, R. (1992), 'Nationalism, Anti-Semitism, and Anti-Feminism in Eastern Europe', *New German Critique*, No. 57, pp. 51-65.
Salecl, R. (1993), 'National Identity and Socialist Moral Majority', in Carter, E. et al. (eds), *Space and Place: Theories of Identity and Location*, Lawrence and Wishart, London, pp. 101-10.
Salt, J. and Clout, H. (1976), *Migration in Post-War Europe*, Oxford University Press: Oxford.
Samardžija, M. (1993), *Hrvatski jezik u Nezavisnoj Državi Hrvatskoj*, Hrvatska sveučilišna naklada: Zagreb.
Schama, S. (1991), 'Homelands', *Social Research*, Vol. 58, No. 1, pp. 11-30.
Schierup, C.-U. (1990), *Immigration, Socialism and the International Division of Labour: The Yugoslav Experience*, Avebury: Aldershot.
Schierup, C.-U. and Alund, A. (1986), *Will They Still Be Dancing?: Integration and Ethnic Transformation Among Yugoslav Immigrants in Scandinavia*, Almqvist & Wiksell International: Stockholm.

Schöpflin, G. (1973), 'The Ideology of Croatian Nationalism', *Survey*, Vol. 19, No. 1, pp. 123-46.
Sekulić, D. et al. (1994), 'Who Were the Yugoslavs? Failed Sources of a Common Identity in the Former Yugoslavia', *American Sociological Review*, No. 59, pp. 83-97.
Shakespeare, W. (1965), *The Life of Henry V*, New American Library: New York.
Sheffer, G. (ed.) (1986a), *Modern Diasporas in International Politics*, Croom Helm: London and Sydney.
Sheffer, G. (1986b), 'A New Field of Study: Modern Diasporas in International Politics', in Sheffer, G. (ed.), *Modern Diasporas in International Politics*, Croom Helm: London and Sydney, pp. 1-15.
Shevill, I. (ed.) (1975) *The Orthodox and Other Eastern Orthodox Churches in Australia*, Anglican Information Office: Sydney.
Silber, L. and Little, A. (1995), *The Death of Yugoslavia*, Penguin: London.
Simat, S. (1992), 'I'm Only Croatian When I Want to Be', *Klokan*, Vol. 3, No. 12, p. 3.
Simmel, G. (1964), 'Conflict', in *Conflict/ The Web of Group-Affiliations*, The Free Press of Glencoe: London, pp. 11-123.
Sitar, S. (1992), 'Enako ponosen na srbsko rodbino in hrvaško domovino: Nikola Tesla', *Srce in Oko*, No. 35, February, Ljubljana, pp. 97-100.
Skrbiš, Z. (1998), 'Making It Tradable: Videotapes, Cultural Technologies and Diasporas', *Cultural Studies*, Vol. 12, No. 2, pp. 265-73.
Slovenian Club Incorporated (1973), *Rules of the Slovenian Club Incorporated*: Adelaide.
Slovenian Research Center of America (1993), *Poročila/Newsletter*, December, Ohio.
Slovenian Second Generation Survey (1994), Adelaide.
Smith, A.D. (1971), *Theories of Nationalism*, Duckworth: London.
Smith, A.D. (1981), 'War and Ethnicity: The Role of Warfare in the Formation, Self-Images and Cohesion of Ethnic Communities', *Ethnic and Racial Studies*, Vol. 4, No. 4, pp. 375-97.
Smith, A.D. (1986), *Ethnic Origins of Nations*, Basil Blackwell: London.
Smith, A.D. (1990), 'Towards a Global Culture', in Featherstone, M. (ed.), *Global Culture: Nationalism, Globalization and Modernity*, SAGE Publications: London, pp. 171-91.
Smith, A.D. (1995), *Nations and Nationalism in a Global Era*, Polity Press: Cambridge.
Smolicz, J.J. (1979), *Culture and Education in a Plural Society*, Curriculum Development Centre: Canberra.
Smolicz, J.J. (1981), 'Core Values and Cultural Identity', *Ethnic and Racial Studies*, Vol. 4, No. 1, pp. 75-90.

Sorel, G. (1941), *Reflections on Violence*, Peter Smith: New York.
Spickard, P.R. (1989), *Mixed Blood: Intermarriage and Ethnic Identity in Twentieth Century America*, The University of Wisconsin Press: Madison.
Stanovnik, J. (1991), 'Preteklost: mera sedanjosti – temelj prihodnosti, *Zaveza*, No. 1, pp. 3-7.
Stevens, M. (1999), 'Terrorism Hits Home', *The Weekend Australian*, 20-21 February, p. 17.
Ströhm, C.G. (1998), 'Where do the Balkans Begin?', *Croatia Weekly*, No. 5 February, p. 1.
Swezey, K.M. (1976), 'Tesla', in Gillispie, C.C. (ed.), *Dictionary of Scientific Biography*, Vol. 13, pp. 286-7.
Švent, R. (1995), 'Begunski usodi naproti', *Dve Domovini/Two Homelands*, No. 6, pp. 43-51.
Tenezakis, M.D. (1984), *The Neglected Press: A Study of Arab and Greek Newspapers and Their Sydney Publics*, Australian Government Publishing Service: Canberra.
Thernstrom, S. et al. (eds) (1980), *Harvard Encyclopedia of American Ethnic Groups*, Harvard University Press: Cambridge.
Theweleit, K. (1987), *Male Fantasies*, University of Minnesota Press: Minneapolis.
Thompson, E.P. (1991), *The Making of the English Working Class*, Penguin: London.
Thompson, M. (1993), 'Greater Croatia', *London Review of Books*, No. 13, May, pp. 10-12.
Tkalčević, M. (1992), *Hrvati u Australiji*, Nakladni zavod Matice Hrvatske: Zagreb.
Tokic, A. (1992), 'My Personal Odyssey for Croatia, *Klokan*, Vol. 3, No. 9, September, p. 11.
Tolstoy, N. (1986), *Victims of Yalta*, Corgi Books: London.
Tomažič, I. (1990), *Novo sporočilo knjige Veneti naši davni predniki*, Editiones Veneti: Ljubljana.
Tölölyan, K. (1991), 'The Nation-State and Its Others: In Lieu of a Preface', *Diaspora*, Vol. 1, No. 1, pp. 3-7.
Tölölyan, K. (1996), 'Rethinking Diaspora(s): Stateless Power in the Transnational World', *Diaspora*, Vol. 5, No. 1, pp. 3-36.
Tönnies, F. (1988) *Community and Society*, Transaction Books, New Brunswick.
Tudjman, F. (1989), *Bespuća povjestne zbiljnosti*, Nakladni zavod Matice Hrvatske: Zagreb.

Tudjman, F. (1992), 'Prologue', in *Borders of Croatia on Maps from 12th to 20th Century*, Muzej za umjetnost i obrt/The Museum of Arts and Crafts: Zagreb, pp. 6-7.
Urbanc, P. (1993), 'Kratek historiat slovenske politične emigracije', *Zaveza*, No. 10, Ljubljana, pp. 72-77.
Vasta, E. (1992), 'The Second Generation', in Castles S. et al. (eds), *Australia's Italians: Culture and Community in a Changing Society*, Allen and Unwin: Sydney, pp. 155-68.
Vičar, S. (1993), 'Balkanska ponudba: še vedno ražnjiči na slovenskih kmečkih praznikih', *Nedeljski dnevnik*, 29 August, p. 3.
Viorst, M. (1991), 'A Reporter at Large: The Yugoslav Idea', *New Yorker*, 18 March, pp. 58-79.
Vitez, V. (1970), *In the Defence of Justice*, History and Life Series: Melbourne.
Viviani, N. (1984), *The Long Journey: Vietnamese Migration and Settlement in Australia*, Melbourne University Press: Melbourne.
Viviani, N. (ed.) (1992), *The Abolition of the White Australia Policy: The Immigration Reform Movement Revisited*, Australia-Asia Paper No. 65, Centre for the Study of Australia-Asia Relations, Griffith University: Nathan.
Vucinich, W.S. (1974), 'Some Aspects of the Ottoman Legacy', in Jelavich, C. and Jelavich, B. (eds), *The Balkans in Transition*, Archon Books, Hamden, pp. 81-114.
Warner, M. (1985), *Alone For All Her Sex: The Myth and Cult of the Virgin Mary*, Pan Books: London.
Watson, J.L. (1977), 'Introduction: Immigration, Ethnicity, and Class in Britain', in Watson, J.L. (ed.), *Between Two Cultures*, Basil Blackwell: Oxford, pp. 1-20.
Weber, E. (1977), *Peasants Into Frenchmen: The Modernization of Rural France 1870-1914*, Chatto and Windus: London.
Woodward, S.L. (1995), *Socialist Unemployment: The Political Economy of Yugoslavia 1945-1990*, Princeton University Press: New Jersey.
Yallop, P. and Rabinovich, A. (1997), 'Gutnick's West Bank Gamble', *The Australian*, 18 February, p. 11.
Yuval-Davis, N. and Anthias, F. (eds) (1989a), *Woman-Nation-State*, Macmillan: London.
Yuval-Davis, N. and Anthias, F. (1989b), 'Introduction', in Yuval-Davis, N. and Anthias, F. (eds), *Woman-Nation-State*, Macmillan: London, pp. 1-15.
Yuval-Davis, N. (1993), 'Gender and Nation', *Ethnic and Racial Studies* Vol. 16, No. 4, pp. 621-32.
Yuval-Davis, N. (1997), *Gender and Nation*, SAGE: London.

Zavod Republike Slovenije za statistiko (1992), 'Popis prebivalstva, gospodinjstev, stanovanj in kmečkih gospodarstev v Republiki Sloveniji, 1991 – končni podatki', *Statistične informacije*, No. 181, 17 June, p. 5.

Zveza slovenske akcije (not dated), 'Politika za Slovence v Avstraliji', Zveza Slovenske Akcije: Sydney.

Žigon, Z. (1996), 'Funkcionalni bilingvalizem in Slovenci v Argentini in Urugvaju', *Dve domovini/Two Homelands*, No. 7, pp. 71-95.

Žižek, S. (1992), 'Eastern European Liberalism and Its Discontents', *New German Critique*, No. 57, Fall, pp. 25-49.